THE
POWYS
JOURNAL

Volume VIII

THE POWYS SOCIETY

President Glen Cavaliero

Chairman Paul Roberts
Vice-Chairman Griffin Beale
Hon. Treasurer Stephen Powys Marks
Hon. Secretary Chris Gostick

The Powys Society is a registered charity, No. 801332

The Powys Society was founded in 1967 to 'establish the true literary status of the Powys family through promotion of the reading and discussion of their works', in particular those of John Cowper Powys (1872–1963), Theodore Francis Powys (1875–1953), and Llewelyn Powys (1884–1939).

The Society publishes a journal and three newsletters a year, and has embarked on a publication programme. In addition it organises an annual weekend conference, occasional meetings, exhibitions, and walks in areas associated with the Powys family.

The Society is an international one, attracting scholars and non-academics from around the world, and welcomes everyone interested in learning more about this remarkable family.

Correspondence and membership enquiries should be addressed to:

Chris Gostick, Hon. Secretary
The Old School House, George Green Road, George Green,
Wexham, Buckinghamshire, SL3 6BJ
(tel: 01753 578632; e-mail: gostick@altavista.net)

THE POWYS JOURNAL

Volume VIII
1998

Editor
J. R. Williams

Contributing Editor
Charles Lock

The Powys Journal is a publication of The Powys Society, appearing annually each summer. Its aim is to publish original material by the Powys family — in particular, John Cowper Powys, Theodore Francis Powys and Llewelyn Powys — and scholarly articles and other material relating to them and their circle. It also carries reviews of books by and about the Powys family and their circle.

The Powys Journal is grateful to the copyright holders of the individual estates: Mr John Powys and Laurence Pollinger Ltd for their permission to quote from the writings of John Cowper Powys and Theodore Francis Powys, and Mrs Sally Connely and Laurence Pollinger Ltd for their permission to quote from the writings of Llewelyn Powys.

MSS for publication, correspondence about the contents of the *Journal*, and books for review should be addressed to the editor, Dr J. R. Williams, *The Powys Journal*, School of Humanities, University of Greenwich, Churchill House, Woolwich, London, SE18 6PF. *The Powys Journal* has a refereeing policy, whereby material is submitted for independent reports, in which the anonymity of the author and the referee is preserved. MSS should, therefore, be submitted in duplicate, or on disk in ASCII or text-only format (as well as in your own wordprocessor) with one paper copy, with the name and address of the author on a separate sheet. MSS will be acknowledged but cannot be returned unless accompanied by a stamped, self-addressed envelope. Authors of printed articles will receive two copies of the *Journal*.

Orders for copies of the *Journal* should be addressed to the Society's Publications Manager, Stephen Powys Marks, Hamilton's, Kilmersdon, near Bath, Somerset, BA3 5TE (tel. 01761 435134).

Cover and title-page design: Bev Craven

Typeset in Garamond
in PageMaker 5 on a Macintosh computer
by Stephen Powys Marks

Printed by Anthony Williams, printer (tel: 0117 986 0431)

ISSN 0962–7057

ISBN 1 874559 20 1

CONTENTS

Timothy Hyman: "Weymouth Sands": John Cowper Powys Introduces Me to a Circle of his Admirers, *1986–90*

EDITORIAL

The current number of *The Powys Journal* explores a wide range of work. The three Powys brothers are all represented, in addition to other members of the circle. The articles and reviews engage with poetry, prose in a variety of forms, and the visual arts. John Cowper Powys is discussed in a series of essays that display diverse approaches and interests. Each item, of course, stands on its own merits; but equally questions arise — following on from the nature of much of the material — about the kinds of relationships that might exist between the work of different writers, between different kinds of writing, and between writing and other art forms. Several of the poems in Jeremy Hooker's collection, *Our Lady of Europe*, reviewed in this edition, explore the nature of painting and sculpture through writing. The poem 'Blinded' begins:

> When I stumbled upon it, I was thinking about seeing:
>   how the eye
> can devour, feeding secretly on all it sees, or chooses to
>   see.
>
> It was in a clearing among the trees. A sculpture carved
>   from a block
> of white stone. It represented a figure which was both
>   beast and man,
> seated at a table, or rather attached to it, for table and fig-
>   ure were
> carved from the same block. (38)

It is a meditation on how we see; the poet stumbles into the poem as though blind because he is 'thinking about seeing'. The object itself becomes secondary; what matters, it seems, is not the artefact but how you think about it. Thus a painting of Saul and David by Rembrandt prompts Hooker to observe not so much the painting, but the condition of loneliness it portrays. David is lost in his creativity, 'absorbed in the music he is making'; Saul, who is close enough to touch 'The beautiful young man':

> … hears it where he sits,
> deep inside himself,
> music he was once part of,
> that sounds now
> eternally distant,
> beyond the ramparts of paradise. (39)

In many respects, the series of articles on John Cowper Powys printed here, though connected by the presence of the author, could hardly be further apart in the way they engage with their subject. The author of one of the articles, Morine Krissdóttir, goes on to review *"I Am Myself Alone": Solitude and Transcendence in John Cowper Powys*, a new book by Janina Nordius which is clearly different again in its approach. So are there worthwhile connections to be made between these pieces, or do they exist properly in a more or less permanent state of isolation, sharing the fate of Saul and David?

Isolation is the theme dealt with in Gamel Woolsey's short story, reprinted here for the first time since its appearance in *The Saturday Evening Post* in 1955. Michael Alsford makes biographical connections from 'The Star of Double Darkness' to Woolsey's personal situation, but he also links this work with the broader cultural phenomenon of science fiction writing in the 1950s and '60s. While the critical and intellectual enterprise revolves around the process of making such connections, however, it is important not to lose sight of the fact that appreciation of the work itself will often be predicated (initially at least) on the sense of isolation experienced by the artist (witness the title of Nordius's monograph); it is certainly not the critic's job to remove that. Alsford therefore never allows us to lose sight of the significance of this theme in Woolsey's work; it is also the note upon which Theodore Powys's story, 'The Sixpenny Strumpet', begins:

> About the time, though the exact date of these happenings is uncertain, when Mr. Spurgeon large in mighty words, with a cigar in his mouth, rode in a fine carriage to the Tabernacle to

preach his sermons, there existed somewhere in the West of England a small village, the people of which were ill fed and neglected. (297)

The difference between Powys and Woolsey is sufficient to suggest that here there can be little if any common ground. Theodore Powys sounds a characteristically sonorous, socially explicit note of bitter irony to emphasise the isolation of that 'small village' where, in contrast to the affluent Spurgeon, 'there was wont to be more dirt than bacon for the poor.' (297) What could be more different from the chatty style of the popular short story characteristic of *The Saturday Evening Post*? The answer is, not a great deal; until, that is, you begin to probe the concerns expressed by both writers, then interesting things may well begin to emerge around the general theme of isolation on a planet that can appear to be so beautiful, while in the event it can turn out to be the loveless environment that T. F. Powys so trenchantly describes. 'The Sixpenny Strumpet' is published now for the first time (with 'In Good Earth', 'God' and 'The Two Thieves') by the Brynmill Press, and is reviewed here by David Gervais.

Making connections in this way remains primarily the concern of the critic; it is how, for example, the excellent Afterword by Ian Robinson and the critical apparatus supplied by J. Lawrence Mitchell for the new T. F. Powys title operate; it is the basis of Rodney Aitchtey's essay, where he explores thematic connections between the work of Robinson Jeffers and that of John Cowper Powys, and then connects both to his own belief in the need for a radical rethink in relation to global pollution. The work that is being discussed, however, will often depend for its effectiveness upon the maintenance of a sense of profound isolation experienced by the writer, this is manifestly the case with respect to Woolsey's story, and it certainly seems to be the case with respect to the T. F. Powys stories referred to above; where John Cowper is concerned, perhaps we should turn to Timothy Hyman's essay in this edition of the *Journal* for more guidance.

Hyman has written a very personal account of his engagement with John Cowper Powys's work, framed by his long-standing enthusiasm for the artist Pierre Bonnard. This latter has been an enthusiasm that in recent months has become a far more intense involvement, culminating in the publication of his book on Bonnard for the Thames and Hudson World of Art series, and, of course, his current article in *The Powys Journal*. Publication of the book coincided with the major exhibition of Bonnard's work at the Tate Gallery (this has now moved on to New York where it continues until late September). Hyman's essay is all about making connections, it is a personal account of the way the two artists have worked for him as complementary voices, and he has a case to make about the chemistry of a relationship that exists between a writer and a painter, with himself (a practising writer and painter) acting as catalyst.

The experience of viewing room after room of Bonnard canvasses is one I shall not quickly forget, and what very soon became apparent to me was how important the issue of relationships is within his work. The most dramatic example of this must be the *Café 'Au Petit Poucet'* with its multiple spaces, part real, part reflection, and the questions it asks of both its own figures and the viewer, about who is looking at who, and from what vantage point. In the same way, though perhaps with less fuss, *The Bowl of Milk* (1919) is an interior that questions the way we relate to objects we might otherwise pass over as unworthy of notice. The table falls away from the window, the objects to its left seem to accelerate the process, slanting downward. The Bonnard cat (a ghostly inhabitant of many of the paintings) tail erect, defies that momentum and moves across and down to the right, eager to receive its milk. The bowl on the table glows in the sunlight that floods in from an outside world, but it is an outside world which — as so often in Bonnard — exists in an ambivalent relationship to a dark, restless, interior world. In front of the table is the figure of a girl about to give the cat its milk (we must suppose), but as the room shifts uneasily about, she appears (not least because of the priestly style of her robe) more as a priestess; she has turned from the light, and her eyes — hidden in shadow — seem to be gazing past us in a state of trance. The eyes (and here I make a connection with Jeremy Hooker's poem 'Blinded') denote an inward gaze that renders the viewer at best a trespasser.

Having drafted this passage, it was interesting to turn to Timothy Hyman's own comments on this picture in his book; it is as it should be, some thoughts we share, others we don't. What matters is the way this painting engages with the ambivalence that resides in a series of interlocking relationships; there are many, but they all come to revolve in the end around a restless dialogue between external and internal worlds, and from here it is indeed only a short step into the restless world (both spiritually and physically) of John Cowper Powys. What Hyman does in his *Journal* article is to bring a distinctively Powysian reading to bear on the paintings, and in the process he offers new and exciting insights into how John Cowper Powys may be read and understood.

Pierre Bonnard: The Bowl of Milk, *1919*

Francis Powys

Francis Llewelyn Powys 1909–1998

Francis Powys was the second son of Theodore Francis and Violet Powys, born in East Chaldon, Dorset, on March 21st 1909. He died near Hastings on May 2nd 1998. A memorial service was held for him and his wife Sally, who had died in 1993, at Mappowder Church on May 30th, and the burial of the ashes of both of them took place in the Churchyard in the grave of his parents.

The favourite cousin of my mother, Isobel Powys Marks, and just three years younger — that is how I think of Francis. I remember meeting him when he and Sally lived in Buckland Newton. From the late 1960s they would come over to my mother's house in Mappowder, four miles away (where she had moved in 1967) or we would go over to them, and they became good friends of Tordis and our two children. Always cheerful, in party mood, when one met him in Mappowder, eager to corrupt the young ones with a sip of his sherry; perhaps more pensive in his own home, where he was surrounded by his great accumulation of books by his father and his uncles (he was the literary executor for J.C.P. and T.F.P.), manuscripts, and many of his aunt Gertrude's paintings.

I remember the many trips which he and Sally and Isobel made to France, the great preparations and real hard work of arranging routes, hotels, crossings, books to read, and then when they came back, Francis's really wonderful photographs — the professional photographer at work, of course, supplying transparencies to many different journals.

I met him before that, too, when he worked in London and lived in Hastings. He worked, I believe, in Foyles, but I remember him in the late 1950s and early 60s when he helped to manage Better Books, also in Charing Cross Road (when it moved a few doors away it become Better Bookz, with a 'z' for some reason), and when it was about to close I was invited to salvage books from its basement. He also opened his own bookshop in Hastings; he had been running it from his own home from the early 1950s, but then took premises in George Street called, very properly, 'The Powys Bookshop' (*see* p. 203). He ran this with his partner Graham Boycott. I paid very few visits there, as it was very much out of my way, but I do remember in the early 60s buying from the bookshop, not only a few Powys books, but more notably, for a song, one of my most valuable and important architectural books, which I treasure still; not, of course, the staple diet of the bookshop of a literary bookseller.

Bookseller, photographer, cousin of my mother, I knew him as these, but he was also an accomplished poet, though he published little. Writing under the name of Laurence Powys, he produced a slim volume, *The Harlot's Burial*, in 1930, then another volume, *Ghost of Marseilles and other poems*, in 1932, whose finely crafted long title-poem echoes his memories, beautiful and painful, of that city during an early period working in France. Lastly, in 1985 a selection of early poems was published by Kenneth Hopkins's Warren House Press under the title of *A Winding Sheet of Gold and other poems*, from which the poem printed below is reprinted with permission.

More recently, in 1987–88 in enforced physical inactivity, he wrote a clutch of new poems; one of these, 'Old Cat Henry' was printed on the memorial service sheet and has also been reproduced in the July *Newsletter*, together with tributes to Francis Powys.

Francis was the last but one of today's elder generation.

Stephen Powys Marks

Sleep

I have of late been intimate with night
And here, alone, outcast beneath the sky
Have learned strange secrets, and the calm moonlight
has taught me awful verities, while I
Have watched the stars steer their uncharted course.
Have watched vast armies trample down the sky

.......And once, I saw, set on a great pale horse,
The Master Death, going on his rounds at dawn,
When the cold half-light of the eastern sky
Spread a slow chill across the silvered lawn.
I closed mine eyes in fear, lest it were I
He sought so early. — Than the blast of dawn
Falls no more bitter time for man to die.
.......And I have taken darkness to my side
For a companion, down long hours awake;
And learned each path, each step across the wide
Star-circled tract of heaven, — a boundless lake
Clustered with lilies .... And there have been clouds
All night in dismal waste, there has been rain,
There has been mist; and the great mournful crowds
Of the night-people, born of war and pain,
And the god-children of Almighty Death,
Souls of the rack, blind with perpetual fear,
Have brushed so close that I could feel their breath,
Could almost touch them, they have been so near.
.......I have heard weeping, cries .... But Oh, to tell
The tales of night, of all the laughter, tears
Of those that walk therein, — it's Heaven, Hell, —
Would take a lifetime — weeks and months and years.

.......I have neglected day, but what of days?
What of these mornings, evenings? To what end
Should I have dealings with the sad day-light?
Why notice days, when darkness is my friend?
— I have of late been intimate with night.

Francis Powys
(from *A Winding Sheet of Gold, 1985*)

SUBI SWIFT

The Eternal Epicene
Images of the Androgyne in John Cowper Powys

No study of John Cowper Powys can indefinitely ignore the handling of sexual themes or fail to notice the dominance of the epicene as a recurring motif. My intention here is to try and explore the importance of the image to Powys and to examine, in relation to the tradition of visual representations of the androgyne, its role as an expression of Powys's sexual themes and preoccupations.

In his *Autobiography* John Cowper Powys wrote: 'Why, the mere bringing together of the word "woman" and the word "naked" a conjunction which is apparently a temptation to many, always fills me with a cold and sickening aversion'.[1] Physical revulsion and 'fastidiousness', aversions to nudity (as described in the *Autobiography*) and to the reproductive process, to bodily functions and the grosser aspects of the human condition, coupled with voyeuristic and sadistic lust, led Powys to evolve and develop an appropriate image on which to focus his 'imaginatized sensations':[2] an image that might accommodate his imaginative vice without demanding, so to speak, physical engagement. The figure on to which Powys was to project this uneasy conjunction of erotic lust and shrinking frigidity was the sylph or androgyne, that eternal symbol of what D. H. Lawrence would have scorned as 'sex-in-the-head' and A. J. L. Busst describes as 'cerebral lechery'.[3]

The *Autobiography* is a testament to Powys's 'nympholeptism', as he called it, an obsession with 'sylph'-like epicenes, and these curiously sexless creatures recur with some persistence in the fiction. Circus girls seem to conform to the androgynous ideal particularly well in the Powysian imagination, realized most fully in the creation of Wizzie Ravelston in *Maiden Castle*. Repeated emphasis is placed on her slender form, her legs, and the colour and texture of her clothing as a means of enhancing the 'imaginative suggestion' of her boyish figure. We see Wizzie in her 'boy's costume' (MC, 352) and learn that her 'boy's attire offered no feminine impediment' (MC, 359) to her movements. Powys's fascination with circus themes can be seen as part of a wider tradition, most notable in the visual arts in the second half of the nineteenth century, which saw the figure of Pierrot, with whom Powys identified strongly, as 'one of the types of our century, of the moment in which we live, or of the moment, perhaps, out of which we are just passing', a tragic-comical embodiment of 'grotesque joy'.[4] The wistful pathos of such images was attractive to Powys and lent itself readily to his circus epicenes. Dolores, in *Wood and Stone*, is an example: an earlier and considerably younger version of Wizzie. Unlike Swinburne's 'Dolores', a hard-eyed, heavy limbed 'Lady of Pain',[5] Powys's creation is, literally, a child, a poor circus orphan aged about twelve. Yet much ambivalence, not to say sexual aberration, surrounds her presentation. She combines the typical Powys androgyne qualities of helplessness and vulnerability with sexual allure.

The strangely provocative yet sexless, tragi-comical demi-monde of the circus girl clearly held much attraction to Powys. It evoked for him an epicene wistfulness, a strange combination of smiling despair and sweetness, which he would translate into metaphors derived from pictorial images. These might be robust Post-Impressionist visions of 'the distended flanks of the acrobat hanging head downwards in the circus',[6] recalling, perhaps, Seurat or Sickert, or those of 'fatal sweetness' inspired by Verlaine:

> attracted irresistibly to that wonderful artificial fairyland, associated for us for all time with the genius of Watteau, wherein pale roses and fountains and yew-hedges are the background for the fatal sweetness of Columbine and the dancing feet of Arlequino.
>
> This Garden-of-Versailles cult, with its cold moonlight and its faint music has become, with the sad-gay Pierrot as its tutelary deity, one of the most appealing 'motifs' in modern art.[7]

This was a world evoked by Pater, too, in 'A Prince of Court Painters', where in Watteau's 'happy valley' one can 'catch in the twilight the shimmer of the dancing feet of the Phantom-Pierrot, and the despair in his smile!'[8]

Staying with Pater, there is much evidence to suggest that Powys's response to androgynous images was an aspect of Paterian thought to which he was especially responsive. He refers repeatedly to Pater's writings on, for instance, 'certain delicately sensuous pictures of Giorgione, or to those long-laboured-over, equivocal revelations of Leonardo's super-human art' to which 'we must go, those of us who are secret amorists' in search of 'this strange quality', 'that rare elusive loveliness'[9] embodied in the androgyne.

In his essay, 'Leonardo da Vinci', Pater writes of a small drawing in red chalk of 'a face of doubtful sex, set in the shadow of its own hair, the cheek-line in high light against it, with something voluptuous and full in the eyelids and the lips' as offering 'the thread of suggestion'[10] in the apprehension of an ideal beauty. Always, suggestion is the key word, such depictions inviting us to respond to expressive possibilities and shades of meaning that transcend the picture space:

> We recognise one of those symbolical inventions in which the ostensible subject is used, not as matter for definite pictorial realisation, but as the starting-point of a train of sentiment subtle and vague as a piece of music.[11]

This quality of suggestiveness was to be found, most especially, in paintings of sexual ambiguity, like *Saint John the Baptist*, which Powys would have seen at the Louvre:

> one of the few naked figures Leonardo painted — whose delicate brown flesh and woman's hair no one would go out into the wilderness to seek, and whose treacherous smile would have us understand something far beyond the outward gesture or circumstance.[12]

And the mystery and ambivalence of such images held within them 'a touch of something sinister', so relevant to Powys's work, epitomised by the 'unfathomable smile'[13] of *La Gioconda* in whose face was enshrined primeval knowledge of evil, of 'exquisite passions', of love, lust and the sins of man.

The 'unfathomable' depths of such a smile were to haunt the fictional response to the Powys androgyne, here embodied by Nelly in *After My Fashion*, 'smiling to herself a quaint elfish enigmatic smile that seemed to separate her in some queer way from all possible lovers and turn her into a mocking sexless thing of childish unapproachableness.' (AF, 102) Similar notations inform the presentation of Mary Crow, in *A Glastonbury Romance*, as she

> smiled one of those deep, mysterious, feminine smiles, that only the greatest poets and artists, such as Dante, Leonardo, Blake, have dared to note, depict and comment on, in their troubled search for the absolute. (GR, 628)

And other references can be found, in the same novel, to the suggestive meaning carried in 'the wavering beginning of a girl's smile' in the art of Leonardo and his ability, as one of the "greatest Realists that have ever lived", to find in women's lips the entelecheia of all Nature's secretest designs.' (GR, 981)

Of particular relevance to Powys's work, too, was Pater's vision of a refined sensibility, a kind of all-seeing, all-knowing deity, evoked in Symons's 'Modern Beauty' and embodied in 'La Gioconda's' face, which, although apprehending mortal lusts and desires, was essentially sexless, just as 'the beauty of the Greek statues was a sexless beauty'.[14] Such images carried the burden of ideal beauty and eternal wisdom while remaining aloof and immaculate in their sexless or sexually uncertain representations.

The connection here with Powys's sexual fastidiousness seems clear enough, and he was able to identify readily with a similar trait in Pater, who, 'because of his fastidiousness, could get his sense-ecstasies only from things several times removed from the chaos of reality'.[15] The theme is carried in such Paterian characterisations as those of Sebastian Van Storck and Watteau, who attract love but do not, as John Conlon[16] points out, return it. They, like the Greek statues, embody 'a moral sexlessness, a kind of impotence, an ineffectual wholeness of nature, yet with a divine beauty and significance of its own.'[17]

Powys lectured on Pater, exhorted his friends to read him, 'You MUST get this 'Imaginary Portraits' ... out of some library ... Pater is wickedly neglected nowadays. He is still my Master. He is still to me ... the beautifullest of all our writers',[18] and was thrilled to know that his son was reading *The Renaissance* and had developed 'quite a mania for reading Walter Pater', encouraging him in his writing 'with great care and labour a sort of child in the house Marius-Florian-Garton [*sic*] kind of 'study' of his own sensations'.[19] He saw his son, too, in Paterian terms: 'there is something like that 'Diaphaneite' sketch of Pater's about him — something tenuous and fragile and a little wistful and yielding', though he thought him 'too childish to be compared with Gaston de Latour and too 'earthy' in a way'. [20]

Rodmoor bears the clear imprint of Pater's influence on Powys's characterisations. In addition to Baltazar Stork, an echo of Pater's Sebastian Van Storck, an obliquely homosexual embodiment of the book's underlying theme of darkness, death and perversion, there is Philippa Renshaw with her 'ambiguous red lips and white cheeks'(Rod, 319), the archetypal Powys androgyne and direct descendant of Pater's Mona Lisa. Her 'slender equivocal figure' (Rod, 42) is emphasised to indicate the nature of her 'defiant sexlessness' and epicene character, 'the boyish outlines of her body' giving her the appearance of 'one of those androgynous forms of later Greek art whose ambiguous loveliness wins us still' (Rod, 49–50). Philippa, and her name too is significant, is described in terms strikingly similar to Pater's. La Gioconda's 'unfathomable smile' is the clear model for Philippa's 'enigmatic smile challenging and inscrutable which seems, more than any other human expression, to have haunted the imagination of certain great artists of the past.' Although closer description of Philippa reveals a look too modern to denote a pre-Christian time, she is yet, as 'a creature of the old perverse civilizations' (Rod, 269), related to the Mona Lisa, who while symbolizing 'the modern idea'[21] also embodies the accumulated layers of history and prehistory.

And the impression Philippa first gives finds us 'tempted to dream that the dust of the centuries had indeed been quickened and some delicate evocation of perverse pagan desire restored to breath and consciousness' (Rod, 50), just as La Gioconda carries the burden of 'the animalism of Greece, the lust of Rome ... the return of the Pagan world'.[22] And the sense of evil, or apprehension of evil, a kind of sexless yet knowing fatality, embedded in Pater's vision of the Mona Lisa, is echoed in the 'equivocal' and 'epicene' image of Philippa, who

> resembled some girl-priestess of Artemis invoking a mocking image of her own defiant sexlessness. With her sorrowful inhuman eyes she suggested some strange elf-creature, born of mediaeval magic. (Rod, 50)

Though Powys stresses the elf or waif-like qualities of Philippa, her gazelle-like youthfulness as she runs through dark woods like a pagan 'masquerading boy', in contrast to the sedentary, even matriarchal, dignity of La Gioconda, she too carries in her 'ambiguous' eyes the expression of a soul in which, as Pater said, resided all 'the ends of the world', all man's hopes and disappointments:

> She might have been taken for a symbolic image of all that is condemned, as this mortal world goes round, to watch and wait and invoke the gods and cling fast to such pathetic relics and memorials as time consents to leave of the days that it has annihilated. (Rod, 57)

A similar presence surrounds another Powys sylph, Tegolin, in *Owen Glendower*, looked on here by Rhisiart:

> as he watched Tegolin's delicate figure in her page's dress and noted its soft curves and the slenderness of her neck compared with all these men, a vague obscure thought... took possession of him. It was something so passive, so receptive ... in Tegolin's pose, something that suggested, compared with the compact and concentrated energies of all these men, the deep, soft, yielding, silent-growing potency of Nature herself! Yes, there was an aura about her, an aura that even these monks were feeling — the greatest mystery in the world! (OG, 118)

Commonly in Powys, the epicene, or sylph, is seen as the holder and conveyor of Paterian suggestiveness and mystery. The androgyne seemed to Powys to embody the ineffable and the mysterious, a kind of metaphysical repository of unnamed desires. His fictional sylphs, like those he sought in parks and on beaches, constantly hint at desire and seem even to offer the hope of sexual engagement, while ultimately always distanced from such engagement by a sexless spirituality. Christie, in *Wolf Solent*, is a major creation of this image of spirituality, a more fully realised embodiment of the qualities prefigured in Philippa. Related, too, to Wizzie, and rather to such Paterian heroes as Watteau, Gaston de Latour, Marius and Denys L'Auxerrois of whom Pater asks: 'who could tell what kind of powers? hidden under the white veil of that youthful form',[23] than to the Mona Lisa, Christie is Powys's fictive response to the 'curious emotional phenomenon' that underpinned his sexuality and informed his female characterisations, voiced here by Wolf:

> He discovered that the peculiar glamour which had always hovered for him like a diaphanous cloud round the impersonal idea of girlhood, had concentrated itself upon the image of Christie … The thought of Gerda' s warmth gave him a voluptuous thrill, direct, earthy, full of honest and natural desire. But he recognized now that there hovered over the personality of this other girl something more subtle than this — nothing less, in fact, than that evasive aura of mysterious girlishness — the platonic idea, so to speak, of the mystery of all young girls, which was to him the most magical thing in the whole world. (WS, 237)

In the conflicts which disable and eventually define Wolf, conflicts between the corporeal and the cerebral, between his needs for physical and spiritual fulfilment, it is to Gerda, whom he marries, that he turns, with brief success, for the former, while in the androgynous Christie he finds the true partner of his intellectual and spiritual needs.

Christie's epicene qualities, evoked, as so often, in pictorial terms, are inseparable from Wolf's perception of her as a spiritual being. 'That evasive aura' surrounding her is embodied in her figure 'so slight and sexless' that it resembles 'those meagre, androgynous forms that can be seen sometimes in early Italian pictures.' (WS, 83) Her attraction and spirituality are seen to reside in her passive, childish form, the very incarnation, to borrow J. Hillis Miller's phrase, of distance and desire. Set against the earthy and conventionally beautiful Gerda, Christie's role as an androgynous spirit is given an early notation in Wolf's remark, 'I wish you were a boy, Christie!' and her reply, 'I used to wish that myself' (WS, 220).

Given the antithesis set up between the physicality of Gerda and the spirituality of Christie, reinforced by careful description of looks and behaviour and underpinned by precise imagery and symbolism,[24] it comes as no surprise that, as in the typical Powysian encounter with a sylph, sexual gratification is presented as tantalisingly near yet impossibly remote. In a central scene in Chapter 10, 'Christie', seduction is suggested, both symbolically and literally. Wolf thinks of little else, 'Will she let me make love to her? Will she let me?', and Christie is seen both as seductress and compliant victim. But, although the scene builds up a heavy and potent atmosphere of sensuality and achieves, symbolically, a climax of a kind, sexual consummation is, as ever, thwarted and subverted by a complex web of psychological and physical evasion and misunderstanding. Undermining the possibility of physical engagement is Wolf's awareness, characteristic of the Powys-hero, of 'the peculiar limitations of his own nature':

> He knew well enough that any great surge of what is called 'passion' was as impossible to him as was any real remorse about making love. What he felt was an excitement that trembled on the margin — on the fluctuating fine edge — between amorous desire for the slim frame of this mysterious girl and the thrilling attraction of unexplored regions of her soul. (WS, 247–8)

Wolf's typical Powysian fascination with marginal experience conjoins with a tendency to idealize and cerebralize the object of desire to a point where sexual engagement becomes not only impossible but, in a sense, redundant. Threatening both Wolf's 'life-illusion' and idealized image of Christie as chaste, the sexual act would disturb Wolf's private mythology, violate Christie's inviolable spirituality, and destroy the ineffable pleasure of indirection by direct action.

Although largely unnoticed by Wolf at this stage, Christie shares

with other Powys androgynes significant elements of darkness and
perversion. Anticipating Tegolin in *Owen Glendower*, daughter of the
evil Mistress Lowri, Christie's background of clearly implied incest
and pornography in the shape of her father's bookshop, tends constantly to undermine her image as physically and spiritually chaste,
while at the same time heightening her mystery and ambiguity. John
Brebner has drawn attention to the 'unhealthy and moribund' atmosphere surrounding Christie in the near-seduction scene, citing the
'tinge of faint rose-carmine' on the 'hyacinthine bloom' of the bluebell
as the imagery of death and decay.[25] The highly-charged atmosphere
of the scene is heightened by the ambivalence of the protagonists and
by the atmospheric and symbolic conjunction of the sickly and the
spiritual, a combination at once seductive and repellent:

> The faint flush that had now appeared in her cheeks, and the
> complicated wistfulness of her expression, disarmed and en-
> chanted him. He stooped down to her and stroked with the
> tips of his fingers the white blue-veined skin under her lace
> wristbands; but as he looked at her now, there was a certain
> virginal detachment about her thin ankles and about those
> lace-ruffled hands which irritated and provoked him by its
> inhuman remoteness. (WS, 249)

Christie can, of course, be no more responsible than Tegolin for an
evil parent. We know, though, that Powys read and admired Ibsen, and
may have taken from him, in addition to the phrase 'life-illusion',
which he found in *The Wild Duck* and placed at the pivotal centre of his
personal philosophy, the idea of parental sin attaching itself to subsequent generations. Regardless, though, of their parentage, Powys's
androgynes tend to embody certain dark forces, sometimes defined
by their actions, more often hinted at by association. The representation of these dark forces in the novels establishes a link between
Powys's vision and the literary and visual expressions of the Decadents.
  Something of this impulse can be seen in the realization of Gladys,
in *Wood and Stone*, who enshrines in her lithe figure and boyish sandals
the characteristics of an epicene flirt and coquette, delineated by

actions that range from amorous teasing to flirtatious cruelty and sadism, the female embodiment of the novel's 'Mythology of Power'. A cruel and spiteful 'spoiled child', Gladys manipulates the loyalties and affections of those who become entangled with her, for her own malicious pleasure, 'to amuse herself; to satisfy her wicked, wicked nature!' (W & S, 69) Her evil is seen to reside, in part, in her relationship with the stone of the novel's title, symbol and manifestation of insensitivity and unyielding cruelty:

> The sun-warmed slabs of Leonian stone, upon which she had so often basked in voluptuous contentment seemed dumbly to encourage and stimulate her in this heathen design. How entirely they were the accomplices of all that was dominant in her destiny ... They answered to her own blond beauty, to her own sluggish remorselessness ... They gave support and weight to all her pretensions.
>
> Thus it had been with an almost mystical thrill of exultation that she had felt the warmth of the Leonian slabs caress her limbs. (W & S, 103–4)

This presents a powerful, and telling, image of the androgyne in erotic communion with the inanimate, resembling, although with different resonances, Philippa Renshaw's erotic response to the oak trees. The unyielding, hard texture of the stone is a significant choice, underpinning Gladys's cruel androgyny and setting her apart from traditional, more 'feminine' images of women basking in 'voluptuous contentment', from less sexually ambivalent visual images as, for example, Correggio's *Io*, Rembrandt's *Bathsheba*, Titian's *Venus* or Ingres' *La Grande Odalisque*, who surround themselves with soft drapes and 'caress' not stone but silk.

Gladys's nature is transcribed in, literally, visual terms when she is painted by the American artist, Dangelis, who, somewhat naively, feels inspired to endow her image with 'something of the superb non-moral 'insouciance'... which one observes in the forms of Attic sculpture, or in the creations of Venetian colourists.' (W & S, 132) 'Bewitched' by the artful and 'wily' Gladys, Dangelis is seen as responsive, particularly, to her childlike behaviour, a common androgynous trait in Powys's work. Quick to notice and exploit this, she acts out the role of 'a romping and quite unscrupulous child', providing the desired display of 'youthful malice, or greed, or sensuality, or vanity' (W & S, 115–16) flicking him with roses or, 'Like a mischievous infant caught in some unpardonable act ... flagrantly and shamelessly' (W & S, 125–6) sticking out her tongue at him. Their curious flirtation reaches its apotheosis during the portrait session in which Gladys's 'boyish' and girlish charms conjoin to evoke a Dionysian ecstasy in the painter as the figure before him shapes itself into the image of Ariadne on the canvas.

Throughout the scene, dramatic tension is created by the sense that painter and sitter have not the same purpose in mind. Gladys's 'want of aesthetic feeling', her waywardness, her self-seeking vanity, seem to threaten, at any moment, the 'thrill of exquisite sweetness', the transfiguring, 'divine joy' (W & S, 238–9) experienced by the artist in perfect communion with his art. Both careless and careful of her effect on the proceedings, Gladys acts out two of her, and other androgynes', favourite and most effective roles, first as the ingenue-coquette:

> The playful girl, her fair cheeks flushed with excitement and a treacherous light in her blue eyes, swung herself upon the rough oak table ... and sat there, smiling coyly at him, dangling her sandalled feet. She still held in her hand the strawberries she had picked; and ... these between her lips, she looked at him with an indescribable air of mischievous, challenging defiance. (W & S, 240–41)

And here, derived in part from Pater's 'Mona Lisa' and in part from Swinburne's 'Hermaphroditus' and 'Fragoletta' or Symons' 'Rosa Flammea' of 'unsearchable lids', becoming, as the sitting resumes, the femme-fatale, calculating, cruel and powerful:

> the languorously reclining model was not in the least oblivious to the effect she produced. This was, indeed, one of Gladys's supreme moments, and she let no single drop of its honeyed distillation pass undrained. She permitted her heavy-lidded blue eyes, suffused with a soft dreamy mist, to rest tenderly on her impassioned lover; and as if in response to the desperate

longing in his look, a light-fluttering, half-wistful smile crossed her parted lips, like a ripple upon a shadowy stream.

The girl's vivid consciousness of the ecstasy of power was indeed, in spite of her apparent lethargic passivity, never more insanely aroused. Lurking beneath the dreamy sweetness of the look ... were furtive depths of Circean remorselessness. Under her gentian-blue robe her youthful breast trembled with exultant pleasure, and she felt as though, with every delicious breath she drew, she were drinking to the dregs the very wine of the immortals. (W & S, 242)

There is a clearly Decadent notation in the language of this piece, the 'langour', 'lethargy', parted lips and heavy-lidded eyes, and 'no single drop of ... honeyed distillation ... undrained' that points to the influence of such writers as Wilde, Symons and Swinburne. A similar influence is suggested in the girl's cruel malevolence. More mentally than physically androgynous, Gladys can be seen as the first, and most sadistic, in a line of Powys sylphs in whose sexual ambiguity reside strains of evil or darkness.

Thuella Wye, in *Maiden Castle*, is a later and more consciously 'modern' variation on the androgyne theme. Again, Powys insists on a precise physical typology, a kind of imaginatively constructed sine qua non to which other aspects of characterisation could be added. Dud's first impression of Thuella emphasises, typically, her androgynous form beneath a black silk gown:

Her chest, her hips, her legs seemed to be thinner than the thinnest boy's, so thin as to resemble the fancy of some perverse sculptor who had turned in fastidious loathing from every normal curve in a woman's body! (MC, 62)

Representationally aligned with perversity and 'fastidious loathing' as set against the 'normal', Thuella's introduction carries with it layers of symbolic meaning that go beyond her 'frail androgynous being'. 'Notorious', and producing in Dud 'an electric shock', Thuella's impact is dramatically heightened by her visually striking and somehow shocking 'scarlet lips', 'the most painted lips he had ever seen!', lips so red that her mouth 'in her white face seemed like a wound, a wound that struck him at once as the outward sign of a complicated tragedy.' (MC, 62–3) At such moments, there is, in the strongly visual presentation of Thuella, something of the 'taint of corruption' which Symons discerns in the art of Toulouse-Lautrec in *Le Clown*, for instance, where 'macabre', 'blood' colours betoken such corruption. A similar fleshly corruption is marked by the 'red mouth'[26] of *La Danseuse* as it is by countless red-lipped tormentors in Swinburne's poetry and even by Tennyson's 'crimson petal'.

Thuella's figure and mouth embody strangeness and passionate intensity; her slenderness is 'weird' (MC, 64) and from her 'crimson mouth' pours forth a diatribe like 'spiritual blood' (MC, 62); her behaviour is variously described as feverishly magnetic, audacious, impulsive, 'caressing and cajoling' (MC, 67). Whether in her role as artist or as seductive lesbian, Thuella is evoked in strongly visual terms. In addition to the crimson lipstick of her first entrance, clothes play an important part in her characterisation and visualisation: 'Thuella's slenderness was accentuated by an extremely clinging olive-green gown of fine silk … With that silk gown clinging to her body she looked exactly like the Lamia of Keats's poem' (MC, 143). Defined here, by her clinging silk, as a seductress, she later appears, with the help of a bizarre and tattered outfit, in a more pathetic and vulnerable light:

> She was less well-dressed for one thing … she wore … the most old-fashioned, faded, frayed, cloth suit that No-man had ever seen … It was of a dirty heather colour … and it had a belt which was so frayed and twisted that it looked as if the girl had used it to drag a restless animal about … In place of her usual boyish cap … she wore one of those big, wide-brimmed, flexible straw hats that … looked as if Gainsborough might have painted it on the head of a great lady. (MC, 205)

The juxtaposition here of startlingly incongruous elements, the Gainsborough straw hat and tramp's suit, heightens the visual poignancy of the androgyne as scruffy, schoolgirl ingenue, far removed from the scarlet-painted vamp in black silk we met earlier. It is in transfigurations such as this that the androgyne is, in Powys's fiction, uniquely able to embody the apparently contradictory roles of the archetypal fantasy figure, the siren-child. Thus Thuella moves from silk-clad femme fatale to guileless waif, from scarlet woman to sexless epicene.

Throughout *Maiden Castle*, clothes are described and discussed in considerable detail, foreshadowing, although with different, rather more mystical resonances, the precise details of costume in *Owen Glendower*. In *Maiden Castle* such details concentrate, for the most part, on the epicene figures of Wizzie and Thuella. The latter's 'long, painter's smock, smeared with stains from her palette' (MC, 324–5), sometimes covered by a shawl, combines, with other specific items of clothing like scarlet stockings and a bright yellow dress, to provide a striking visual image of a 'modern', Post-Impressionist painter. By such devices, Powys is able to explore, through figures of sexual ambivalence, themes that are seen to radiate out from and refer back to this ambivalence: on female sexuality and emancipation, and the relationship between women and art, art here represented by Wizzie's circus work and by Thuella's abstract, modernist 'responses' to experience. Clothes play an important part in exploring and defining such themes; they are seen as a source of mystery, attraction and division, as emblems of sexual allure, ambivalence, entrapment and freedom, signifying, above all, a kind of sublimated sexuality by which the clothes themselves become fetishistic conveyors of, or substitutes for, sex itself, thus offering a visual pointing to the androgynous theme:

> The glamour of her muteness, the glamour of her relation to him, turned everything she wore into a delicately withdrawing mystery. He felt as if he wanted to make love to her boots, her stockings, her waist-band, her funny hat! The mystery of her evasive inscrutability flowed through all these things, flowed inwards through them into her infinite feminine soul, receding, receding, yielding, yielding, so that of their heavenly 'seduction' there was no end! (MC, 103)

Clothes, as a 'sacred barrier between a man and a woman' betoken, in this way, as does the androgyne herself, a distancing and indeed a substitution of the sexual act with the ineffable pleasures of erotic contemplation.

★ ★ ★ ★

Powys's first fictional representation of the androgyne occurred in 1915, in *Wood and Stone*, and, as a sexual preoccupation, owes its visualization in his work not only to personal preferences but to a voluminous body of visual and literary work, with which Powys was familiar, which addressed itself to this theme. Much of what we know Powys read relates to the late nineteenth-century's preoccupation with exploring sexual themes and, in particular, to *fin de siècle* curiosity about sexual aberration and perversity. Powys's reading of Barres, D'Annunzio, Goethe, Whitman, Poe, Verlaine, Balzac, de Gourmont, Baudelaire, the de Goncourts, Gautier, Pater, Swinburne, Wilde and subsequently Jung, are all relevant here. It is interesting to note that although Powys came to know 'the alliterative melodies of Swinburne' while at university, and dedicated poetry to him, it was not until he came down from Cambridge, in 1894, the year of Pater's death, that he 'so much as even heard of Walter Pater'.[27] He had not, at that time, heard of Oscar Wilde, either. But it is clear that the young, newly-graduated Powys, a morbidly fastidious ascetic, tormented by sadistic guilt, was to see and read much in the eighteen-nineties that was to colour and shape his thought and work. His impressionable early manhood, his first published poetry (in 1896), and the beginnings of his career as a lecturer, all coincided with that singular period, the eighteen-nineties, when Wilde and Beardsley were at the height of their fame, and when Decadent obsessions with 'almost everything perverse', an 'appetite for the strange, abnormal and unhealthy in art',[28] were to find gratification in the paintings of, for example, Gustave Moreau and Simeon Solomon.

It is interesting, in view of Powys's morbid eroticism, so marked in *Rodmoor*, and his literary taste for, amongst others, Tennyson, some of whose poetry is not without a certain heavy-lidded, morbid sensuality, to note Powys's response to Pre-Raphaelite art, which, in its closing stages and much deviated from its original course, links with later, more Decadent movements. Powys was familiar with the Moxon edition of Tennyson's *Poems* (1857), for which Rossetti produced five illustrations, including *Sir Galahad at the Ruined Chapel*. There is no record of Powys's response to these particular illustrations, but on the Pre-Raphaelite appropriation of his much-loved Dante he had a great deal to say:

> (Dante's) influence upon modern art has been so morbid and evil. The odious sensuality of the so-called 'Pre-Raphaelite School' — a sensuality drenched with holy water and perfumed with incense — has a smell of corruption about it that ought never to be associated with Dante's name ...
>
> His illustrators ... O these sentimentalists, with their Beatrices crossing the Ponte Vecchio, and their sad youths looking on! All this is an insult — a sacrilege — to the proudest, most aristocratic spirit who ever dwelt on earth.
>
> Why did not Aubrey Beardsley stop that beautiful boy on the threshold? He who was the model of his 'Ave atque vale!' might have well served for Casella, singing among the cold reeds, in the white dawn.[29]

This recalls Powys's initial reaction, before William Gaunt's *The Pre-Raphaelite Tragedy* brought about something of a reappraisal, 'a purely physical prejudice', to Pre-Raphaelite figures, 'as if their bodies were not fresh and nice and healthy and clean'. Such a response recalls, too, the decision of Messrs W. H. Smith, in 1894, not to stock George Moore's novel, *Esther Waters*, 'because of a certain Pre-Raphaelite nastiness'[30] and 'Thomas Maitland's' (Robert Buchanan) famous attack on 'The Fleshly School of Poetry' with its 'morbid deviation from healthy forms of life, the ... sense of weary, wasting, yet exquisite sensuality'.[31]

Powys's response to such art is intriguing and paradoxical, pointing to what Philip Stephan calls the 'perverse logic of decadence, which was fascinated by what it loathed'.[32] Such a fascination is apparent in Powys's fiction and is central to his handling of the androgyne theme. The heavily morbid atmosphere of *Rodmoor* is underpinned and given a sexually perverse resonance by the specifically morbid eroticism of Philippa. A creature in darkly erotic communion with fungus stalks, 'her face whipped by... wet leaves', she is an image of 'mad desire' as she flings herself amongst the 'sea-deformed and wind-stunted' trees in an orgiastic act of abandonment:

> Releasing her fierce clasp upon the rough bark of the tree, not however before it had bruised her flesh, the girl dug her nails into the soft damp leaf-mould and rubbed her forehead against the wet moss. She shuddered as she lay like this, and as she shuddered she clutched yet more tightly, as if in a kind of ecstasy, the roots of grass and the rubble of earth into which her fingers dug. (Rod, 51–2)

The textual detail and self-flagellating impulse of such a piece points to that 'perverse logic' which led to Powys's fascination with the 'Morbid and evil ... the odious sensuality' which, at the same time, he disliked and associated with Pre-Raphaelite art. And he shared with the Pre-Raphaelites an abiding fascination with prostitutes and waifs, whose roles in his fiction bear similar symbolic overtones to those evoked in Pre-Raphaelite painting, particularly in representations of sexual ambivalence. There is evidence of Pre-Raphaelite influence too, in the medievalism of *Owen Glendower*, particularly in the description of the androgynous Tegolin, with 'her white face and mass of blood coloured hair ... a Salome in a church-window' (OG, 80) and her precisely-noted clothing of long dresses with pointed sleeves and low slung belts, pointed toes and braided hair.

If Powys's response to the Pre-Raphaelites was marked by a certain paradox, the 'perverse logic of decadence' was more clearly stamped on his attitude towards aestheticism. On the one hand, Powys seemed anxious to distance himself from the main thrust of the aesthetic movement. The phrase 'supporting art', for example, inspired him to think of a comical visual image of 'Theophile Gautier or Someone' literally 'supporting Art' in the form of a great tipsy Goddess'.[33] More seriously, he suggested that 'the arrogant snobbishness of the art-for-art's-sake code poisons and blights' cultural development, damning

> Writers like Huysmans, Maurice Barres, the de Goncourts, Baudelaire, D'Annunzio, Oscar Wilde, and the particular kind

of half-brutal, half-barren sophistication, represented by the garish over-crowded stage of Huneker's exotic 'little flowers,' [who] tend to throw a rank withering death-odour over the natural up-shooting, the fresh green growths, of a sensitive mind's development.[34]

In his fiction, Powys picks up and develops the theme of such dislike in *After My Fashion*, where the *fin de siècle* style of Richard Storm's past work in France is seen as a source of world-weariness, disillusion and morbidity. His return to England is, more than anything else, the result of his wish to escape the 'artificial fragilities' (AF, 10), the 'feverish tension' (AF, 28) and the 'dangerous lure of ... perfect skin, like cruel white satin' (AF, 23) that marked his life in Paris. His affair with the dancer, his friendships, his work as a poet of 'easy charming verses, with a faint fragrance of morbidity' (AF, 9) and his biographical work, The Life of Verlaine, described as 'the poet of the demimonde' (AF, 78), are seen to be intellectually draining and disabling, stultifying and corrupting creative freshness and vigour. In his criticism, too, Powys attacks aestheticism's dedication to subtlety and sophistication, here blamed for Charles Lamb's neglect and declining reputation:

I have myself in the circle of my acquaintance more than half a dozen charming people, of the type who enjoy Aubrey Beardsley, and have a mania for Oscar Wilde, and sometimes dip into Remy de Gourmont, and not one of them 'can read' Charles Lamb ... The mistake our 'aesthetes' made, these lovers of Egyptian dancers and Babylonian masks, is that they suppose the simplicity of Lamb's subjects debar him from the rare effects. Ah! They little know![35]

Powys's attitude to aestheticism might be thought to be summed up when, aiming with absolute precision at the heart of what might be called the movement's creed, he writes:

It is all very well for us to talk of 'burning with a hard gem-like flame,' when, as a matter of fact, we move along, dull as cavemen to some of the finest aesthetic effects in the world.[36]

As a response to a codified system of values of formal critical doctrine, this is convincing enough, and typical of Powys's attitude to any such formulations. But, I suggest, if aestheticism's posturing and 'form' did not appeal to Powys, much of its 'content' did. Not only is there the evidence of his admiration for Pater, but we know that, against a background of *Yellow Book* sets at the Chicago Little Theatre, Powys lectured enthusiastically on Wilde and Verlaine, as well as Pater. He read widely such authors as these, associated with the Aesthetic movement, and others like Huysmans, Gautier, de Gourmont and Swinburne. Powys even, on occasion, looked the part, as a photograph, described by his nephew, shows:

> It's the only photograph I know of my Uncle Jack smoking, his left hand held up in the air in the most langorous and most sensuous of semi-decadent mannerisms: a real Edwardian or even Yellow Nineties gesture. (Never forget that he sprang from that background.)[37]

Although Powys could scarcely be described as a Decadent, there was much in that movement he was to find stimulating and seductive. Of D'Annunzio, for example, he said:

> He teaches a shameless and antinomian hedonism, narrower, less humane, but more fervid and emotional, than that taught by Remy de Gourmont.
>
> In "The Triumph of Death" we find a fierce smouldering voluptuousness which recalls the frescoes on the walls of ancient Pompeii. In "The Flame of Life" we have in superb rhetoric the most colored and ardent description of Venice to be found in all literature.[38]

Of Oscar Wilde's *Salome* he wrote of

> the most richly colored and smoulderingly sensual of all modern tragedies. One actually touches with one's fingers the feasting-cups of the Tetrarch; and the passion of the daughter of Herodias hangs round one like an exotic perfume.[39]

This suggests a response not unlike that of Symons to Beardsley's

Salome illustrations, their 'bodies ... faint and eager with wantonness', noting their spiritual intensity and transfiguring, perverse beauty.[40] For Symons, the same perfume of 'corruption' and 'perverse ecstasy' permeates the drama as it does the designs, and, for all his distaste for bodies that were not 'fresh and nice and healthy and clean', it was a perfume which Powys found hard to resist.

Part of the attraction of the Decadents for Powys was, I believe, to be found in its treatment of sexual themes and, in particular, aberrations. Disliking a Zolaesque realism in sexual representations or the 'sardonic realism'[41] of James Joyce, Powys was drawn to works like the de Goncourt novels and the importance they attached to morbid hypersensitivity,[42] to Gautier's *Mademoiselle de Maupin*, to such de Gourmont works as *Une Nuit au Luxembourg* with its strong emphasis on sensations, and to Balzac's *Seraphita*, all of which offered a rather more exotic array of sexual alternatives. Of particular relevance, too, was the poetry of Swinburne,[43] widely read by Powys, whose *Poems and Ballads* were, as Morse Peckham puts it, mostly concerned with 'one theme, the eroticism of submission and domination, with sadism and masochism':[44] an erotic mixture of no little interest to Powys. And, of course, central to such Decadent sexual permutations was the image, so close to Powys's heart, of the androgyne. Chris Snodgrass has written of the hermaphrodite as coming

> to represent in the *fin de siècle* not only the incorporation and confusion of male and female, spirit and flesh, good and evil, and other contraries, but also self-reflective, incestuous desire ... it represents both completion and sterility, unified totality and imprisoning stasis.[45]

This has great relevance to Powys's thought and work, the characteristically *fin de siècle* response to the androgyne, summed up by Snodgrass, corresponding closely with Powys's own needs, conflicts and preoccupations.

Brian Reade has written of the 'stream of French literature dealing with hermaphroditism' and has drawn attention to the predominance of epicene figures in romances like *Seraphita*, *Mademoiselle de Maupin*, 'a source-book for homosexuals of either sex for many years', and in such Swinburne poems as 'Hermaphroditus' and 'Fragoletta', all works, as already suggested, that Powys knew:

> O Love! what shall be said of thee?
> The son of grief begot by joy?
> Being sightless, wilt thou see?
> Being sexless, wilt thou be
> Maiden or boy? [46]

Reade's observation that in such literature the preoccupation with 'hermaphrodite ideals sugaests that femininity in any sort of excess was unsatisfactory'[47] accounts, in large measure, for its attraction to Powys. Given his aversions and proclivities, the androgynous images cited above, together with such others as Goethe's Mignon, Pater's Winckelmann and even Hardy's Sue Bridehead must have provided a welcome and seductive confirmation of his own sexual, imaginative and creative impulse.

The images of the androgyne in Powys's work indicate that he was influenced by both literary and visual manifestations of the theme. In addition to Leonardo's *St John the Baptist*, he doubtless saw Araldi's *Virgins and Saints* at the Louvre, both works of marked sexual ambiguity. Arthur Symons and A. J. L. Busst both draw attention to Huysman's appreciation of *Virgins and Saints* (which he wrongly attributed to Bianchi), noting the emphasis Huysmans placed on the painting's androgynous character as central to its appeal.[48] Another work Powys must have seen in Paris was Chénavard's *Divinia Tragedia* at the Musée du Luxembourg, a painting which, as Busst points out,

> is dominated by the figure which the catalogue describes as: 'l'eternelle androgyne, symbole de l'harmonie des deux natures ou principes contraires' ... indicated not only by its prominent position in the top left-hand corner, but also by the fact that, among all the gods and goddesses of the world, this person alone is given a sort of halo.[49]

And it is likely that amongst nineteenth-century images of the androgyne, Powys will have seen, in addition to Pre-Raphaelite versions, some outstanding examples in the art of Moreau and Solomon. The blurring of the sexes in Solomon's art, what Swinburne called 'a supersexual beauty',[50] corresponds closely to androgyne images in Powys's work, particularly in a certain moral ambiguity; as Swinburne put it, 'it is often hard to say — hard often to make sure whether the look of loveliest features be the look of a cruel or a pitiful soul.'[51] The suggestive qualities of Solomon's art and its ambiguous fusing of the perverse, the abnormal and the cruel with 'infinite tenderness, ... sad illimitable pity ... sweetness'[52] bear a marked resemblance to the presentation of such Powys androgynes as Philippa, Persephone and Thuella. Symons wrote of a 'queer, orchid-like colour and exotic and enigmatical expressiveness' in such Solomon paintings as *Lady in the Chinese Dress* and the 'morbid delicacy' of, for example, *The Sleepers and the One that Waketh*, a quality that immediately recalls Philippa's nocturnal ecstasy, so like, in its morbidly perverse nature, Solomon's painting, described here by Symons:

> Three faces, faint with languor, two with closed eyes and the other with eyes wearily open, lean together, cheek on cheek, between white, sharp-edged stars in a background of dim sky. These faces, with their spectral pallor ... are full of morbid delicacy.[53]

In substituting the three figures of Solomon's painting with those of Philippa, Brand and the complicitous trees, one finds a striking literary parallel in terms of morbid suggestiveness and unnamed perversion.

The art of Moreau is evoked, too, by Powys's response to Wilde's *Salome*, noted earlier. The 'smoulderingly sensual', exotically per-fumed world of Wilde's drama found visual expression not only in Beardsley's designs, but in such Moreau paintings as *Salome Dancing Before Herod* and *The Apparition*, both heavily suggestive with what Huysmans called 'l'impression de l'onanisme spirituel'.[54] Symons described Moreau's painting as 'sexless and yearning', rendering 'the legends of sex with a kind of impotent allurement',[55] underpinned by the androgynous images of, for example, the head of St John the Baptist in *The Apparition*, or the figure of

> the hermaphrodite or eunuch who stands sabre in hand at the foot of the throne, a terrifying creature, veiled as far as the eyes

and with its sexless dugs hanging like gourds under its orange-
striped tunic[56]

in *Salome Dancing Before Herod*. Such figures were central to Powys's
androgynous representations and indicate a correspondence with
visual examples, pointing to shared preoccupations, impulses towards
perversion, and suggestive overtones.

Certainly, in Powys's fiction there is much evidence of visual, as well
as literary influences. Gladys Romer's Grecian knot and bronze circlet
(W & S, 237, 240), for example, resemble, as does her youthful, Grecian
appearance, the 'small Greek head with plaited coils of dark-brown
hair'so enchanting in Sibyl Vane's portrayal of Juliet in Wilde's *The
Picture of Dorian Gray* (1891). Both images recall Powys's description
of his 'ideal sylph', a show girl he once saw, 'like the lovely figure on a
Grecian urn'.[57] And all represent, too, images of perfection through
distance, typical of the appeal of the androgyne. Thus, Gladys is seen
as closest to perfection when posing, in costume-disguise, for a
painting. Sibyl, whose name is not without significance, represents an
ideal when, in costume-disguise, she acts on stage, and the 'ideal sylph'
manifests her ideal charms in the role of 'supernumerary ornament'
who 'did nothing during the whole performance but simply stand
there'.[58] Both Powys and Wilde stress the androgynous charms of
their characters (it is significant that Sibyl is especially charming when
playing Rosalind: 'in her boy's clothes she was perfectly wonderful'[59]), both require an idealizing distance: a stage or an artist's couch,
from where they might, with perfect safety, admire or, as Dorian Gray
puts it, place their ideal incarnation on 'a pedestal of gold'.[60]

The importance of Greek and Italian art in evoking androgynous
images is an interesting aspect of Powys's work. We see it, for instance,
in his use of water lilies (see, for example, *Maiden Castle*, 310, 417) to
denote androgyny, a symbol found in the paintings of Leonardo da
Vinci. We have seen it in his response to Leonardo's 'strange faces of
women full of dim doubt and faint scorn'.[61] And it points, above all, to
Pater's influence. Powys was particularly responsive to, for example,
Pater's 'A Study of Dionysus' in *Greek Studies*, writing of his 'memory
of Pater's bleeding, wounded, naked, flagellated Dionysus so oriental

and so soft and so much in women's clothes',[62] and taking from Pater's 'nympholepti' the cue for his own nympholeptism. And as Pater's Persephone's descent into Hades inspired Powys's Persephone Spear in her underworld seduction, so was Philippa Renshaw's 'boyish outlines' and 'ambiguous loveliness' inspired by 'those androgynous forms of later Greek art' (Rod, 49) which Pater evoked as images of an ideal, sexless beauty.

Powys frequently sought to establish a link between his androgynous images and early Italian art, a connection not limited to his fiction. Frances Gregg, a young epicene with whom he was much in love, was tantalisingly attractive in boy's clothes on a visit to Italy in 1912, 'a regular Mona Lisa':[63] 'Such a curious smile, at once mocking, tender, reproachful, derisive, contemptuous, and wistful, crosses her mouth — you know her mouth?'[64] And the thought of the poet Shelley evokes a similar image: 'His beautiful epicene face, his boyish figure, his unearthly sensitiveness, haunt us ... They allure and baffle us, as the smile on the lips of the Mona Lisa',[65] as does Dostoievsky's Alyosha, who

> makes me think of Walter Pater's 'Diapheneite', and of those strangely guileless and spiritually incorruptible figures of Raphael who look, in their inherent purity, so immune to all obsessions from the underworld of our nerves! [66]

In his fiction, Italian art is something of a unifying motif in the depiction of the androgyne. In *Wood and Stone*, Dangelis seeks to establish a correspondence between his portrayal of Gladys and 'the creations of Venetian colourists' (W & S, 132). In *After My Fashion*, Nelly, 'but for her English dress', resembles 'some early Florentine's conception of Psyche waiting for her invisible lover' (AF, 32), the reference here to the myth of Eros and Psyche heightening the androgyne theme, and Canyot's model, 'a handsome girl from Siena', typifies that particularly Italian combination of 'a certain glowing and yet chaste voluptuousness' (AF, 197), here recalling Veronese. It is a visual motif that Powys develops throughout his fiction, enriching the image with pictorially suggestive points of reference.

In *Wolf Solent*, Christie's 'slight and sexless' figure, her 'smoothly-parted hair' and 'quaint, pointed chin' not only evoke the 'androgynous forms' (WS, 83) of early Italian art; her and Wolf's words and actions in the 'seduction' scene are themselves translated into pictorial enactment, as John Brebner has pointed out. Our impressions, he suggests, are 'guided by a *pastiche* of words which seem to transmute the human lineaments of this episode into the sacred figures of medieval or renaissance art.'[67] In *Maiden Castle*, Thuella is seen in the dawn light to resemble 'one of the coldly beautiful inhuman angels who used to prop up the austere Madonna' (MC, 478). She not only looks like an image from Italian art, her own painting recalls 'the lineaments of Pico della Mirandola' (MC, 417). In *A Glastonbury Romance*, too, Persephone's 'slender hips and the waist like that torso' (GR, 673) are shown to bring to mind an example of Italian sculpture. In such ways, the image of the androgyne is given a pictorial and art historical context from which it derives an impression of permanence and continuity as an ideal of mystical and erotic suggestion.

Returning to more contemporary, and Decadent, visual images to which Powys responded, we can find in the work of Aubrey Beardsley an important link with the androgyne. Powys and Beardsley had, curiously, a certain amount in common. Both were highly literary and well-read, both endured poor health, both were fascinated by sexual perversion and the abnormal, and both tended to direct their art towards an exploration, intensification and elaboration of one essential theme, of which the search for a Platonic ideal, in its androgynous form, was a central motive force. Powys knew Beardsley's art well, he mentions such work as his illustrations for Malory and for Pope's *The Rape of the Lock* (Rod, 125), and even wrote an essay on him for *Suspended Judgments* which was, rather mysteriously, withdrawn before publication.[68] The outstanding example of Beardsley's impact on Powys is to be found in the androgynous vision which appears before Sorio in *Rodmoor*:

> I seemed to see a living human figure outline itself against the wall of my room … It was a human form … but it was unlike all human forms I've ever beheld—unless it be one of those weird drawings … of Aubrey Beardsley. It was neither the form of a

boy nor of a girl, and yet it had the nature of both. It gazed at me with a fixed sorrowful stare, and I felt that I had known it before, somewhere, far off, and long ago. It was the very embodiment of tragic supplication, and yet, in the look it fixed on me, there was a cold, merciless mockery.

It was the kind of form ... that one can imagine wandering in vain helplessness down all the years of human history, seeking amid the dreams of all the great, perverse artists of the world for the incarnation it has been denied by the will of God ...

... I know what I thought of then. I thought of that 'Secret Rose Garden' where the timid boy-girl thing — you know the picture I mean ... is led forth by some wanton lamp bearer between rose branches that are less soft than her defenceless sides. (Rod, 18)

The reference here is surely to *The Mysterious Rose Garden*, an ink (over pencil) drawing of 1894. Contained in this vision are all the qualities, so carefully delineated by Pater in his 'Leonardo da Vinci', embraced by the eternal androgyne: the 'sorrowful stare', the expression at once tragic and mocking, the embodiment of artistic striving, a centuries' old dream, 'expressive of what in the ways of a thousand years men had come to desire'.[69]

It is interesting to note the way in which Powys superimposes, as it were, a specific visual image from Beardsley on to a literary experience. Immediately prior to the appearance of the vision, Sorio reads de Gourmont's *Le Livre des Litanies*, picking out the 'Litany of the Rose' for special emphasis:

Rose au regard saphique, plus pâle que les lys, rose au regard saphique, offre-nous le parfum de ton illusoire virginité, fleur hypocrite, fleur de silence. (Rod, 17)

The vision emerges from these lines as if the words themselves take physical shape in an imaginary transmutation. The figure itself, importantly, enshrines the typically androgynous connotations of good and evil representing, as it does, a figurative amalgamation of Sorio's son, Baptiste, a 'boy-girl' 'angel' and Philippa Renshaw, a 'girl-boy' devil.

41

De Gourmont's 'Litany of the Rose' had an especial attraction for Powys, who warmed to its 'strange, ambiguous, sinister, and lovely appeal, the full appreciation of which is an initiation into all the "enclosed gardens" of the world'.[70] It was an attraction paralleled closely in Beardsley's art, to which Powys seems to have been, perhaps against his will, irresistibly drawn. Verlaine's poetry, too, made Powys think of Beardsley, inspired here by 'Fantoches' in Fêtes Galantes, which he thought 'worthy of an illustration by Aubrey Beardsley.'[71]

Much has been written[72] on the role of the androgyne in art and literature, particularly in its late nineteenth-century manifestations. Its significance to Powys was, as I have tried to show, wide-ranging and central to his work and thought. It marks his fascination with the *demi-monde*, with idealized waifs and prostitutes, and with the margins of life,[73] particularly sexual life, an ambiguous underworld of marginalised experience and desire:

> You see, quite apart from being 67, all my dangerous temptations are those of THE EDGE, — the brink, the margin, the fringe … I have always been a VOYEUR, a cerebralist, a wicked-imaginer; and my real vice (I mean the one that makes my knees knock together) is SADISM, but sadism of the edge, the verge, the border, the fringe, the brink.[74]

The image of the androgyne in Powys's work is also, as suggested, a response to physical fastidiousness and sexual revulsions. It is perhaps significant, in this respect, that Pater claimed that 'the way to perfection is through a series of disgusts':[75] a theory particularly suited to Powys's sensibilities. The sexless, epicene charms of the androgyne can be seen as a unique and satisfying antidote to 'ordinary women', who, as Dorian Gray says, 'never appeal to ones imagination',[76] and to motherly, domineering and aggressively-female women, frequently depicted in the fiction, of whom Mrs Solent is a prime example. Such women were, it seems, with a mixture of admiration, fear and awe, not only a source of physical revulsion in Powys, but also seen through their sexual demands and procreative instincts, to maim and disable male freedom, spirituality and 'life-illusion'. It is a fear echoed in certain Burne-Jones paintings, most notably *Demophoon* (1870) and

The Depths of the Sea (1887). 'Normal' women, then, were destructive, ruled by 'possessive instinct' (MC, 225) or worse, just as 'normal' sex was equated with entrapment, a premise informing such relationships as that of Rook and Ann in *Ducdame* and Wolf and Gerda in *Wolf Solent*, amongst others, or with instant frigidity: 'The merest approach to normal sex behaviour quelled my excited desire like blocks of ice, froze it dead, like that cold water that my nurse used to throw over me'.[77]

Ignoring the probable culpability of the nurse in dashing any hope of 'normal' sexual development, we can find in the image of the androgyne a symbol of 'abnormal' sex uniquely able to embody the idea of parthenogenesis, which Powys found attractive in two ways. On the one hand it circumvented, so to speak, what Powys regarded as the horrors of consummation and paternity:

> 'There's something grotesque ... about the relation of father and son. It's outside nature.' For a moment he struggled desperately to find a rational defence for his loathing of the process of generation.
>
> '*Parthenogenesis* is the natural thing! That's why the act of love is monstrous and ridiculous. Lust isn't comic. Lust is grave and sacred. And there's nothing but poetry in conception. It's the act of paternity that's so horribly humorous. Monstrous and comic. That's what it is. An interference with the beautiful processes of parthenogenesis.' (MC, 174)

On the other, it codified what Brebner has described as Powys's term for the 'sex-imagination relationship',[78] a relationship which he saw as a potent creative force. Unfulfilled desire and sexual fantasy, of which the androgyne is the supreme symbol, were to Powys a major source of imaginative and creative power. What Busst has called 'cerebral lechery' thus endowed androgyne images with potent spiritual and creative powers while at the same time confirming Powys's own cerebral and androgynous sexual impulse and enabling him more readily to reconcile and accommodate the conflicting parts of his nature. 'The truth is,' Coleridge said, 'a great mind must be androgynous'.[79] It was a view echoed by Virginia Woolf when she claimed that 'everyone is partly man and partly woman'[80] and shared by Powys, who constantly identified himself with the poet Teiresias and called himself by every female epithet from 'extremely fussy old woman'[81] to sentimental servant-girl'[82] and 'literary Doll Tearsheet':[83]

> this Punchinello-Proteus, old-Miss-Betsy soul of mine can derive extraordinary pleasure from feeling itself to be a *young girl*. This girlish metempsychosis is the one that I enjoy toying with in my imagination most of all ... I derive a quaint sort of genuine erotic pleasure from turning my withered elderly shanks into girlish limbs ... In my non-human cult for impossibly slender sylphs I resolve myself — like all true contemplative ecstatics — into the element I *contemplate*.[84]

The androgyne was, in addition, a means, as G. Wilson Knight has pointed out, of counteracting the sadistic with the seraphic,[85] a symbol of 'Saturnian' sex that transcended conventional limited and limiting sexual definitions. However visually seductive, the androgyne was thus able to diffuse the sadistic impulse or at least direct it towards the relative safety of the imagination. Such diffusion was important to Powys; he felt it to be a prime responsibility of the artist, and the mark of 'supreme' art, to control and transcend 'destructive' or sadistic energies:

> in a great many quite famous works of art there will be found an element of sadism. But it will always remain that in the supreme works of art this sadistic element has been overcome and transformed by the pressure upon it of the emotion of love.[86]

Thus the sadistic impulse is transcended by love in Powys's poem 'The Ship' where, as Paul Roberts has pointed out,[87] the boy-girl figure is transfigured into the God of Love:

One stood
On the edge of the little pier,
A boy — a boy in his solitude!
A girl — a girl in her fear!
No boy — no girl; a god, a god!

> And I hoisted the sails of my ship;
> And Cruelty, with Love on board,
>   — Your finger on your lip!
> Went sailing, sailing over the sea.[88]

And, perhaps most importantly, as an erotic image associated with and inhabiting a dimly-outlined, ambivalent, suggestive fantasy world, the androgyne was especially close to the imaginative process, so important to Powys. Richard Gaul, in *Weymouth Sands*, speculating on the 'essential mystery of beauty', and its relationship to the imagination, though addressing here wider philosophical considerations, seems, in the 'half-created and half-discovered' realization to suggest the way in which such a 'half-created and half-discovered' figure as the androgyne might embody that 'essential mystery':

> For what was beauty if not a manifestation in the midst of objective reality of something half-created and half-discovered by the craving of our human organism? (W Snds, 99–100)

Particularly alluring, too, in androgynous images was the element of detachment, of the impersonal, so crucial to Powys's erotic sensibilities. Gaul touches on this when he finds

> that he *had* learnt one very serviceable piece of erotic knowledge — namely the important part played in the various stages of lechery by the element of the impersonal. (W Snds, 338)

The attraction of polished limbs, in this case Peg's, arouses a frisson of pleasure only as long as the impulse is voyeuristic and not reciprocated. This sustained preoccupation with 'erotic virginity', with impersonal lust, a kind of masochistic looking and longing, is informed by an overriding desire:

> what I really wanted was not a woman with normal feelings, for such a woman I was dedicated to hurt, but some kind of an Undine or Elemental, entirely devoid of the natural instincts of womankind,[89]

and accounts for the appeal of such androgynous creations as Nelly, in *After My Fashion*, who speaks for all Powys sylphs when she claims:

'I'm awfully detached from my body' (AF, 41). The seductive allure of such epicenes resides, crucially, in such detachment, in the singularly one-way erotic engagement:

> The sight of Peg's polished limbs gleaming so beautifully in that pearl-soft sunshine, when he had first contemplated them had been an intense amorous delight ... full of a delicious tremulous satisfaction, that diffused itself over the whole surface of the shimmering water. But the moment he recognized that the girl knew he was looking at her *in that way*, and that she, too, was deriving pleasure from it, the thing came over him with such over-powering force as to be shaking, agitating, destructive of peace, creative of disturbing desire. (W Snds, 338)

The erotic point, then, of the androgyne is that she is the focus of 'cerebral lust', participating by suggestive presence alone. Fear of consummation, disgust at female and 'normal' sexuality, a need to transfer sexual energy from procreation to artistic creation, as Storm puts it, to have his name 'perpetuated not by children but by poetry' (AF 177), all conspired, in Powys's work and thought, to create in the figure of the androgyne the only endurable sexual incarnation.

Yet the fictional implications of this dependence are far from facile or satisfying. We frequently see the negative and damaging consequences of such a singular eroticism, particularly in the form of a life-denying sterility. It is a theme that permeated Powys's private life, part of 'a desperate insane obsession' in which his

> own subjective definition of the power of sex would always be *vice*, that is to say an abstract impersonal sterile lust, entirely divorced from what is called 'love' and selecting the objects of its desire without regard for either beauty or mental sympathy,[90]

and was reflected again and again in the fiction. In *Maiden Castle*, for example, the theme of sterility is carried in Dud's impotence and Jennie Wye's repressed sexuality, echoing Wolf's fear of consummating his relationship with Christie. To these might be added, amongst

IMAGES OF THE ANDROGYNE IN JOHN COWPER POWYS

many others, the much-emphasised barrenness of Rook's mistress, Netta in *Ducdame*, Sylvanus's dedicated cerebral lechery in *Weymouth Sands* or Dud's extraordinary cerebral love-making, for ten years to a dead wife. Such fictional representations are rarely portrayed as ideal, exemplary or even tenable, but rather as a source of emotional disablement, limiting or damaging potential for any lasting fulfiment, and pointing to a very real tension between physical necessity and emotional peace.

For all its inevitable limitations, however, the androgyne does emerge from Powys's fiction as a vital, indeed the only, erotic solution, the only hope of reconciling the particular assortment of 'manias', 'disgusts' and desires with which he presents us. No other image could so well accommodate erotic desire, impersonal lust, with the need for detachment and non-engagement. It represented, for Powys, the only tenable manifestation of that 'last fine shade'[91] which he so dearly sought.

NOTES

1 John Cowper Powys, *Autobiography* (London: Picador, 1982), 481. (All subsequent citations from this edition.)
2 *Autobiography*, 388.
3 A. J. L. Busst, 'The Image of the Androgyne in the Nineteenth Century', *Romantic Mythologies*, ed. Ian Fletcher (London: Macmillan, 1967), 43. (All subsequent citations from this edition.)
4 Arthur Symons, *From Toulouse-Lautrec to Rodin* (London: Constable, 1929), 181–2. (All subsequent citations from this edition.)
5 Algernon Charles Swinburne, *Poems and Ballads* (First Series) (1866), (London, 1917), 154.
6 John Cowper Powys, *The Meaning of Culture* (London: Village Press, 1972), 73. (All subsequent citations from this edition.)
7 John Cowper Powys, *Suspended Judgments: Essays on Books and Sensations* (London: Village Press,1975), 212. (All subsequent citations from this edition.)
8 John Cowper Powys, *Visions and Revisions: A Book of Literary Devotions* (London: Village Press, 1974), 178. (All subsequent citations from this edition.)
9 *The Meaning of Culture*, 71.
10 Walter Pater, *The Renaissance: Studies in Art and Poetry*, ed. Donald L. Hill (California U. P., 1980), 90–91. (All subsequent citations from this edition.)
11 *The Renaissance*, 93.

[12] *The Renaissance*, 93.

[13] *The Renaissance*, 97.

[14] *The Renaissance*, 176.

[15] John Cowper Powys, *Dorothy M. Richardson* (London: Village Press, 1974), 32.

[16] John Conlon, *Walter Pater and the French Tradition* (Bucknell, 1982), 108.

[17] Walter Pater, 'Diaphaneite', *Miscellaneous Studies* (London: Sphere, 1924), 253.

[18] John Cowper Powys, *Letters to Nicholas Ross* (London: Village Press, 1974), 9. (All subsequent citations from this edition.)

[19] John Cowper Powys, Letters to His Brother Llewelyn, Volume 1, ed. M. Elwin (London: Village Press, 1975), 346.

[20] *Letters to His Brother Llewelyn*, Volume 1, 291–3.

[21] Walter Pater, *The Renaissance*, 99.

[22] *The Renaissance*, 98.

[23] Walter Pater, *Imaginary Portraits* (London, 1914), 60.

[24] See John Brebner, *The Demon Within: A Study of John Cowper Powys's Novels* (London: Chatto, 1973), 64–71. (All subsequent citations from this edition.)

[25] *The Demon Within*, 70.

[26] *From Toulouse-Lautrec to Rodin*, 7.

[27] *Autobiography*, 181.

[28] George Moore, *Confessions of a Young Man* (London, 1888), 40 & 60.

[29] *Visions and Revisions*, 40–41.

[30] Cited by Timothy Hilton, *The Pre-Raphaelites* (London: Constable, 1979), 9.

[31] Derek Sandford, ed., *Pre-Raphaelite Writing* (London: Thames and Hudson, 1973), 38.

[32] Philip Stephan, *Paul Verlaine and the Decadence 1882–90* (Manchester U.P., 1974), 130. (All subsequent citations from this edition.)

[33] John Cowper Powys, *Letters to Louis Wilkinson 1935–1956* (London: Village Press, 1974), 93. (All subsequent citations from this edition.)

[34] *The Meaning of Culture*, 121–2.

[35] *Visions and Revisions*, 83–9.

[36] *Visions and Revisions*, 84.

[37] *Powys Notes* (The Powys Society of North America, Fall, 1985). From a presentation given by Peter Powys Grey to the Powys Society of North America during their Inaugural Conference, June 1985.

[38] John Cowper Powys, *One Hundred Best Books* (London: Village Press, 1975), 35. (All subsequent citations from this edition.)

[39] *One Hundred Best Books*, 59.

[40] *From Toulouse-Lautrec to Rodin*, 183–4.

[41] J. F. McDermott & K. B. Taft, eds., 'James Joyce', from 'Modern Fiction', *Sex in the Arts: a symposium*, ch.3. Reprinted in *The Powys Review* 11 (1982/3), 57.

[42] See *Paul Verlaine and the Decadence*, 25.

[43] Powys dedicated his first collection of *Poems* (1896) to Swinburne. And Frederick Davies recalled that during the last two years of his life, Powys would frequently burst into quotation of Swinburne's poetry, in particular 'Sapphics' (from *Poems and Ballads*, 1866), of which he knew several stanzas by heart.

[44] Morse Peckham, *Beyond the Tragic Vision: The Quest for Identity in the Nineteenth Century* (Cambridge U. P., 1981), 315.

45 Ian Fletcher, Assoc. Ed., 'Swinburne's Circle of Desire: A Decadent Theme', *Decadence and the 1890s* (Stratford-upon-Avon Studies 17, London, 1979), 82.

46 'Fragoletta', *Poems and Ballads*.

47 Brian Reade, *Sexual Heretics: Male Homosexuality in English Literature from 1850 to 1900* (London: Routledge Kegan Paul, 1970), 14. (All subsequent citations from this edition.)

48 See *From Toulouse-Lautrec to Rodin*, 95–6, and *Romantic Mythologies*, 52–3.

49 *Romantic Mythologies*, 24

50 Edmund Gosse and Thomas James Wise, eds., *The Complete Works of Algernon Charles Swinburne*, Volume 15 (Bonchurch Edition, 1926), 453. (All subsequent citations from this edition.)

51 *Complete Works of Swinburne*, 456.

52 *Complete Works of Swinburne*, 457.

53 *From Toulouse-Lautrec to Rodin*, 150.

54 J. K. Huysmans, *Certains* (Paris, 1889), 19.

55 *From Toulouse-Lautrec to Rodin*, 163.

56 J. K. Huysmans, *Against Nature (A Rebours)*, trans. Robert Baldick (Harmondsworth: Penguin Books, 1966), 64.

57 *Autobiography*, 242.

58 *Autobiography*, 242.

59 Oscar Wilde, *The Picture of Dorian Gray* (Harmondsworth: Penguin Books, 1966), 87.

60 *The Picture of Dorian Gray*, 89.

61 *Complete Works of Swinburne*, 156–7.

62 *Letters to His Brother Llewelyn*, Volume 2, 225.

63 *Letters to His Brother Llewelyn*, Volume 1, 97.

64 *Letters to His Brother Llewelyn*, Volume 1, 116.

65 *Visions and Revisions*, 135.

66 John Cowper Powys, *The Pleasures of Literature* (London: Cassell, 1938), 98–9.

67 *The Demon Within*, 67.

68 I have been unable to find any trace of this essay or to discover why it was withdrawn.

69 *The Renaissance*, 98.

70 *One Hundred Best Books*, 33.

71 *Suspended Judgments*, 214.

72 See Brian Reade, *Sexual Heretics: Male Homosexuality in English Literature from 1850 to 1900*; Bram Dijkstra, 'The Androgyne in Nineteenth-Century Art and Literature', *Comparative Literature* 26 (1974), 62–73: a discussion of the social motivation behind the resurgence of the ideal of the androgyne, seen mainly as a revolt against bourgeois values; A. J. L. Busst, 'The Image of the Androgyne in the Nineteenth Century', *Romantic Mythologies*, ed. Ian Fletcher: an excellent essay on the androgyne.

73 See Jeremy Hooker, *John Cowper Powys* (Cardiff: University of Wales Press, 1973), 30–31.

74 *Letters to Nicholas Ross*, 17.

75 *The Renaissance*, 81.

76 *The Picture of Dorian Gray*, 60.

77 *Autobiography*, 398.
78 *The Demon Within*, 229.
79 Cited Carolyn G Heilbrun, *Towards Androgyny: Aspects of Male and Female in Literature* (London: Routledge Kegan Paul, 1973), xx.
80 *Towards Androgyny*, 115.
81 *Autobiography*, 274.
82 *Autobiography*, 507.
83 *Letters to Louis Wilkinson*, 142.
84 *Autobiography*, 274–5.
85 See G. Wilson Knight, *The Saturnian Quest* (London: Methuen & Co., 1964), 58–61.
86 John Cowper Powys, *The Complex Vision* (London: Village Press, 1975), 171.
87 In a Paper presented to The Powys Society at a London meeting on 7 December 1985.
88 John Cowper Powys, *Mandragora* (London: Village Press, 1975), 139.
89 *Autobiography*, 602.
90 *Autobiography*, 34.
91 Arthur Symons, 'The Decadent Movement in Literature', *Harper's New Monthly Magazine* (November 1893).

The following editions of John Cowper Powys's novels were used:
Wood and Stone (London: Village Press, 1974).
Rodmoor (London: Macdonald, 1973).
Ducdame (London: Village Press, 1974).
Wolf Solent (Harmondsworth: Penguin Books, 1964).
A Glastonbury Romance (London: Picador, 1975).
Weymouth Sands (London: Picador, 1980).
Maiden Castle (London: Macdonald, 1966).
Owen Glendower (London: Picador, 1978).
After My Fashion (London: Picador, 1980).

MORINE KRISSDÓTTIR

The Diary of a Man who Walks

In August of 1933, when John Cowper Powys was living at Phudd Bottom in up-state New York, a friend asked if she could paint his portrait. Despite his professed loathing for his own image — what he called his 'anti-narcissistic mania' — Powys readily agreed. The sittings did not go well, and finally he told the artist, Gladys Ficke, that

> I look like Faust when he could not bear the sight of the Earth-Spirit he had conjured up.[1]

This chance remark summed up something I had long intuited but had no real evidence for, until recently, when I was given access to all the diaries as well as many unpublished letters. That is this: that Powys, like Faust, was a magician and a word-smith whose triumphant act was to summon up the Earth-Spirit, the Earth Mother — the Creative Being at the Centre of the Universe. And having by his powers of imagination 'conjured her up', Powys walked on, walked away from the terror of the vision.

James Joyce, in his notes for his play, *Exiles*, gives a cryptic gloss on the male protagonists, Richard Rowan and Robert Hand, as rivals and twins, as doubles going in opposite directions.

> Richard — an automystic
> Robert — an automobile

This in turn reminded me of the many myths, legends, traditions which explore the Faustian enigma: the twin desire for the centre and the urge to escape from it. There are multiple variations of this fundamental theme of inversion: the myth of Odin, the Wild Hunt, the Basque fable of the Abbot's dogs, Bergman's film, *The Seventh Seal*. Ludovico Dolce, the sixteenth-century Italian playwright and poet, describes the archetypal scene in *Le Transformationi*. There is a small lake in a clearing in the wood. A man is kneeling motionless before it, gazing at himself in the mirror-like surface of the water. In the woods behind him a hunter with a pack of hounds circles restlessly in pursuit of his prey.

Powys often refers to Demeter, the Mother Goddess, in his diaries. He identifies her with 'static contemplation': the mystical gaze into the mirror-lake in order to see or to seer the self within.

> I took Black over Bridge to those trees by the Red Wohn Bridge Orchard that I particularly like because their trunks end in such nice roots. Below them today the snow had melted. Therefore I kiss the great mother, that Chthonian Demeter whose image in the British Museum is my secret Idolatry and from whom I learn a particular device of contemplation — static — which is important to me.[2]

But that desire to practise static contemplation was countered by an equally strong anti-narcissistic desire *not* to see, an imperative to keep moving, to walk on.

> I thought of Demeter and tried to practise that Contemplation I had prayed to her for in the British Museum. It is funny how restless my mind is and how it seems to require walking ...[3]

The 'centre' has many symbols — the clearing in the wood, the earth spirit, the mystic mother-goddess — but it is also symbolized by 'home', by childhood, and the landscapes of childhood.

Readers of his autobiography are familiar with the details of John Cowper's childhood and his close-knit upper-middle-class Victorian upbringing. Intimately identified with the apparent sense of security and stability was the landscape of that childhood, the west country of England. It is in childhood that the surrounding environment assumes a numinosity, sinks into the memory. Gaston Bachelard uses the term 'felicitous space', and by it he means the affective bond, the emotional feeling-bond between a person and a place.

Much of Powys's best fiction is a celebration of this felicitous landscape of childhood, but in fact, Powys left England, close family ties, childhood places, as quickly as was feasible. He went to America and deliberately chose an itinerant life of circuit lecturing.

In the front of Powys's 1930 Diary there is a printed list of 102 'principal cities' in America. Above the page he has scrawled 'I have been in every one of these places except those crossed out.' Only 21 were crossed out. From 1905 to 1930 he must have given thousands of lectures in these big cities as well as in innumerable small towns from coast to coast. A lecture in a strange hall, questions by strangers without configuration, a supper in an anonymous café with a book for company, a few hours writing in an empty hotel reception hall, a night train caught, a few words with a black porter and sleep. Only to awaken to another hotel in another city and another audience. His life for long periods in America was the archetypal image of solitude and movement. He wrote in his *Autobiography*: 'I see myself … as a sort of vagabond play-actor wandering through the world with a Jew's harp under my Master of Art gown … .'[4]

In many ways constant travel suited something very strong in his character that is not often mentioned by his critics and disciples — his extreme restlessness. His marathon walks tend to be identified with his love of the natural world, a communion with the earth. So in a sense they were, but equally they satisfied a need that was not emotional but physiological. If he did not have a period of fast walking, he would feel as if he were swelling inside. 'I have got that curious sensation of being swollen in my hands & legs & swollen in my head too which I get when I long to walk fast and for a certain distance!'[5]

There is a Giacometti drawing entitled 'L'Homme Qui Marche'. This stick figure is, for me, the essential John Cowper — back hunched, arms held so close to his body as to be part of it, legs and feet grossly elongated and wide apart. The face and eyes are hardly there. The impression is not of a man but of a-man-who-walks.

Powys would walk, even if it brought on intense ulcer pain, as it often did. A self-inflicted wound. Walking or travelling by train, always the on-looker, the voyeur.

> I find the greatest difficulty in really enjoying Nature unless I
> am walking and really walking pretty fast. For then I get my

glimpses quick & take them in <u>imaginatively</u> whereas to contemplate in a static state is to my nature terribly difficult. I am a restless man ... <u>To</u> <u>take</u> <u>life</u> <u>in</u> I prefer to be <u>passing</u> <u>through</u> it like a pilgrim whose real goal is beyond life. There is something that makes the tips of my fingers tickle & gives me actual distress in having to stand or sit for long in the same place. ... I think to read a novel on a train-journey is one of my greatest joys for <u>then</u> the very landscape itself <u>moves</u>; & I read, & then catch a <u>glimpse</u> <u>as</u> <u>I</u> <u>pass</u> <u>by.</u>[6]

This restlessness, this auto-mobility, is a necessity for the exilic personality and I have finally accepted that Powys was the quintessential exile. Exile freed him of his past so that he could recreate his past in his writings. Carlos Fuentes, in his introduction to Arthur Lundqvist's *Journeys in Dream and Imagination* notes that 'displacement is the action of literature, whether this means leaving one's village, ... abandoning the world of the gods..., or finding one's way back home.... In displacement, substitutions between what we were, what we are, and what we hope to be, take place — or rather — take leave.'[7]

The word exile derives from the Latin 'to leap' 'to jump out of'. For Powys there were two kinds of jumps: the leap across a small stream near Weymouth as a child, which he always failed, — which ominously, in memory, he continued to fail, rehearsed his failure — and the 'mean jumps' concocted by his lecture-manager Arnold Shaw, which he never failed, which he successfully made for 25 years. America offered John Cowper an escape from the conventions of his up-bringing; it allowed a tactful separation from an incompatible wife; probably the opportunity to distance himself from this close family clan of the Powyses, about which so much has been said in reverential tones. A chance to prove himself the prophet he was not in his own land, an escape from the centre to the periphery.

In March 1921 he met Phyllis Playter. The unpublished love letters to her chart his growing craving to spend more time writing and less lecturing. He continued his arduous tours during the period from 1923 to 1929 when they lived together in New York City, but by 1930 the success of his first great novel, *Wolf Solent*, liberated him from the necessity of lecturing. In rural up-state New York, Powys bought a cottage he named Phudd Bottom, where he and Phyllis lived until 1934.

Two questions arise from this move. Why, during this period, did he not write about the landscapes, the people, the customs of America that he had observed closely for so many years? He refers to the possibility often enough. He certainly had the material. The oblique answer is contained in an unpublished letter to Dorothy Richardson written 19 January 1930.

> I've lived here for 25 years, lady, did you know that? For a quarter of a century. No one knows the <u>nuances</u> of America better than I do — none as well! But do you think I'll write about it? Sideways I always must — for I must see England like a daydream, a brown study, an onanistic (forgive me) ecstasy.[8]

America, specifically, Phudd Bottom, was a kind of Calypso's isle, a zone of intermediacy in which he could recreate his Ithacan home. I've noted before that everything at Phudd became a substitute for 'elsewhere' and the elsewhere was home — the West Country. Phudd hill looks like Montacute hill, the little stream in front of their cottage reminds him of Weymouth bay. The fact that they were totally dissimilar in reality was irrelevant; they were necessary mediums. The long daily walks recorded in the Diary exposed him to sights, sounds, weather conditions, smells which would trigger in his mind sudden upsurges of childhood memories. He wrote 'In this place … all my past began to be Retrouvé — Le Temps Retrouvé.'[9]

As he was struggling with the writing of *A Glastonbury Romance*, Powys was also re-reading Joyce and Proust — quintessential exiles — for an article on modern fiction.

The critic Walter Benjamin suggests that for Proust, exile created 'not only a new space to exercise one's being but a medium through which to re-imagine one's beginnings.'[10]

'One's beginnings' is both a place and a time. The novels Powys wrote in America are what another exilic writer, Vladimir Nabokov, calls 'the whereabouts and whenabouts of memorial space'.

Nabokov's hero in his novel *Ada* is the psychiatrist Van Veen who writes 'visionary treatises on mental landscapes embedded in the texture of time'.[11]

In the Introduction to the 1961 edition, Powys describes *Wolf Solent* as a 'Book of Nostalgia, written in a foreign country with the pen of a traveller and the ink-blood of his home'.

The second question is, therefore, if Powys was so nostalgic for home why did he not then return in 1930, once he had made enough money in America to be reasonably sure he could henceforth make a living by writing?

There were a number of practical reasons. There always are. But the reason that mattered was that for some artists, exile frees the imagination: time and distance are necessary to actuate it. Joyce, Nabokov, Dante, Proust, are more at home in the remembered spaces of their works than in their homelands. Writing of the desire for home becomes a surrogate for home; the onanistic daydream of England indeed.

This is the significance of Powys's self-imposed exile to America. It allowed him to recreate a place from which time had barred him, but into which the sovereign imagination could force re-entry. But in another sense he is not desiring a return to the landscape of his real childhood, but the landscape of his imagined childhood. So instead of 'going home', he wrote in America some of his finest books that evoke in obsessive detail, all the sights, sound, smells of the England of his childhood: *A Glastonbury Romance*, *Weymouth Sands*, and *Autobiography*.

When Geard, the Glastonbury magician, drowns in the flood, his last image is of Montacute: 'He was lying in the green spring grass of the Park at Montacute; and an incarnate Sweetness that was his daughter and yet not his daughter was running to meet him with outstretched arms.'[12]

The Landscape of Childhood — Es ist ein Land Verloren. Or in Geoffrey Hill's poem:[13]

> There is a land called Lost
> at peace inside our heads.

Unfortunately, this lost land, when found and retrieved, is never at peace. The very imagination that allows the outsider, the voyeur-exile, to recreate the lost paradise of childhood, insists on identifying it also with the mother — with Demeter and her daughter Persephone, identifying it with the underworld, with drowning in that mirror lake.

So to the adult exile that maternal landscape has great ambivalence, great tension. I go back again and again to his novel *Weymouth Sands* because it sets up so magnificently the ambiguity of Powys's mystical search for the lost centre, the lost feminine half.

Weymouth was for Powys a concentrated symbol of the Golden Age as a child might know it. It was inextricably bound up with his ecstasies, 'the ravishing transports of happiness' as a small boy. Now superimposed on that world of glinting summer sunlight are the perceptions of a benighted adult. The two voices are magnificently caught in the final chapter entitled 'Lost and Found'. The Powys-hero, Magnus Muir, is clambering over the sea-rocks of Portland until:

> ... until, feeling exhausted, he sank down on a rough lime-stone slab, over-grown with sharp indented rock-shells and gazed into a rock pool.... Here in this enchanted fissure, he could see purple and amber-coloured sea-anemones, their living, waving antennae-like tendrils swaying gently, as the tide swell took them. And tiny, greenish fish with sharply extended dorsal fins darted to and fro across the waving petals of those plants that were more than plants! But it was at the motionless shells at the bottom that he now gazed with his strongest sense of the past. ... he could see one involved mother-of-pearl shell, with a tiny seaweed actually growing from its surface.
>
> Suddenly ... against his will the shell-like radiance of his lost girl's flesh and blood, that incredible transparency her face used sometimes to assume, shot through his senses like an arrow, an arrow of sea-pearl!
>
> Up he sprang and fleeing desperately from those rocks, as a lost soul might fly from an oasis in its perdition where the memories cut its feet, he made his way across Chesil, across the road, across the railway, till he came to the shallow mud-flats of

the Fleet Backwater.... Across this Waste Land drifted the stricken man....[14]

The lost soul flees from the rock pool, the reflecting lake, flees from the centre to the circumference, flees to the sovereignty of exile. The cursed hunter — perdu — escapes to the periphery, to the waste land which has no memories to hurt him. But he cannot stay there.

★ ★ ★ ★

The hunter-exile's perspective is from the outside looking in. He is the Jamesian small boy with his nose pressed against the glass of the sweet-shop, the Kafkaian child banished by his father from the bedroom to the balcony because he is whimpering for water. These are the anxious memories of the exile witnessing an inside action from the outside. Thus the hunter will flee, but he is drawn back inexorably from the outside to the inside, the voyeur wanting desperately to become the clair-voyeur. The auto-mobile becomes, once again, the auto-mystic. The hunter's double, his twin, is the man who kneels by a still lake in the centre of the forest gazing into the mirrored surface of the water, willing entry into the shadow reflection of the feminine within.

The cycle begins again. The place from which the cursed hunter is exiled is the place of origin: *die Erde, die Begrundung*. But often the ground, so to speak, gives way. Whimpering for water in the waste land, the Grail-searcher is in danger of finding it and being sucked down into the water, drowning in the black unconscious. The only way of out-foxing the black-out is to run away. The obverse of the anxiety of the outsider-voyeur desiring to get *in*, to merge with his feminine shadow-soul, is the relief of the exiled hunter in getting *out*. Back and forth, back and forth from centre to circumference, circumference to centre; the beat of the pattern is relentless, remorseless.

★ ★ ★ ★

By the time Powys was writing his great Wessex novels, his *Bild* of childhood and its landscape was bound up not only with his life-long worship of Nature, but of the earth-spirit: the feminine self which he so assiduously cultivated.

Like Faust, he 'built his inward world ... intent on rising to the level of spirits'. The earth spirit answers Faust's call with the words: 'I have felt a mighty pull from you, you have long been sucking at my sphere'. Faust averts his face: 'Schreckliches Gesicht': 'Terrifying Vision'.[15]

For Powys too, She would often become a terror. He writes in the *Autobiography* that between the ages of 21 and 30

> Everything I looked at in Nature ... presented itself to me as a repetition of the feminineness of [his dog] Thora! ... I loathed the thought that so many of the trees and the flowers possessed feminine organs. The thing went so far with me that I became panic-stricken lest I myself should develop feminine breasts ... I began to feel as if there were no longer any real solidity left in Nature, as if, whichever way I turned, the firm substance of the earth would 'go in'.[16]

The impression carefully left by the *Autobiography* is that this 'mania' was an isolated phase in his earlier life and that later, Nature once again was the loving Mother. But now that we have the diaries available we see that this phobia of being sucked in, absorbed, of becoming feminine, continued all his life. Years later, with another dog (this time male) he makes even clearer the complex connection between anti-narcissism and looking at self; the shadow reflected in the lake and the horror of black-out; of feminine breasts and of walking away.

> I went to Grouse-Gate where I roused a grouse. Here I <u>leant</u> on gate & looked at the green path, at the railings and chicken-wire & at the little larches. Here I <u>forced</u> myself to contemplate Nature.... And coming home I <u>forced</u> myself to enjoy the sun in my bones & with my knees and hands & skull like a gorilla. And I forced myself to enjoy my own <u>Shadow</u>. This forcing myself to enjoy my own shadow and to <u>lean motionless</u> on gate meant of course that I was flouting & defying my Anti-Narcissistic Mania according to which I run

away oh so quick & always <u>from</u> <u>myself</u>. Thus — <u>as</u> I <u>knew</u> <u>would</u> <u>happen</u> — tho' <u>I</u> <u>foxed</u> <u>the</u> <u>blackout</u> — yet there remained even <u>in</u> the <u>black-out</u>, those queer nervous and quite <u>mad</u> physical-psychic feelings of all my pulses beating & a sort of swelling of interior Breasts![17]

The link between biography and art is a vexed one and I will not attempt here to make a connection between Mother Nature, real mothers or fictive mothers. Powys, when he came to write his *Autobiography* also avoided it. He wrote in his diary on August 15th 1933: 'I have decided to begin on this lovely day — the Day of the Assumption — my *Autobiography*. In that Assumption of the Mother of God — all Women "who lead us Upward & On", as it says at the end of Faust, call to us from some Heavenly Dimension & thus it will not be necessary for me to mention one single of them in my *Autobiography*.'

This line of reasoning is what one of my students called 'a far-out sequitur'. I call it walking away.

However, it is interesting that while he says that the Mother calls from some Heavenly Dimension, often enough in his novels the love of mothers for their sons is not beneficent, but possessive. They hold the hero to themselves, to their centre, when he is seeking the freedom of the periphery. In the Wessex novels this mother–son relationship is rather menacing but controlled. In his later novels, when so much pours out, the imagery of the possessive human mother is directly linked with devouring sexual animal nature.

In the novel *The Inmates*, the hero, John Hush, becomes obsessed by Nancy Yew's possessive love for her half-witted son.

> He couldn't expel from his consciousness that possessive, in-drawing, in-sucking, maternal eye of the mother of Seth ... that eye wherein this much-praised 'love' could be observed, in the serpentine coils of its devouring insatiability, swallowing its offspring's freedom to live a life of its own and exciting itself to swallow the more voluptuously as its own pity for the helpless thing's struggles draws forth more maternal saliva to smooth the path of its re-enwombing.[18]

John the author has the mother killed by falling from a height onto a sharp-edged stanchion. I have always thought of this fictionally unnecessary death, this gratuitous sadism, as the product of a semi-senile imagination. Then I read the 1930 diary and came across the following passage about John's sister Marian and her son Peter:

> Marian's devotion to Peter is an infatuation. It always makes me tremble & shiver with dread. These desperate and passionate loves of mothers for only sons…. One feels that if a mother and son are absorbed in each other like two lovers it doesn't matter what the outside world feels.[19]

Obviously the dismembered was remembered, obsessively, for more than 20 years. Or perhaps he was not thinking of his sister and her son at all but of another mother and her son.

★ ★ ★ ★

Why did Powys leave Phudd Bottom, where the constraints on his imagination were so creatively released? The diaries make it very clear that Powys loved Phudd Bottom. It was a necessary 'elsewhere'. Nonetheless, just as JCP was driven to America thirty years before, something now drove him back to England. There were practical reasons for leaving but the two reasons which I should like to discuss have little to do with practicalities. They have to do with his creative, imaginative life and his myth of himself as the onlooker, the exile.

It is surely significant that the book which Powys read and reread throughout his long life was Homer's *Odyssey*. He once wrote that he read it daily as a breviary. Powys knew his *Odyssey* at least as well as James Joyce did. So he understood the spatial frame of an exile's story, which is from centre to periphery and return. The myth of exile is in fact the myth of exile *and* return.

I am reminded of Samuel Beckett's novel *Molloy*. Molloy, in his search for his lost mother, moves away from his mother's room. He finds himself in a forest (or more precisely, like Powys, on the edge of the forest). He is in exile but he is free. However, he cannot stay there. Indeed he feels he is not 'free' to do so; that to stay is to go 'against an imperative'.[20] Interestingly, Powys also uses the word 'imperative' in

61

a diary entry for January 16th 1934, as he argues with himself about leaving America.

> As I stood down by the Alders River beyond Spinney on which the sun shone so strong as it rushed so black and glittering between its snow-banks there came over me another Inspiration or rather a powerful Impulse a Magnetic Imperative towards my Book about Merlin and Taliessin & Ceridwen & Welsh Mythology.

The second reason for leaving America is perhaps a little more difficult. In the extensive literature of exile in the western world, exile from the homeland is almost always associated with physical pain. In Paradiso XVII of the *Commedia*, Dante wails 'You shall leave everything you love most dearly; and this is the arrow which the bow of exile shoots first.'

Magicianship played an essential role in the Powys myth as his novels, letters, and diaries amply attest. It meant many things, but it was, at least in the beginning, an arduous exercise in control, of not drowning in the feminine self or other. Gradually it became at Phudd a qualified submission to pain in order to become a seer.

I have discussed in the introduction to *Petrushka and the Dancer* the relationship between pain, creativity, magicianship and sovereignty. I believe that Phudd was the place of exile where learning through, or in spite of, pain occurred. It was at Phudd that he truly learned to be a magician. Although he would often tell this story of learning in a semi-humorous way, his struggles with the gods of Phudd were intentional echoes of the heroic battles of Odin or Merlin to win wisdom.

The wounding bow of exile: Sophocles's late play *Philoctetes* is the myth of the hero with an incurable wound. In the case of Philoctetes it was an ulcerous heel, in the case of Powys it was an ulcerated gut. The Greek hero was on his way to fight Troy with the magic bow given him by Heracles, when, while making a sacrifice to the goddess, he is bitten in the heel by a snake. The wound makes him a non-hero. He is abandoned by his companions and spends 10 years in a cave on an island. The wound never heals: the ulcer comes and goes. In a significant image, Philocetes says of the bursting ulcer — linking pain and exile, coming home and leaving again; pain and the female wound: 'She comes home again from time to time as if she were fed up with her wanderings.' Then, as the pain passes, 'The grief of my wounds leaves off.'[21]

In André Gide's variation of the story, Philoctetes becomes convinced that his exile on the island, while full of pain, has enabled him to perfect himself. He says: 'I have come to know more of the secrets of life than my masters ever revealed to me. And I took to telling the story of my sufferings, and if a phrase was very beautiful, I was by it so much consoled; I even sometimes forgot my sadness by uttering it.'

With Gide we come close to a further implication: the idea that genius and disease, like strength and mutilation, may be inextricably bound up together. (Less seriously, we may have stumbled on the reason for Powys's extraordinarily long novels.)

By the time Powys left Phudd, he truly believed he had gained magical powers and that these powers had given him the sovereignty of words, independence from the Mother. He could go back to the centre without the danger of being swallowed. Phudd was no longer necessary and he left as abruptly as he had come.

He and his companion, Phyllis Playter, returned to England in June 1934, staying firstly at Rat's Barn, Chaldon, to be near his brothers Llewelyn and Theodore, and his sisters Gertrude and Katie, before moving permanently to Wales in July 1935.

They could so easily have stayed on in Dorset, and indeed, were pressed by circumstances and his family to settle there. Phyllis loved Weymouth and was comfortable in Dorchester, Powys had happily begun a new book, it was the very landscape of his lost childhood. The return should have worked, but in fact failed miserably; it was a devastating, even destructive year. As James Joyce noted, 'a nation exacts a penance from those who dared to leave her, payable on their return.'[22]

Henry James was one of John Cowper's and Phyllis's favourite authors and it is probably not a coincidence that they read several of his novels during their four month stay at Rat's Barn. James was another exile who returned 'home' — home in his case being America. There are some interesting parallels in their experience of return.

63

James was nostalgic for his homeland of America and in 1904 left England to spend a year there. Initially he was happily re-united with his brother's family, and a trip to Boston revived old memories, but he finally realized that he now belonged in neither country: 'I saw, moreover,' he wrote, 'that I should be an eternal outsider.'[23]

Powys's Dorset year was spent in the gradual acceptance that he too was an eternal outsider, that the past is always irrecoverable and paradise-land, by definition, 'ist verloren'.

The landscape he returned to was not the landscape of childhood he had recreated in his novels. Instead Powys was confronted by money worries, legal problems, sick and quarrelsome relatives, work-disruptive visits from the post lady, the shepherd, the local colonel, the coalman. In a letter to Richardson he refers to himself as 'a Returned Native' and to 'alien encounter after encounter'.[24] And these aliens could not be ditched by taking the next train, as he had done so often in his land of exile. Nor could Phyllis protect him from these encounters as she had at Phudd, for now she too was an alien.

However, as James wrote in *The American Scene*, it was not all loss. Like Powys, James had just written three major novels in quick succession (the *Ambassadors*, *The Wings of the Dove* and *The Golden Bowl*), and he felt the need of new material. James also believed that the return of the native would release new creativity because he would be returning to familiar boundaries with a fresh inward and outward eye.[25] Presumably Powys too felt that his return from the circumference to what is/was the centre would release a new creativity. It is significant that upon his return to England he began a novel about Maiden Castle (the place he calls in his diary 'my ancestral home') and that he calls his hero, modelled closely on himself, Dud No-man.

As I've noted, Powys knew his *Odyssey*. In Book ix line 366 Odysseus has entered the cave of the man-eating Cyclops. The one-eyed monster asks his name and Odysseus, the wanderer, instead of saying I am Odysseus [Ὀδυσσεύς] says he is Οὖτις — meaning nobody, no man. Just as the naming of names is a mechanism of sovereignty and consciousness, divesting oneself of name, fame, and identity is necessary in the approach to the boundary between self and non-self. By calling himself no-man, Odysseus is allowed past the threshold guardian and crosses the boundary into no-man's land.

This is not the place for an analysis of Powys's novel, *Maiden Castle*, but it could only have been written by an exile struggling with the attraction–repulsion rhythms of an exile's return. In the course of the novel No-man finds his lost father Urien, and in their encounters, Powys explores the exilic themes of wounding, doubling, split-selfhoods, circle and circumference. Moreover, as does Homer, he sets the scene at the junction of the human and the monstrous — the earthwork Maiden Castle. Maiden Castle is a metaphor both for a return to that centre which he has longed for, and the entrance to the otherworld which he fears. Like the cave of the Cyclops it both attracts and repels the wanderer.

In one scene No-man and Urien are walking on the earthwork and Urien articulates the basic premise on which a lost paradise is regained:

> Everything's in the mind. Everything's created and destroyed by the mind.... Don't you feel this whole great fortress ready to shake, shiver, melt, dissolve? Don't you feel that you and I are behind it, making it what it is by the power of our minds? Don't you feel it floating, with all its bright grass, on the dark under-sea of our terrible ——[26]

The human crosses the border of bright grass into the monstrous dark sea. Urien says of the image that has just been dug up in the excavations — a bull with two human torsos impaled on its horns — '*You've* had, Mr No-man, haven't you, … visions of life that suggest our being impaled on the horns … of darkness?'[27] and discusses the necessity of impalement as a prelude to 'breaking through' to 'take by storm' the Secret that is Life beyond Death.

In the end No-man cannot follow his magician-father. He walks away, just as Odysseus escapes the cave of the Cyclops clinging to the underbelly of a ram.

Powys had great difficulty with this novel. He made several abortive starts on it at Rat's Barn and got on only a little better when they moved to Dorchester. Urien dies mad, and Powys himself became fully aware in the Dorset year that insanity lurks in the confusion of nostalgic and temporally linear worlds. It was not finished until he had 'walked on' once again — this time to Wales where he lived from 1935 until his death in 1963.

Why Wales? His brother Bertie was, quite correctly, irritated by John Cowper's insistence on the 'Welshness' of the Powyses. Certainly there were Welsh ancestors on his father's side, but in truth the blood connection was dilute. Literal truth never gets one very far with John Cowper's motivations.

There were two worlds that constituted his universe of meaning, the world of childhood memories and the world of ancestral memories. While Powys was still at Phudd, he knew that the world of childhood memories had been written through and that he must now confront the other world of which Wales was a symbol.

His first major novelistic confrontation with this world was *Owen Glendower*. Roland Mathias, in an important critical essay, says it is unsuccessful as a novel and speculates why.[28] Mathias suggests that it was a mistake for Powys to choose a political subject; that the places he describes, such as the hill fort of Dinas Bran and Mathrafal are, uncharacteristically, sketchily described; and that the few 'natural effects' he does use are not fully developed. Mathias cites the image of the goosander as an example of the latter.

I refer to this article partly because I want to make the point that the diaries clarify much that has puzzled critics of the past. First of all, it was not Powys but Phyllis who decided he should write about Glendower (15 May, 1935: 'She wants me to write a Romance about Owain Glyndwr'.) She had become concerned that his characters and plots were becoming totally implausible and that to write a novel about a person and a time that had an historical and political reality would give Powys a necessary container. (20 June, 1935: 'She says this present book about Dorchester goes back to *Rodmoor* & is a curving back in a <u>cycle</u> to where I began & <u>not</u> an advance! She says there <u>must</u> be Reality & an interpretation of Reality for a book to be <u>really great</u>.').

Secondly, Powys never attempted to know the landscapes of Wales as he knew the West Country. Dinas Bran and Mathrafal are 'sketchily described' because, as the diaries indicate, Powys only visited them once. Wisely, in his next novel, *Porius*, he situated the action literally in his own backyard at Corwen.

The 'purely visual image' of the sea-bird which Mathias finds unsatisfactory occurs in the chapter 'The Goosander'. Owen stretches his head through a stone slit in the great wall of Harlech Castle and catches sight of 'some great somnolent sea-bird rocking up and down on the illuminated tide' and to Owen's 'moon-drugged fancy the eye of this bird met his own.' The rocking sea-gull and Owen, both solitary, mingle their thoughts.[29]

The image of the sea-bird — Powys calls it both a sea-gull and a goosander — may be 'undeveloped' in the novel but the diary makes it clear how images and memories coalesce in an artist like Powys. In August 27, 1929, Powys was returning by ship from England to America. 'Tuesday, August 27, 1929: Last night out of my porthole thro'; which I stuck my head for a long while I saw the moon not only yellow but orange, no red!' Then on the 1st December, 1934:

> I saw a sea-gull floating on the waves that were the colour of Jade, very beautiful. The T.T. last night burst out against the waves of our sea as compared with those of the American Ocean … she said our waves were like a tiger licking its prey. But this sea gull floating on the sea gave me a passionate inspiration…. Remember the Seagull I shall say to myself.

He had indeed remembered. 10 years later, on July 14th, 1939, he mailed the 'Goosander Chapter' to the typist. But that is not the last of the image. In the next chapter, Powys has Owen decide that he had let his soul be caught in the urge to power and that he should give up the struggle even as victory is in sight:

If I had the will … to let this supreme chance of victory go, it would be proof to me forever that my soul *is* outside my body, and *is* able to be as free as that goosander I saw on the waves![30]

The goosander thus becomes an image of the solitary freedom of Owen's soul. While the diaries are immensely important in tracing the source and meaning of his symbols, Mathias is nonetheless correct in the sense that increasingly many of Powys's images became private, and, like 'emily-coloured hands', incommunicable at an artistic level.

Owen Glendower opens with Rhisiart ab Owen en route to Wales from Oxford where he had been a student. Rhisiart is intent upon seeing the hill-fort of his ancestors, Dinas Bran, and becoming secretary to Owen Glendower. Mathias points out that Rhisiart is like Wolf, in *Wolf Solent*, who departs London as precipitously, for Ramsgard. 'Both ... return to the land of their fathers without their mothers' approval.'

Wales was the landscape of ancestral memory, and the ancestor was paternal. It was the landscape of his father — the father. Mathias suggests that the rough and masculine landscape of Wales never gave Powys 'the degree of sustenance' which he obtained from the Dorset landscape with its rolling curves — Mathias refers to Dorset's 'swelling feminine breasts'. It is true that as soon as Powys was there, so to speak at the circumference of the world, he is longing for the centre, and tries to convert Welsh history and mythology into feminine mysteries. The old ambivalence. But if Powys felt 'deprived' of the dugs of Dorset, there was no obvious reason why he could not have left Wales and returned. He chose to remain.

★ ★ ★ ★

The theme of the 1997 Powys Conference was 'Between Two Worlds'. I thought initially that the two worlds were England and Wales with America between. But I have come to believe that Wales itself was the 'between' — the borderland — a place that allowed Powys continual movement between centre and circumference, 'forever making a double flight'.[31]

I have recently been reading a book by John Murray called *Reiver Blues*.[32] It is set in the early 1990s on the border between Scotland and England. Samuel and Vanessa Beatty live in a Cumbrian pele tower and teach further education on all subjects under the sun on both sides of the border. Sam is also a Sanskrit scholar and Vanessa a Cambridge-trained Arabist. Sam is worried by money problems and by reality impinging on his world of imagination. One day he makes the mistake of buying a *Guardian* and is terribly upset by reading the foreign news about atrocities between Serbs and Albanians, Tutsis and Hutus. He says desperately to his wife, 'the whole of Europe, Africa and Asia is butchering in the name of some bloody Border or the desired borders or the ideal separations or perfect apartheids'. Then he decides he will 'try to feel less of the haunting parallels if I can'. She asks what parallels, and he replies: 'The Border. The Border parallels. Here we are right on the border. We live in England but work in Scotland. Where we live, the farmers … have a very typical North East Cumbrian dialect. They say gan for go and mait for might. Now then, if we move two hundred yards into Roxburgh they say gang and micht just like in the Broons. But all within a minute distance of each other the phonetics change so drastically. Isn't it incredible how two hundred yards can transform a whole world?'

'But it's not so sudden or as dramatic as that' said Vanessa, who was a linguist if not a philologist herself. 'There's a fluxing continuum, a slow gradation, in fact an absence of definite opposites. For example I know a shepherd at Sorbitrees whose mother is English … and whose father is a Scot … He might say 'micht' or 'mait' or even use both in consecutive clauses. The … shepherd is the answer to your conundrum. He *is* the Border, don't you follow? The Border is a fiction, because when you attempt to get there, when you attempt to get to the finest divisions of it, it's precisely like Zeno's Arrow. There is no point at which it is.'

In a sense, Beatty's argument is that of Urien's in *Maiden Castle*. A border is or it isn't; you either break through or you fail to break through. A border is a barrier, like the huge stone in front of the door imprisoning Odysseus in the Cyclop's cave. It is not debatable. His wife's argument is closer to Powys's eventual conclusion: the erection of a boundary does not alter the possibility that there is no boundary.

Dorothy Richardson wrote a long letter to John Cowper Powys on August 15th, 1944, and asks: 'Isn't it time, wouldn't you like, to get back to England? Or do you feel at home in an undiluted Celtic twilight?' He responds to her question in a revealing postcript to a letter dated August 23rd 1944.[33]

> No you see
> I've got a
> a curious mania for
> antiquity in

continuity in one
spot of the
earth's surface
if I can claim with
almost absolutely
certain certainty
a share
   by
blood-heredity
   in
this particular
   continuity
      &
it goes
  back
   to
Total Obscurity
   and
Mythology
  fading
   away
   too
slowly to be
  caught at any
point for certain
   between
reality & unreality
   and
between history
   and
   legend.
This ever receding
   landscape
      &
   mirage
(reality & unreality!)

I can pursue
here
as
nowhere else

Between. Between. This is Powys, pursuing what he knows cannot be caught — caught between. Margins — marginality. Wales was an 'elsewhere' but, as someone has said, an elsewhere is no more possible than a formerly.

What is the between? What is the connection between circumference and centre, between alienation and threshold, between limen and borderland, between schizophrenic non-borders and interlace? I was in Northern Cyprus last spring. There the border is guarded jealously by young soldiers, themselves exiles from their motherland of Turkey, who stand at every cross-road, defending fiercely nothing but the fears of their imagination. As did Powys. As do I. As do we all. Each town in Northern Cyprus has two names — Greek and Turkish, so you can call it whichever one you want. The naming of names. But why stop there? Why not three names, ten names, a name for every solitary individual's imagination. Everything may be transformed into anything else, since nothing is really anything.

Despite his argument that 'two hundred yards can transform a whole world', Beatty in *Reiver Blues* equates the border with himself. He calls the English–Scottish border (it could be the English–Welsh border or the border between mother and father, centre and circumference, reality and unreality) 'debatable lands' and he calls himself 'debatable'.

I doubt if Powys knew finally what was centre and what circumference. Or if they were the same or if he was only using names — singing in the solitude. Not sure if he was the reiver or the reeved — the one who plunders across the border or the one who is severed, divided, cleaved. The reiver bereaved.

And I doubt if I will ever know, despite the many years of slipping across the borders of his mind, whether Powys was a mighty magician or a lost child terrified of 'going in'; mad or on the borderline; a clown or a holy fool; a writer of margins or a marginal writer. It is debatable.

71

NOTES

1 If a quote from Powys's diaries appears in *Petrushka and the Dancer* (M. Krissdóttir; Manchester: Carcanet Press, 1995) the page number will be noted. Otherwise only the date will be given. This quote is from 30 August 1933.

2 Diary, 15 February 1931.

3 Diary, 13 August 1929.

4 *Autobiography* (London: John Lane The Bodley Head, 1934), 368.

5 *Petrushka and the Dancer*, 9.

6 Diary, 8 November, 1934.

7 Arthur Lundkvist, *Journeys in Dream and Imagination* (New York: Four Walls Eight Windows, 1991), 16.

8 Gloria Fromm in her book *Windows on Modernism* (Athens, Georgia: University of Georgia Press, 1995), originally intended to publish 15 of the 20 letters from John Cowper to Dorothy Richardson, which are in the Beinecke Library at Yale University, but editorial decisions and high copyright fees obliged her to omit most of them. I wish to give particular thanks to Harold Fromm who facilitated my use of the letters not published.

9 *Petrushka and the Dancer*, 48.

10 Benjamin. 'The Image of Proust' in *Illuminations*, Harry Zone (New York: Schocken, 1968).

11 *Ada or Ardor: A Family Chronicle* (London: Weidenfeld and Nicholson, 1969).

12 *A Glastonbury Romance* (London: John Lane The Bodley Head, 1933), 1171.

13 'Ave Regina Coelorum' in *Collected Poems* (Harmondsworth: Penguin Books, 1985).

14 *Weymouth Sands* (London: Macdonald, 1963), 551–3.

15 Goethe, *Faust*, I, ll. 483–93.

16 *Autobiography*, 222–3.

17 *Petrushka and the Dancer*, 322–3.

18 *The Inmates* (London: Macdonald, 1952), 199–200.

19 *Petrushka and the Dancer*, 42.

20 *Molloy* (New York: Grove Press, 1955).

21 ll. 757–58:
ἥκει γὰρ αὕτη διὰ χρόνου πλάνοις ἴσως
ὡς ἐξεπλήσθη.
and l. 765:
τὸ πῆμα τοῦτο τῆς νόσου τὸ νῦν παρόν,
Translation by Professor John Bligh, Greek classicist, who pointed out to me that the feminine demonstrative 'this' which begins the phrase refers to the noun wound which is feminine. He also pointed out that the usual translation 'returns' is not accurate; that it is 'she comes home again.' Edmund Wilson has an interesting analysis of this play in *The Wound and the Bow: Seven Studies in Literature* (Cambridge, Mass: Houghton Mifflin, 1941).

22 *Exiles* (London: The New English Library, First Four Square edition, 1962), notes, 150.

23 *The Notebooks of Henry James* (New York: Oxford University Press, 1947), 26.

24 Letter to Dorothy Richardson, 16 November, 1934.

25 Henry James, *The American Scene* (London: Chapman and Hall, 1907).
26 *Maiden Castle* (Cardiff: University of Wales Press, 1990), 241.
27 Ibid., 154.
28 'The Sacrificial Prince', in B. Humfrey (ed.) *Essays on John Cowper Powys* (Cardiff: University of Wales Press, 1972), 233–61.
29 *Owen Glendower*, II (New York: Simon & Schuster, 1949), 645.
30 Ibid., 695.
31 Ibid., 889.
32 *Reiver Blues: A New Border Apocalypse* (Newcastle-upon-Tyne: Flambard Press, 1996), 88ff.
33 Richardson's letter in *Windows on Modernism*, 507–8. JCP's letter unpublished.

CHARLES LOCK

T. F. Powys: Fables and the Silence of the Person

To weep into stones are fables. [1]

No reader of T. F. Powys can fail to be shocked, on occasion, by the horror; and few can fail to be much more shocked by the pleasure that the reader is apparently asked or expected to derive from that horror. In 'Death and its Desires', an essay written in 1933 but published only posthumously in 1987, William Empson writes:

> If one takes [T. F.] Powys simply as providing cultured and tasteful entertainment his [method] is not annoying at all .... [But] if he has tricked you into feeling that he is telling some profound truth about life then I think you need to become angry ... and discover that on the contrary the stuff is nasty. [2]

'Nasty' is an interesting term in the critical vocabulary: in certain cases it can be a term of praise, when applied for examples to the stories of 'Saki' or the novels of Ivy Compton-Burnett. Such writers do indeed offer, in Empson's formulation, 'cultured and tasteful entertainment'. But in writers from whom we expect to learn profound truths about life, nastiness is no longer a term of praise: in Rudyard Kipling, for example, whose late short stories seem to resonate in some of T. F. Powys's work. Reviewing Kipling's *A Diversity of Creatures* (1917), Arthur Waugh wrote of 'Mary Postgate' — now recognized as one of Kipling's greatest stories — that it 'leaves a bad taste in the mouth'.[3] The same could have been said of *Mr. Tasker's Gods* and of any number of stories and episodes characterized in certain circles as 'Theodorean'. Nastiness, we may understand, is redeemable by wit; it remains unpleasant, even threatening, if the narrative voice seems to be telling us profound truths. The conventional distinction between pleasing and instructing is here decisive: nastiness as occasion for cultivated wit and entertainment is acceptable, even admirable; but nastiness as a mode of instruction is distasteful, almost pornographic. It is worth noting that the short story has been the distinctive genre for this aesthetic/ethical equivocation, from Kipling and 'Saki' to V. S. Pritchett and William Trevor; and that in precisely this matter of tone and wit the debt of Flannery O'Connor to T. F. Powys would bear investigation.

T. F. Powys has a way of leading his readers to suppose that he is instructing them, telling some profound truths about weighty themes: life and death, God and the devil, good and evil, time, speech, silence, and death again. Wit is the way, and the way out of portentousness and the distasteful exploitation of nastiness. It could be stated that the failure — to whatever extent — of T. F. Powys is a failure of wit: that is, a failure of the reader to recognize the tonal undercutting of the grand themes. Of course one cannot condemn those readers who find in *Mr. Tasker's Gods* or *Innocent Birds* a brutality and a nastiness somewhat in excess of any redeeming wit. But one can note the similar pattern of reaction to some of Flannery O'Connor's work. Empson's judgment is worth retaining, for it is made in principled opposition to Christian theology: we have every reason to suppose that both T. F. Powys and Flannery O'Connor believed in the evil that they so nastily presented. About 'Saki' or Compton-Burnett one would have no such confidence. It may be that we prefer nastiness to be gratuitous, that we might not only laugh, but laugh it away.

Fables, published in 1929, two years after *Mr. Weston's Good Wine*, may be seen as an explanation, an apology or a reply to the critics of that most successful of all T. F. Powys's works. For *Fables* set out an answer to the critical question provoked by *Mr. Weston's Good Wine*: what is the status of fable or allegory in modern literature, for a contemporary of Joyce or Woolf or Lawrence? In 1931 *Fables* was 're-issued under the curious title of *No Painted Plumage*'4 — curious because the source of what appears to be a quotation had not been identified, and because the title has a purely negative or privative charge. *Fables* is unique in Powys's work as a generic rather than thematic title, and we might suppose that *No Painted Plumage* restores consistency, pointing to some thematic unity in the stories. However, even the revised title refuses to be thematic, but is rather a gloss on the nature of fables: stories which can be dressed up, bitter truths made sweet, stern morals made palatable, adult lessons presented to children. These stories will not be of that kind. They will be fables that self-consciously resist the moral, and the decorative sweetening: anti-fables.

The title comes from Thomas Gray's 'Ode on the Spring' (1742), itself a teasingly paradoxical presentation of a 'moralist':

> Methinks I hear in accents low
> The sportive kind reply:
> Poor moralist! and what art thou?
> A solitary fly!
> Thy joys no glittering female meets,
> No hive hast thou of hoarded sweets,
> No painted plumage to display …[5]

The accusation against the moralist continues for two more lines, and then is suddenly turned back — reversed:

> On hasty wings thy youth is flown;
> The sun is set, thy spring is gone ——
> We frolic, while 'tis May.

The odd sharp switch of the last line comprises both the moralist and the sportive ones among those who frolic: both are flies. And as the title of a book, *No Painted Plumage* has its verbal frolic, its pun on plumage and the pen. Fables and allegories are conventionally thought of in terms of inward and outward, marrow and rind, core and covering, kernel and shell: of a hard moral encased in a soft seductive story. The plumage of these fables is not painted, which is to say that it is hardly plumage at all, for figuratively speaking, all plumage is painted: ornamental, decorative, superfluous, deceptive. These fables are without additional sweeteners, are rendered in all their bitterness. As 'anti-fables' they are about the very nature of fables, of the fabulous, of the didactic.

Both *Fables* and *No Painted Plumage* are titles about the form of the stories within. *No Painted Plumage* is not a thematic title. It is also worth insisting on the exceptional case in T. F. Powys's practice as a writer, that the stories gathered in *Fables* had not previously been published separately in periodicals. The stories here gathered are to be read as one sequence, in one volume, as Kenneth Hopkins remarked: 'from their special nature as fables the book has a unity and cohesion no random gathering of separate tales could have, and it gains by being read straight through....'[6] We shall be considering the value of that unity; only in passing can we muse on the financial cost to T. F. Powys of the volume publication of stories that would surely have been appreciated in magazines, and much better remunerated therein.

It is on the contents page that the distinctive coherence of the volume is made explicit: each title contains 'and' and there are no verbs or adjectives except 'Blind Hen' and 'Holy Crumb'. There is a single exception: 'The Withered Leaf and the Green', the single story involving two similar things, leaves, distinguished only by their attributes. The remaining eighteen titles arouse our curiosity in narrative as well as classificatory terms: what might they have in common, the clout and the pan, the ass and the rabbit, the dog and the lantern, the hat and the post, the bucket and the rope, the corpse and the flea, the spittoon and the slate, the coat and the crow, the hassock and the psalter, the candle and the slow-worm? We can of course see a number of spatial connections between these items, but the temporal or narrative connections are often obscure. Slightly different are the titular collocations one of whose terms is a proper name: Mr. Pim and the Holy Crumb, John Pardy and the Waves, The Stone and Mr. Thomas, John Told and the Worm, Darkness and Nathaniel, Mr. Tapper and the Tree. And one title combines two things as unlike as a raven and a writing-desk: we are baffled by the spatial as well as by the temporal links between the Seaweed and the Cuckoo-Clock. Unlike the Mad Hatter, however, the fable does provide an answer to the riddle implicit in its title.

Traditional fables have titles whose obscurity is dispersed when we consider not the thing but the attribute, not the grasshopper and the ant in themselves, nor the fox and the crow, but the moral qualities or characteristics for which those creatures are known. And with traditional fables we always know already what those attributes are: could there ever have been a naive reader who was mystified by the title 'The Tortoise and the Hare'? The title implies the moral, and the narrative itself merely fills in the details. Powys's fables, by contrast, perplex us by their titles, and offer few morals even at the end, unless we call them immorals.

'Fable' comes from the Latin *fabula*, meaning a simple tale or act of telling. Behind *fabula* is the Greek word *hyponoia*, meaning an under-thought, or hidden thinking, from which one word the two literary concepts of *fable* and *allegory* both derive.[7] To this origin the opening paragraph of the opening fable pays tribute:

> Often the true feelings of human kind are hidden away, tucked into a bottom drawer, pushed under a pile of mouldy letters, or let to lie in an old cast-off shoe.

And the second paragraph explains the method of fables, as they have been told from the time of Aesop, to give voice to the inanimate, to conceal human motivation within non-human stasis:

> But it sometimes happens that the utensils of a house, that have a way of speaking, as every housewife knows — a bowl, maybe, or a flat-iron, or a rusty gimlet left in a corner — know the true state of the case and have a word to say.

Thus the fable is itself fabulized, rendered self-conscious of its own procedures. These fables are not stories told by a human narrator in a disguised, concealed or oblique form, whether in order to evade the censor ('Aesopism' was its name in the Soviet Union) or simply to make the moral memorable or palatable. In the fables of Aesop or La Fontaine we find a clear division: after the animals have acted and spoken, the human narrator speaks, and points the moral, that moral purpose which justifies the narrator's telling of this story.

Powys's *Fables* are subtly different. For that most common device of fables, the attribution of voice and human feelings to animals and inanimate objects, is no longer a code or a crypt by which a direct message can be communicated obliquely or surreptitiously. In the Powysian fable, or anti-fable, the fable speaks without a human narrator; and what the things say is not what any narrator would have supposed things to say, if they had voices and thoughts and feelings. What they say is what humans refuse to say. Or what they say only to themselves, what is to be heard only by the things around them. Inanimate objects absorb words and thoughts which humans dare not utter, and those inanimate objects then take it upon themselves to speak on behalf of humans. In the etymological sense, things become prophetic.

T. F. Powys was of course writing in the bright noonday of Freudianism, and some of those visitors to East Chaldon were closely associated with the circle of Freud's English followers. The narrative conceit of *Fables* is that things themselves speak, and of their own volition, of the feelings and fears and desires which humans repress. The inanimate has been cunningly confused with the unconscious. There is no human narrator to point the moral of the fable, nor any human reason why these things should have spoken. And, conversely, what humans say to each other is, by gloomy implication, false, hypocritical, insincere: only the neglected and rejected things, the meanest household objects learn the true state of the case, and — as 'if these should hold their peace, the stones immediately would cry out' (Luke 19.40) — so when humans are silent or dishonest, things will speak.

We should not, then, assume that the author is asking the reader to believe that each fable will reveal the true state of the case, or that T. F. Powys has privileged access to profound truths about the human condition. Instead we should admire the wit by which the idea of a fable has been subtly modified. No longer a consciously anthropomorphic use of animals and things, the Powysian fable is an allegory of the unconscious, of all those words and feelings which we suppress, are unuttered or — as we say — 'taken out' on things. As Freud taught, whatever is repressed will return, whatever is silenced will find a voice.

The figure of this fable as allegory is *prosopopoeia*, personification, the attribution of voice or feeling or characteristic to a non-person, whether animal, thing or abstraction. Personification operates most simply at a grammatical level, in the distinction registered between 'who' and 'which', as decreed by Partridge: '*which* refers to things only; *that* to things and persons; *who* to persons only.'[8] Partridge goes on to insist that '*that* is not a syntactical synonym of either *which* or *who*. ... The discrimination between *which* and *that* and between *who* and *that* is one of the marks of a stylist.' And T. F. Powys was certainly that.

It may have been noticed that in the opening paragraphs of the first story, 'The Pan and the Clout', there is a *that* where we might expect a *which*: 'the utensils of a house, that have a way of speaking ...' *That* is going to be made to do a great deal of work, relatively speaking, as in the third paragraph:

> Upon a rubbish heap in a corner of a garden that has long since been given up to weeds and to desolation, an old pan dwelt together with a torn dish-clout, that had made its home in the pan in order to protect itself against the wind and the weather. These trusty old household servants were never tired of an argument, and what interested them most were the feelings of mankind one to another.

That is used consistently and repeatedly, not only for stylistic but also for figurative reasons: *that* does not determine whether its antecedent is a thing or a person. The conspicuous absence of *which* or *who* (there is a single *who* on p. 5: 'said the clout, who hated young girls') creates an unsettling sense of fluidity between the animate and the inanimate:

> Mr. Keddle ... [was] still to enjoy the pleasant taste of his breakfast, *that* was followed by a pipe of mild tobacco. As he puffed at his pipe, *that* he always took with his last cup of coffee, he would look in an interested manner at the pot in *which* the porridge had been cooked. (7)

The *thats* here seem contrived: a stylist of Partridge's school would, I think, find it hard to justify the use of *that* rather than *which* in these two sentences. And in the second of these sentences we do find a *which*, one of very few in the entire volume: the word occurs only in those prepositional phrases — *in which, on which, during which, at which* — wherein or in which '*that* is not a syntactical synonym'. And 'the pan *in whom* the porridge had been cooked' would lack all subtlety. Throughout this volume there is not a single instance of *which* being used where *that* is a syntactical synonym.[9]

We should therefore not be surprised to find that the first occurrence of *which* — 'the pan in *which* the porridge had been cooked' — has its figurative and narrative point. For at once the pan interrupts the clout, whose words these have been:

> 'Prithee, friend,' inquired the clout, 'was not the pan you?'
> 'How otherwise, if the pan were not I, could I have told you this tale?'
> 'You might have invented it,' replied the clout curtly.
> 'It would not be proper,' said the pan, 'to prove an argument by fiction.'
> 'It was Plato's way,' remarked the clout.
> 'The more fool he!' cried the pan angrily. (7)

We might take this as merely ironic, the pan unaware of its own role in a fable told by a modern Plato. It is much more interesting to suppose that in this passage, so early in the volume, T. F. Powys's fables are being firmly distinguished from those of Plato or Aesop.

The traditional fable knows what it is about; personification is its figurative mode, instruction and entertainment its purpose. Like allegory and *hyponoia*, a fable depends on a clear knowledge and understanding of what it is that is being spoken about in coded and cryptic terms. In a fable, foxes must exemplify cunning, and wolves ferocity; a fable has no further interest in the specific characteristics of individual animals. A story entitled by paradox 'The Naive Fox' or 'The Gentle Wolf' would have to be a story, or a novel, a narrative explanation of non-conformity to type.[10] Powys's titles puzzle and perplex us because they fail to evoke stereotypical or traditional qualities or attributes. As we have seen, the nineteen titles contain hardly any adjectives, and the nouns seldom have clear or conventional associations or values. We do not associate clouts or pans with anything in particular, and certainly with no moral or didactic role in a fable; presented with *hyponoia*, we have very little guidance as to what is going on 'above'.

In two ways, then, Powys's fables differ from the traditional and canonical exemplars of the genre. The telling of the fable is assumed to be brought about without human agency or purpose, indeed, in spite of human desires to hide and suppress such thoughts and words in the bottom drawer or a cast-off shoe. This we can call the Freudian difference. Secondly, the Powysian fable has no clear moral because we do not have a secure sense of 'the real world' of which the fable is a code. The crypt is the cellar, the underground of hyponoia, a figure of the unconscious. But there is in *Fables* no key, whether to the code or to the crypt. Traditional fables and allegories require that we have a clear sense of the world: that knowledge, of cunning or ferocity, then serves as a key to a story about a wolf or a fox. Code, crypt, oblique, indirect: all these terms depend, as literary devices, on the reader's access to a key, to an open world, to a straightforward manner of representation.

We assume that what is overt, clear and direct can serve as a key for what is hidden, obscure, oblique. But if the unconscious can tell us about the conscious, then the mechanics of the fable must be inverted: it is the process of fabulation itself which can tell us about how the 'real world' is constructed. What if — so Powys's fables ask — the figure of *prosopopoeia* is not just an idle passive ornament or device of story-tellers and moralists, but is itself determinative of human cognition, of our understanding of what it is to be human? That is to ask: what is it to be a person without personification?

The keys are to be looked for not among symbols but among tropes, in, for example, the figure of catachresis, understood as 'dead metaphor'. We can sense the metaphorical verb in the sentence 'an old pan dwelt together with a dish-cloth' but not in 'the clock is sitting on the mantelpiece' or 'the book is lying on the table'. *Sitting* and *lying* are here catachretical verbs; we could introduce catachretical nouns by mentioning the *face* and *hands* of the clock, or the *spine* of the book. Nouns and verbs know of no such firm distinction between the animate and the inanimate as is known to relative pronouns. It is through the inevitable and involuntary trope of catachresis that Powys exposes the pretensions of traditional fable, its unjustifiable assumption that there is a fixed and inviolable distinction — as between *which* and *who* — between humankind and everything else; and that there is a clear and available understanding of the real world that is prior to and quite independent of the figurative representations of fable.

William Empson makes the further point that the narrative and figurative method dissolves the distinction between life and death: 'The Fables use an idea of the rudimentary and corpselike consciousness of all matter ... which allows the state of death to be treated as a humble but profound sort of life, the life most pleasing to God, and a conscious satire on the triviality of the living.'[11] The phrase 'the sort most pleasing to God' may be Empson's sour gloss on Christianity, but it still makes a sound etymological link between humanity, humation and humility (not to mention humour).[12] In 'John Told and the Worm' a rare word is ascribed to the worm: 'I fear I cannot convert you to humilitude.' (155) Death confronts us with the absence of sentience, the dis-animation of the body, the shift from the human to humation: inhumation as a figure of *hyponoia*, mediated by the cryptic. And such a link resists and prevents the swift sudden transition of death, from the person *who* to the corpse *which*: not the polarity of life and death, but a spectrum, a gradation of degradation.

Powys has learnt something from Hardy, whose graveyard poems, 'Channel Firing' or 'Voices from Things Growing in a Churchyard', use the Ovidian device of metamorphosis together with the fabular trope of personification:

> I, these berries of juice and gloss,
>   Sir or Madam,
> Am clean forgotten as Thomas Voss....
>
> The Lady Gertrude, proud, high-bred,
>   Sir or Madam,
> Am I — this laurel that shapes your head;
> Into its veins I have stilly sped,
> And made them of me....
>
> And so these maskers breathe to each
>   Sir or Madam

83

Who lingers there, and their lively speech
Affords an interpreter much to teach....

'These maskers' is a specific gloss on personification, for the early meaning of the Latin word *persona*, and still the sense of the English 'persona', is mask. In Hardy's graveyard all things are masks, and all former persons are maskers: and every inanimate thing can be a mask for an animate 'thing'.

That Hardy sets his variations on the trope of personification within a graveyard is consonant with Theodore's apparent morbidity. In neither writer — if we attend to the figurative — is death the negation of life: rather, death is the wavering porous margin between the animate and the inanimate, not an impermeable border but a space between, a space in which one can figuratively wander back and forth, most simply and inconspicuously by substituting both *which* and *who* for *that*. It requires no great leap to move from that — and *that* — to the notion that it is the inanimate that is truly animated, and that that which we suppose to be animated — persons — are mere puppets in the figurative hands of higher powers. That move is made by Hardy in *The Dynasts*, and is implicit in all of T. F. Powys's work: 'It is much better, I have found, to love a chair than to love a person; there is often more of God in a chair... .'[13] Exemplary is the anecdote told by Sylvia Townsend Warner:

I remember him coming back from one such [nocturnal] walk, but sooner than usual, and looking troubled. 'I heard a noise in the hedge. I said to myself, It's only a rat. But then I thought, Who made that rat?'[14]

Powys modifies the conventions of the fable in two ways. The first — by which the crypt is the key — we have loosely termed Freudian. The second we may think of as tropic: things are personified, and persons, including the narrator, can be figured as puppets. We must not reduce to 'whimsy' these explorations in the trope of personification, whether in Hardy or in John Cowper Powys, whose *A Glastonbury Romance* (1932) contains a thinking corpse and a talking tree.[15] In Theodore's *Fables* we hear in the thoughts and voices of things something altogether more rich and strange than the generic licence of the conventional fable; above all, we are alerted to the extraordinary discrepancy between our linguistic dependence on catachresis and our rational assumption that a rigid distinction exists between the animate and the inanimate.

'The Clout and the Pan' concludes with the pan's account of Mr. Keddle's new situation underground: 'he is happily surrounded by his own gossips — the clods of earth — and he has already addressed a lively centipede as "My brother".' (13–14) The next story plays less with the general instabilities of figurative language than with the extreme and singular metaphor of transubstantiation. John Toole, speaking from underground in the churchyard, asks Mr. Pim, the church clerk, to 'get a word wi' thik crumb of bread that [sic] be the Lord on High....' (20) Of the standard animate form of being, only Mr. Pim is present in church when he hears himself called:

'Mr. Pim!'
The clerk of St. Nicholas looked into the pulpit, he looked down the church aisle, but could see no one.
'Mr. Pim!'
His name was spoken very near to him.
'If thik little crumb be changed into God, mayhap 'tis 'E who do speak,' observed Pim.
'And why not?' said the Holy Crumb; 'surely I have as good a right to speak as any other person.' (22)

The right to speak goes with personification or, in this case, divinization. By contrast, symbolism — of which the doctrine of the Eucharist is the most highly-charged instance — is oddly mute. A thing can 'stand for' a person, or God, or an abstract entity, but that thing in its function as a symbol acquires no right to a voice. We might think of traditional personification as symbolism plus voice; Powys's personifications — unlike Aesop's fox — insist on voice at the expense of symbolism: 'crumb', for example, lacks the symbolic value of 'bread'.

Not only voice is implied by personification, as we learn when Pim asks, on behalf of Toole, that at the Last Judgement God should 'look

85

over' both of them (or overlook, or pass over, or consign them to the Calvinist 'preterite'):

> 'John Toole and I ... do ask Thee to let we two bide in ground at last day.'
> 'But you're not dead yet.'
> 'I do owe God a death,' said the clerk. The Crumb smiled. (23)

To these three words — 'The Crumb smiled' — we must ask two questions. Why? Because the Crumb spots the allusion? How? With the lips, of course, those same lips with which the Crumb has been speaking.

In *Fables* we find exposed, repeatedly and almost systematically, the tricks by which, in spite of the ambiguities, instabilities and vacillations of language, we are still persuaded to maintain the proprieties and respect the fixed borders of rational discourse. Is a fable a fiction? Or do fables not show us that it is 'the real world' that is the fiction that we labour to construct and maintain?

The third story opens with the rhetoric of consensual assumption: 'As every one knows, such a simple thing as a green leaf is born with a voice.' (31) If inanimate things, whether corpses, crumbs or leaves, all potentially have voices, we must question any statement made by one of those things about the finality of death. The Withered Leaf pronounces:

> 'we are mocked by all things, except death, which is the only truth, and therefore, because the truth is the most terrible, it is the most to be avoided.' (36)

Death could be 'the only truth' only if one could not speak in or from death. Theodore's writings play on the tension between death as silence — and silence as the only truth — and the irrelevance of death to personification. And if death is a fundamental or foundational truth, it need not be morbidly so. 'Death' may be 'merely' the name we give to that which makes possible the distinction between the animate and the inanimate, the body and the corpse, the person and personification. Death is the axis of differentiation, the very principle of tropes.

We have already noted that the most teasing, riddling of all the titles in *Fables* is 'The Seaweed and the Cuckoo-Clock'. Miss Hester Gibbs is fascinated by the mysteries of matrimony, yet she is irritated by the lack of difference between most of those pairs so contracted:

> She would wish that far stranger weddings happened in the world than anything that she saw or heard of at Madder. She needed much more than plain Madder life to interest her — some events more like a proceeding that had happened in a book of fables that she had once read, where a little mouse wished to be joined in holy wedlock with a lioness, who, unluckily going out to meet her little dear before the wedding, chanced to set her foot upon him. (43–4)

Hester has made a virtue of dissimilarity:

> 'There is nothing in the least exciting in marrying anything that so much resembles oneself. The natural differences between male and female are but dull matters and hardly worthy of any person's serious attention.' (45–6)
>
> '[W]e must go further, too, than wed a young ewe-lamb to a wolf, for after theconsummation of such a wedding the bride herself would simply become the last dish at the feast. It is also a mistake to do anything so simple — as is the custom in the East — as to marry the well to the bucket, for we must bring odder things together than these, if we have a mind to some fun.' (47–8)

'The Well and the Bucket' is not quite the title of one of these *Fables*, but if it were, it would fit among those whose spatial connections are clear. Unlike such titles as 'The Spittoon and the Slate' or 'The Clout and the Pan', we can see in 'The Well and the Bucket' or (an actual title in *Fables*) 'The Bucket and the Rope' a temporal, narrative link as well as the spatial one. Hester is interested only in marrying two objects lacking both spatial and temporal relations, both contiguity and causality.

After her parents' death Hester Gibbs arranges everything in the house so that 'no two things were placed together that were the least alike'. Only the clock is unmatched:

When she supposed everything was married in her house, Hester had unfortunately forgotten the clock. He had always told the correct time — this was perhaps why she had forgotten him, for had be but stopped or gone fast or slow she would have taken the hint that his heart was troubled. (49)

As long as a clock tells the correct time, keeps time, it can be identified with Time — and what is there that could be least alike to Time? Only when a clock malfunctions, when it fails to keep and to be identified with Time, would it be seen as an object itself, a fragment looking for wholeness. Hester's first candidate as a bride for the clock is a rabbit, her second, a bone found in the churchyard. The rabbit is too early potted, and the bone pleads that her life-long virginity should not be violated in death. Hester goes down to the sea, and hears a soft and plaintive voice:

Going to the rock from which she believed the sound came, Miss Gibbs saw a long strand of seaweed.... The reason of the seaweed's sadness was at once apparent to her. The tide had gone far out, and the sea, her husband, had quite deserted her. (52)

As soon as we reach for a comparison between Time and the sea we of course threaten the marriage; but though we can make many such metaphoric appeals — to the ocean of time, tide and time, the rhythm of the waves — we can make no easy analogy between the seaweed's relation to the sea and the clock's relation to time. They seem to meet Hester's criterion of marriage-worthy dissimilarity:

[S]he performed the holy marriage rite to the clock and to the seaweed, and, making a pretty ring of the seaweed and winding her amorously around the clock, her husband, Hester went to bed, leaving the pair to their joyful embraces.

'No, none of them can ever quarrel,' said Miss Gibbs, as she placed her reading-lamp near to her pillow [we note the dissimilarity in this contiguity], so that she might read a page or two of the Scriptures — 'no, none of them can ever quarrel, for the whole joy in matrimony lies in contrast.'

Powys's learning is here most lightly worn, delicately plumed, for this strange fable conceals a dispute between St Augustine and Meister Eckhart. Augustine terms *regio dissimilitudinis*, region of unlikeness, the irrational place in which one is cut off from God: 'And I found myself far from you, in *regio dissimilitudinis*.'[16] For Eckhart, by contrast, dissimilarity and differentiation are not lapses from order, unity and identity but the very mode of creation and of identity. In elucidating Eckhart, Denys Turner writes of 'the differences between different kinds of difference' in ways that could be exemplified by the various titles of *Fables*:

> The difference between a sheep and a goat seems relatively unproblematic, because we find it easy to say what they differ *as*.... But what do chalk and cheese differ as? ... We can only say vaguely that ... they differ *as* material things. Not that this is [an entirely] vacuous piece of information, as we may see if we compare this difference with that between a time of the day (say, 8.30 in the evening) and a wedge of ripe Stilton.[17]

Sheep and goats differ as animals in an obvious way — uninteresting to Hester — as men and women differ as humans. Chalk and cheese differ greatly but not (as Turner fails to note) at the phonetic level: it is the alliterative likeness that invites us to cite them as the proverbially unlike. By contrast, *seaweed* and *cuckoo-clock* are resonantly different in their phonetics. As for 8.30 p.m. and a wedge of Stilton, we can only note the difficulty of imagining radical dissimilitudes — for Stilton is often eaten after dinner, at, say, 8.30 p.m. Contiguity is not likeness, but it provides a context, a frame, a simple narrative: 'At about half-past-eight the Stilton appeared.'

Turner goes on to explain that for Eckhart 'no two things can be totally different from one another; there has to be some sameness for them to be different at all. To be different from each other, two things have to belong ... to the same community of difference.... [T]o be a distinct individual means entering into that community of difference which constitutes creation.'

All things, insofar as they are individual, and identifiable as separate entities, share in the Creation: for Eckhart, no two things can be beyond the imagination's power to draw comparisons, to find like-nesses.

This may help us to explain the violent and destructive ending of 'The Seaweed and the Cuckoo-Clock', in which the sea-weed returns to 'her old lover', and the clock is smashed. After having enjoyed some months of bliss in Hester's home, the pair decide that they should live for a while among the seaweed's old friends; so it is arranged that the clock shall be stolen by a thief who, being pursued by Hester, will then drop it or him on the beach. The only prohibition is the seaweed's: 'you must endeavour not to call "Cuckoo", for that cry my former husband has a distaste for.' There is no further explanation of the cause of this distaste, except of course that the clock has cuckolded the sea, and in that we find a connection, a likeness between the cuckoo-clock and the cuckold-making seaweed. The principle of dissimilarity by which Hester judged them fit to be married would no longer be valid. On the beach the clock is already fearful:

> 'I would prefer to see the warm fire … that was so happily married to Miss Gibbs's Sunday umbrella…. I would rather have Hester's tea-caddy, the wife of the door-handle, as a neighbour'…. And, forgetting his promise at that moment, in preparing to strike the hour he unluckily cried 'Cuckoo.'
>
> No sooner had that unfortunate call been heard by the sea than the first wave of the incoming tide swept over the pair. The seaweed became moist and glad, she left the clock and swam lightly away. The next wave came, and with a fierce roar of triumph dashed the poor clock against a stone, so that he was broken to pieces. (58–9)

Once two unlike things have been brought together, as the seaweed is wound around the clock, their unlikeness is already modified by contiguity. Augustine's *regio dissimilitudinis* is matched and challenged by the unlimited metonymy of creation. Creation is the broadest and most inclusive 'community of difference' within which likeness and unlikeness can be negotiated. There is, within creation, no irreducible unlikeness: the clock and the seaweed end as they do in mockery of Hester's belief that they are radically unalike, in contrast to a man and a woman, who might be named, let us say, Theodore and Violet. Difference is just as interesting and valuable — as constituting identity — in the finest discriminations as in the most general 'set' of creation. And identity — the identity even of a crumb — is the minimal condition for personification and speech.

This philosophical argument is approached again in 'John Pardy and the Waves'. One might guess that this title promises a narrative of the same order as a marriage between a ewe-lamb and a wolf, that the narrative consummation will involve the consumption of one by the other. We are therefore surprised by the fable's conclusion, that men and waves are almost identical:

> 'We, who are waves, know you, who are men, only as another sea, within which every living creature is a little wave that rises for a moment and then breaks and dies. Our great joy comes when we break, yours when you are born, for you have not yet reached that sublime relationship with God which gives the greatest happiness to destruction.'
>
> 'I am interested in what you say,' said John Pardy, 'and I have half a mind to join in your revels; but tell me, if I come to you shall I have the same pleasure in destroying others as I am likely to have when I am destroyed myself?'
>
> 'You may sink a ship,' answered the waves, 'and with good luck you may become a tidal wave that will drown a city.'
>
> John Pardy walked into the sea. (90)

This is the story of the dialectic, of the striving of the Many for the One, an aspiration and a narrative of philosophy that runs from Plato's *Parmenides* through Plotinus and Eckhart to Hegel. The many, the individual, is seen as an epiphenomenon of the One. Destruction, absorption, loss of identity and individuality — these are the defining figures of dialectical thinking whose other names are synthesis, agreement, resolution. And the dialectic presumes to a heroic mode, of sacrifice. John Pardy sacrifices himself, not as an end in itself (the pure form of sacrifice) but for subsequent advantage (the tactical sacrifice of gamesmanship), in order to participate in destruction. As a view of western civilization this is not a pleasant story. The one redeeming or at least consoling thought is that which is carried over from 'The Seaweed and the Cuckoo-Clock', that there is no irreducible difference, not even between the destroyer and the destroyed.

Thus we find ourselves once more on that fluid boundary between the animate and the inanimate, between life and death, the difference that makes identity possible. If one says 'Destroy and you will be destroyed', it sounds like a slogan of conventional morality or even common sense. This fable says: 'Be destroyed, and you will destroy.' No doubt there are some readers who think Pardy is merely foolish or psychotic to believe the promise made by the waves. But within the 'logic' of these fables, there is no reason to doubt that Pardy will 'become' a wave, nor that he will enjoy the destruction of others as much as his own. From the dissimilarity between 'John Pardy and the Waves' we have moved through similarity to contiguity and identity.

Two other fables, 'The Hat and the Post' and 'The Stone and Mr. Thomas', insist on our attention as we pursue the workings of personification. Any hat placed on any post has the effect of personification: personification and speech are inevitably present in the mere contiguity of hat on post. The relationship between Mr. Thomas and the stone is somewhat different. The gravestone marks the place of the body, but the corpse is invisible and after twenty-five years has mostly rotted, together with the coffin, into the mould (111). Yet after fifty years the stone is still legible and has clearly taken the place of Mr. Thomas. At this interval after his death, the sexton moves the stone — 'as a miller moves a sack of beans' — and props it up against the churchyard wall. Digging the plot again for a fresh burial, the sexton then finds Mr. Thomas's skull, which he casts on to 'the rubbish-heap, near to the gravestone that leaned against the wall':

> Of one thing we may be certain — while a man is often utterly forgotten by others of his kind, he is not likely to forget himself. Though it had lain dead for fifty years the skull of Mr. Thomas still retained all the pride that had belonged to him as a man.
>
> He was not a living thing now, and so he could not boast about that .... (113)

The man can no longer boast, but the gravestone, not being dead, is not so constrained:

> [The sexton] heard Mr. Thomas's stone say that it was both surprised and ashamed that an earthy skull should show so great impertinence as to appear again above ground and to lie next to such a stone as he.
>   '... who would have thought that it should have come again only to offend the delicate sensibilities of a chaste stone? for mortal man — such as it [!] was once — is born only to be buried.'

Now the skull is provoked into voice:

> 'I was neither born nor buried ... to please you. I am company, I hope, for your betters. To think that I should be insulted by a mere stone, put at my head to mark my last resting-place....'
> (115)

The stone argues from the strong position of survival and visibility:

> 'Whoever comes to this pretty place must notice me, but who can care, or can wish to care, about a buried man?'

And the skull or 'all that was left of Mr. Thomas' becomes increasingly desperate in his indignation:

> 'Should a dead stone, cut and hauled out of a vulgar quarry, vie with a man who has once been a temple of the Godhead? Are all my past joys and sorrows to be set aside as nothing, and a paltry carved stone to be set up in their place as a thing of more importance than I? ...
>   '... 'tis a pity that those who knew me ... should ever have writ my name upon an ugly stone. I know now that all fond attempts to save a man from oblivion tend only to raise up something that is thought of rather than the man himself.'
> (117–18)

This is the oldest argument against idolatry, one which Plotinus's disciple and biographer Porphyry reports of Plotinus himself. He had forbidden that a bust be made or death-mask taken of his features, for

Plotinus wished not to be remembered in a dissimilitudinous way: that is, by a permanent copy of a perishable body. He wished to be perpetuated only in his ideas, not even in his written words, for his handwriting was slovenly and he refused to revise what he had written.[18]

The twist in Powys's fable is that here words endure not in the realm of ideas but in stony materiality. Even words engraved in stone are subject to decay, as Thomas Browne knew: 'Gravestones tell truth scarce forty years.'[19] And Mr. Thomas's stone has a curious and unusual citation, of Jesus's words to the Centurion (Matt. 8.13): 'Go thy way, and, as thou hast believed, so be it done unto thee.' (120) This stone has been moved from its place — has gone its way — and the boastfulness of its claims is no guarantee that it will not one day be broken up and put to a different and lowly use, as in Hardy's 'Levelled Churchyard':

> 'Where we are huddled none can trace,
>   And if our names remain,
> They pave some path or porch or place
>   Where we have never lain!'

What, in deed and in effect, is the difference between the skull and the stone? Neither, surely, is identical to Mr. Thomas, though both may be identified by his name. Between a talking skull and a speaking stone we have such an excess of personification as to cast doubt on the very idea of the person, that is, on the pure essential person independent of voice or image or body or text. This fable seems to tell of a sign that usurps the place of that to which it referred. But it is not — we must insist — the skull to which the name on the stone refers. What is referred to and commemorated by the stone no longer exists, and the skull has already usurped the place of 'Mr. Thomas'. The latter, being dead and absent, lacks the vocal ability to protest at the skull's imposition, as the skull can protest at the stone's. But if 'Mr. Thomas' as pure person had a voice with which to make his complaint, would not that voice be taken and mistaken for 'Mr. Thomas' himself? What lacks sign and utterance — the pure essence of a person — can then hardly be said to exist at all.

This fable elaborates the unjustifiable assumption that a fable can be decoded in terms of something 'real' and 'present'. Our knowledge of 'the world' and of 'persons' is always a knowledge of signs, names, voices — the very ingredients of fable. A name is already a personification. Can there be a person without a name? 'Mr. Thomas' (these quotation marks are mine, for the impossible entity whose identity has been usurped by both the stone and the skull) might be jealous of his skull, as his skull is jealous of the stone. But he might as well be jealous of his name. The true name of 'Mr. Thomas' is ' —— ' — and even the dash could be thought to have 'usurped' the 'person'. There can be no person without personification. In its tropes language betrays any clear distinction we might attempt to think between the human and the non-human, between the animate and the inanimate. '—— ' may well be the soul's secret name for itself in its immortality, but the gravestone, or the name in any of its written forms can proclaim, without fear of contradiction from the nameless, voiceless '—— ': 'I am the lasting, the tangible result.' (118)

Mr. Bonnet, the human protagonist of 'The Hat and the Post', has the peculiar idea — unique in these fables — that only humans can speak:

> Human beings are glad to be alive.… There are some who are glad to be alive because they are possessed of the faculty of speech. These like to hear themselves talk because they know that so many things — the tables and the chairs, the watches, the pots and pans, the moss in the fields and the flints in the road — have nothing to say for themselves. (125)

Mr. Bonnet may be taken as a representative of the recalcitrant reader — that is, as the spokesman for the reader who, though a person, has no voice in the text. Mr. Bonnet would speak for those readers who have no time for fables. Though Mr. Bonnet allows that animals 'might learn to talk under the proper tuition':

> he despised most utterly the ordinary objects that one meets in country walks, because they had no tongues …
> It seemed to him one of the errors of the grand Creator that

He hadn't given the clods and sticks a voice with which at least to say a good-morrow to a gentleman who liked talking … (127)

Mr. Bonnet would tell the daisies very prettily that he was wise and they foolish, and would inform the holly exactly what his weather-glass was doing in the parlour at home, and because the holly made no reply, Mr. Bonnet would remark in a rage that the bush was a dunce. (128)

Mr. Bonnet speaks to his wife 'about the total absence of wisdom in gate-posts and chalk stones' (129). Then, on one of his walks, he stops 'to regard with a vast contempt a large post …' Removing his hat to wipe his forehead, he places his hat on the post:

No sooner had he done so than he found it was impossible for him to take his eyes off the post that he had crowned. Something strange had happened: the rude post seemed to have become another Mr. Bonnet.

As the post is personified, so Mr. Bonnet is rendered somewhat mute ('deaf as a post', 'between you, me and the doorpost'):

Mr. Bonnet had never in his life been at a loss for a word, and he never remembered any one addressing him before he had spoken to them. But curiously enough, he now began to think that the post meant to speak to him.…

… the post that he had regarded so contemptuously began to address him in almost the same tone of voice that he himself was wont to use to other people.

'Pardon me, Mr. Bonnet,' observed the post, 'for interrupting your gentle reverie, but I would like to say that when you last spoke to me you were not very kind.… You told me that I had no tongue to speak with and was a low thing, of no consequence in the world.… But now that you have set your hat upon my head I can talk with the best.' (131–2)

We note that the top of the post is now a head, and will remain so even if Mr. Bonnet takes back his hat. The post goes on to a consideration of the valuation that Mr. Bonnet places on speech:

'Your only pleasure in speaking is to show yourself that you are not yet nothingness, and when you are nothingness, you will express yourself just as well by being nothing. That is all you open your mouth to do, only to show that you are not a corpse.' (133)

Mr. Bonnet is transformed into a post — 'He seemed like a post that might sprout' (133) — and loses the desire or capacity to speak. Seeing the young girl Lily, to whom he has often spoken 'in long ponderous sentences, in each of which he had hung words like great beads', Mr. Bonnet simply and silently — without thought of lust or hint of violation — helps her in her task:

> Mr. Bonnet stood before Lily but could say nothing. Lily burst out a-laughing, and he, without knowing what else he could do to [sic] such a happy creature, shouldered her sticks and carried them for her into Madder village, without saying a word. (134)

In 'shouldering' the sticks, Mr. Bonnet is in silent contiguity with wood: not only has he been re-figured as a post, but even his name — bonnet/ hat/ head — is inverted. The sticks are now above the Bonnet.

In a brilliant essay of some forty years ago, 'The Meaning of "Literal"', the late Owen Barfield (1898–1997) argued that the literal meaning of a word is always developed from a metaphorical meaning.[20] The implication of this argument is that all literal meanings are dead metaphors, catachresis, and that meaning is achieved not with respect to single essential entities but through 'communities of difference'. Barfield cites Bruno Snell who, in considering Homeric metaphors, argues that a human could not think of a stone anthropomorphically unless he had also thought of a human as a stone, 'petromorphically'. Thus, the personification of an object necessarily entails an 'objectification' of a person. As Eckhart wrote: 'In making a thing the very innermost self of a man comes into outwardness.'[21]

When we talk of the trunk, limbs, or crown of a tree, we may think that we are seeing the tree in terms of a human figure. But when we speak of the trunk, limbs, or crown of a person, we are also thinking of a person in terms of a tree. If a post with a hat on can appear to be a person, the person must also feel himself to be a post. There are no simple references or literal meanings, because a literal meaning assumes the possibility of a knowledge of things in themselves. Language determines that our cognition works always by likeness and difference. Catachresis is the unavoidable figure of the differential.

Death is not only absence, nothingness. It is also the very principle of differentiation. Between two things there must be a space, a gap, a nothingness. The primordial distinction, as Meister Eckhart understood, is that between the Creator and Creation. Creation is thus a community of difference in which any two created things — cuckoo-clock and sea-weed, raven and writing-desk — can be likened to or associated with each other.

In 'The Blind Hen and the Earthworm' we learn wisdom from the worm:

> 'We live gratefully and, when we die, we remain in the soil that nourished us and become a part of the gracious food of the earth. One of the first lessons that we are taught in our childhood is that of humilitude. We are told that we are nothing, and we are glad to believe it.'
>
> 'Surely that's easy,' said the hen, 'for a worm!'
>
> 'But 'tis with that nothing that God works,' replied the other. (219–20)

The hen learns humility from the earth, as Mr. Bonnet learns it from a post. One of the characteristics of humility is silence, yet both post and poet must speak, or else, like Mr. Bonnet, we might despise silence. Silence would be nothing, and we would not have understood the value of nothing. For nothing is not the deprivation of something, but the gap, the space that makes for difference, the line that makes a distinction, the silence that carries voices and holds them apart. T. F. Powys spoke of that silence, into that nothing: in the theme and figure of death he is not indulging a fascination with morbidity — let alone 'nastiness' — but inscribing a celebration of nothingness, of that which makes possible distinction, difference, articulation.

In about 1933, four years after *Fables* was published, T. F. Powys entered a textual silence, and wrote nothing more in the twenty remaining years of his life.[22] *Fables* conceals the assurance of its own fate among readers, implies its own contentment with neglect. Nothing can be suppressed — as, and though, 'nothingness' has been suppressed — for there is no suppression that is not an interment, an encryptment:

> Often the true feelings of human kind are hidden away, tucked into a bottom drawer, pushed under a pile of mouldy letters, or let to lie in an old cast-off shoe.

The comfort of nothingness is that it is always and necessarily cryptic, and therefore that catachresis is its figure. The dead and buried metaphors of catachresis are brought back to life, and brought into the light, by personification: whatever is interred, repressed, hidden, abandoned, silenced, will out, one night or day, as Fables.

NOTES

[1] Sir Thomas Browne, *Hydriotaphia or Urn-Burial* (1653), ch. V.

[2] William Empson, *Argufying*, ed. John Haffenden (London: Chatto & Windus, 1987), 542. Empson's interest in T. F. Powys was presumably related to his close friendship with Sylvia Townsend Warner in the late 1920s: see Claire Harman, *Sylvia Townsend Warner: A Biography* (London: Chatto & Windus 1989), 74, and *The Diaries of Sylvia Townsend Warner*, ed. Claire Harman (London: Chatto & Windus, 1994), 56.

[3] Review in *Observer*, cited in R. L. Green, *Kipling: The Critical Heritage* (London: Routledge, 1971).

[4] Frank Kibblewhite, 'Introduction' to T. F. Powys, *Fables* (Brighton: Hieroglyph, 1993), [vii]. With the exception of 'The Hill and the Book' added to the Hieroglyph edition of *Fables* – as suggested by Kenneth Hopkins, *The Powys Brothers* (Norfolk, 1972), 214 – the pagination and setting of the 1993 edition are identical to those of the 1929 Chatto & Windus first edition and all subsequent reprints, including those under the title *No Painted Plumage*. Further references to *Fables/No Painted Plumage* will be given parenthetically in the text.

[5] Editors tell us that Gray's '*No Painted Plumage*' recalls Milton's 'From branch to branch the smaller birds with song Solaced the woods and spread their painted wings' (*Paradise Lost*, Book VII, lines 433–4) and Pope's 'Windsor Forest', line 118:
'See! from the brake the whirring Pheasant springs …
Ah! what avail his glossie, varying Dyes,
His Purple Crest, and Scarlet-circled Eyes,

The vivid Green his shining Plumes unfold;
His painted Wings, and Breast that flames with Gold?'
Gray's wording is closest to Dryden's 'A Goldfinch there I saw with gawdy
Pride Of painted plumes', lines 106–7 of 'The Flower and the Leaf' in Dryden's
Fables (1700); this fable's title seeming to anticipate those of T. F. Powys's
Fables. Virgil is the source behind Gray, Dryden and Milton: *pictae volucres* oc-
curs in Georgics iii, line 243 and in the Aeneid, Book IV, line 525.

6 Kenneth Hopkins, *The Powys Brothers: A Biographical Appreciation*
(Southrepps, Norfolk: Warren House Press, 1972), 162.
7 For a thorough account of theories of allegory see the important study by
Marius Buning, *T. F. Powys: A Modern Allegorist* (Amsterdam: Rodopi, 1986).
8 Eric Partridge, *Usage and Abusage* s.v. '**which** and **that**'.
9 A rare exception demonstrates the point: 'although Agnes allowed John Pardy
to get his feet into her house, which he was very glad to do ...' (81): here *which*
is relative to a verbal phrase, not to an object. *That* relates only to an antecedent
object; it cannot relate to an antecedent verbal phrase.
10 A memorably malicious instance of such a paradoxical title is Graham Greene's
The Quiet American. That such a sense of paradox can in time be utterly lost is
evident in the naming of 'the Samaritans': 'The Good Samaritan' was once an
intriguing and shocking collocation.
11 *Argufying*, 545.
12 In *La Scienza Nuova* (1725) Giambattista Vico develops the etymology to argue
that 'humanity' begins with and is defined by inhumation, when man values his
fellow-beings sufficiently to protect them after death: hence the myth of
Antigone. Oddly, Thomas Browne makes no appeal to etymology in *Urn-Burial*
(1658), one of T. F. Powys's favourite works.
13 T. F. Powys, *Soliloquies of a Hermit* (London: Melrose, 1918), 5.
14 Sylvia Townsend Warner, 'Theodore Powys at East Chaldon', in Belinda
Humfrey, ed., *Recollections of the Powys Brothers* (London: Peter Owen, 1980),
135.
15 J. C. Powys's 'extreme' personifications are not found before *A Glastonbury
Romance* (1932), and it might be supposed that he was inspired by *Fables* (1929).
Kenneth Hopkins reports that it was Llewelyn who first prompted Theodore:
'Write about anything; write about that log of wood and that old boot.' (*The
Powys Brothers*, 163)
16 St. Augustine, *Confessions*, VII. x (16).
17 Denys Turner, 'Meister Eckhart: Dualist or Monist?' *Eckhart Review* (Spring
1997), 41–2.
18 Porphyry, 'On the Life of Plotinus and the Arrangement of his Work,' in
Plotinus, *The Enneads*, trans. S. MacKenna, ed. J. Dillon (Harmondsworth: Penguin, 1991), cii, cix.
19 Browne, *Hydriotaphia*, ch. V.
20 Owen Barfield, 'The Meaning of "Literal"', in *The Rediscovery of Meaning and
Other Essays* (Middletown, CT: Wesleyan U.P., 1977), 32–43.
21 Franz Pfeiffer, *Meister Eckhart* (1857), translated by C. de B. Evans (London:
Watkins, 1924), 195 (Sermon LXXVII, 'The Image in the Soul').

22 See Peter Riley, 'T. F. Powys at Mappowder: A Consideration of his fiction in the light of twenty years of non-writing', *The Powys Review* 3 (Summer 1978), 17–31; Marius Buning, 'Mappowder Revisited: T. F. Powys's Reading in Retirement', *The Powys Review* 7 (1980), 78–86. In Gerard Casey's *Night Horizons* (Ghent, NY: Phudd Bottom Press, 1997), 85, Theodore is cited as saying in his last years: 'The soul is the waiting silence in us that is free.' To value waiting over event, silence over speech, leaves little to be said, or written.

Theodore Powys and Susie at Beth Car

THEODORE
a rondeau

Without harm, he walked the seven-gated lane
daily; heedless of sea fret or chill rain
or well-whetted tongues, his mind ingrowing
and nurtured by his coming and going
treading the same paths again and again.

Churchyard mound, pit and yew were his refrain
The cramped lives behind the cracked window-pane.
Kindly, his words belied his bestowing,
Without harm, he.

Housed under high hill, his life was plain
Only his fears wove an intricate skein.
Death's thread was scarlet, his constant knowing,
with disillusionment's bitter showing.
Hedge-priest of poverty he must remain
without.

Judith Stinton

H. W. FAWKNER

Atmospherium
Affectivity and Presence in *Wolf Solent*

In *Wolf Solent*, the word 'something' has a curious power. The author deploys the suggestiveness of this power with great care and deliberation. Lenty Cottage has 'something' peculiarly neat about it (144). There is an abject 'something' about T. E. Valley's humility that excites Wolf (145). During a walk to Blacksod, filmy clouds and blue sky conjointly produce 'something' into which Wolf seemingly plunges his mind and hands (151). There is *something* actually in Nature, ... *something* that required nothing save earth and sky for its fulfilment' (151; emphasis added). Nevertheless the 'something' transcends not only nature but also love. 'How could this ecstasy be called love? It was more than love. It was the coming to the surface of *something* unutterable' (153; emphasis added).

I will argue that in *Wolf Solent* the 'something' is of philosophic importance. By this I do not simply mean that it is a strategic unit in Wolf's or in John Cowper's life-philosophy. For the philosophy of a work of fiction is never a mere expression of someone's life-attitude. One must distinguish between philosophy and life-philosophy. Nor do I mean that the philosophic importance of the 'something' has to do with academic philosophy, with some school of adequate philosophic ratiocination. I mean rather that in the work of fictional art, the artefact's 'philosophy' is this side of philosophy as well as art ... this side of thought as well as creativity. The 'something' does not belong to thinking. Nor does it belong to art. It belongs rather to itself as it were. The novel *Wolf Solent* is itself a major instantiation of this 'something' to which the word 'something' in this very fictional enterprise invisibly points.

★ ★ ★ ★

104

I will suggest without any further ado that in *Wolf Solent* the philo-sophic importance of the word 'something' has to do with a question-ing of presence. By questioning I mean some enduring, elaborate process of metaphysical interrogation. In *Wolf Solent* there is a *doubting* of presence. The doubting of presence surfacing in *Wolf Solent* is internal to the general doubting of presence in the post-religious, supernihilist culture of the West. By presence I mean *Parousia*. In Greek philosophy the *Parousia* is a grand self-presence of presence in itself — just as in theology the absolute is a grand absolutizing of the absolute in the absolute. The 'something', pre-cisely by being smaller and more elusive than the *Parousia*, is in *Wolf Solent* more transcendental (more immanent) than the *Parousia*. There is, as it were, a perpetual conflict or incompatibility between the immanence of presence and the immanence of 'something'. The 'something' tends to be victorious in this contest on account of its slenderness — just as Christie Malakite, because she cannot be a love-presence, is closer to loving, loveliness, and lovemaking than Gerda, than the very image of the *Parousia*.

The 'something', even when it is negative, brings Wolf close to Gerda in the instant that celebrates their loveless lack of proximity. 'She looked him straight in the face with an ambiguous tilt of her soft, rounded chin. *Something* had come between them — *something* that troubled him seriously, though not with the sense of any unscalable barrier' (158; emphasis added). We see here that the artefact's philoso-phy is reluctant to posit a dialectical opposition between 'something' and *Parousia*. Although the 'something' and presence cancel each other out, it is not impossible to slide from the one to the other, to slip out of the one into the other. The *Parousia* and the 'something' are adjacent. Why is this so?

★ ★ ★ ★

One way of understanding this nexus is to consider a special type of earliness. This earliness does not suggest prematureness; nor does it really suggest a process of foreshadowing or anticipation. Ordinary earliness occurs in time. This other earliness does not. It is rather the earliness that gives birth to time in the first place. When John

Cowper's fiction projects this special earliness into the affectivities of landscape, erotic love, and nature, the natural loveliness of nature and woman — of the *Parousia* as such, of *being* — give way beforehand to a more solemn, awesome, and imponderable loveliness. Now nature is no longer felt as something that simply affects us. Nor is it a natural womb, an aboriginary dwelling or origin. In fact no words, no contortions of language, no human or inhuman expressivity can do it justice ... with the possible exception of the word 'something'.

'Do you want me to whistle for you?' she asked, in a low, docile voice.

The words reached his ears from an enormous distance. They came travelling to him over rivers, over forests; and as they took shape in his consciousness, *something* quite different from what he had felt for her swelled up in his throat. He took her head between his hands and kissed her as he had never in his life kissed any woman. (163; emphasis added)

The transition from the *Parousia* to the 'something' is at this point the typical Cowperist transition from the human to the faceless — from what an ontological inquiry would call the ontic to the ontological. As she moves away a few paces to do her blackbird singing, Gerda's face ceases to be a human face. The facelessness that she now exhibits is not one that Wolf needs to perceive. For perception now too has sunk away, affectivity finding its strength this side of perceptions, this side of sense impressions, this side ... in fact ... of life.

And he knew, without *seeing* that it was so, that her expression as she whistled was like the expression of a child asleep, or of a child happily, peacefully dead.

And, though it was into the night that she now poured those liquid notes, the tone of their drawn-out music was a tone full of the peculiar feeling of one hour alone of all the hours of night and day. It was the tone of the hour just before dawn, the tone of that life which is not yet sound, but only withheld breath, the breath of cold buds not yet green, of earth-bound bulbs not yet loosed from their sheaths, the tone of the flight of swallows across chilly seas as yet far off from the warm,

pebbled beaches towards which they are steering their way.
(163)

The 'not yet' of the 'not yet green' of buds is not simply a 'not yet' pointing to budding greenness. The 'not yet' of bulbs 'not yet loosed from their sheaths' is not merely a vegetational 'not yet' pointing with grand anticipation to a developmental hereafter, to some wondrously vegetative consummation, to the perfectly achieved presence-to-itself of absolute blossoming. Instead the 'not yet' of 'earth-bound bulbs' points to itself. 'Yet' does not suggest something negative, a part of time still to be delivered. 'Yet' points to that which has escaped from such delivering ... to that which has escaped from life in the very act of seeming to herald its arrival. The 'not yet', and not merely the bulb, is 'earth-bound' ... lodged like the encompassing-invisible 'something' in pure earliness *without future, without life*.

It is tempting to add: without hope. For to be earth-bound in the happiest possible sense is to be wickedly shut up in the earth itself, like William Solent in his coffin. Within the imaginative parameters of *Wolf Solent*, this earth-condition is not morbid. The parameters of the imagination are not the parameters of the psychologist. The deathlike 'not yet', precisely by occurring alongside rather than within the *Parousia*, is not expressive of some Freudian 'death-wish', for it expresses affectivity, not psyche ... affectivity as that which is *not yet* psyche. This affectivity is the *atmospherium* of the 'something' in *Wolf Solent*.

An atmospherium is an optical device used to display images of clouds and other meteorological phenomena on the inside of a dome. In charting the affectivity and hence also ontology of *Wolf Solent* we may begin with the entirety of the imaginative atmospherium, subsequently locating the 'something' in certain junctions and points, or else we may begin with the 'something' and subsequently work out the atmospherium as its affective but by no means concentric extrapolation.

★ ★ ★ ★

We have seen that the 'something' and the 'not yet' conspire. The condition of possibility for this conspiracy is the removal of the 'not yet' from time. The 'something' collaborates in this abstracting of time from itself ... as when the narrator comments that a certain brief passage of time 'seemed to Wolf *something* more than time and different from time' (162; emphasis added). The 'something' is a form of affectivity. 'There came over him a *vague feeling*, as if he had actually invaded and possessed *something* of the virginal aloofness of the now darkened fields' (162–3; emphasis added). Here the vagueness of feeling is not an indeterminacy in emotion, in affect. It is instead the complete atmospherium of the 'something', an absolutely specific instantiation of feeling's highest possible truth. This highest possible truth is pure affectivity as such, the self.

Like a planetarium, an atmospherium is a showing of light. Truth in *Wolf Solent* too is a showing of light. The showing of light is not on show for mankind. Light here shows itself only to itself — which means that the one who has not beforehand been illuminated by the radiancy of the 'something' is excluded from its atmospherium ... this atmospherium being ultimately nothing but the self itself, pure affectivity as such in the invisible diffusion of its slender ray. In this way, the showing of light in *Wolf Solent* is thematized as 'something' that is irradiated this side of humanity, this side of the *human* self. The atmospheric self is in a sense not even a prehuman self, for in the highest possible affective context, mankind as such does not count.

As atmospherium, Gerda in this way does not even have to be present in order to be absolute, in order to be lovely and true in the truest possible ways of love. When the metamorphosis of love's clearest thrill shapes her being as the tonality of a supernal blackbird, there is strictly speaking no *change*. Gerda does not alter. Her nature is simply recognized by Wolf as indistinguishable from the faceless 'something' of a before-presence that has priority over presence. The 'imaginary city' that ideally evolves out of such perfection is an invisible dwelling *seen* in a vision of the concrete experiencing of the first lighting-up of light. In the very 'first lighting of lamps', the 'something' takes the prehuman form of a 'formless presence' ... enabling 'something' to be 'someone', 'some girl', 'some boy' (169). Like 'something', 'some', does not foreground uncertainty or indefinition. It is rather the definitive certainty of their felt affectivity that enables 'someone' and 'something' to emerge as reality. 'The lights of a certain imaginary city' are ultimately nothing less than the lights of Blacksod seen by the lovers as they make their way home in the aftermath of the romance of complete affective encounter. Blacksod joins up with Wolf's childhood visions of an illuminated town which

> was always associated with the first lighting up of lamps, and with the existence, *but not necessarily the presence*, of someone … some girl … some boy … some unknown … whose place in his life would resemble that first lighting of lamps … that sense of arriving out of the cold darkness of empty fields and lost ways … coming along a dark road to where lamps are lit! (169– 70; emphasis added)

★ ★ ★ ★

'Something' is now 'someone', and the someone is 'not necessarily' someone's 'presence'. Yet it would be a fatal mistake for the critic to view the incompletion of 'presence' as a form of absence. Such hasty interpretation would be utilizing a simple presence-versus-absence continuum. On such a continuum, a certain diminution of presence translates as an absolutely equal increment of absence. Following this misguided line of analysis, we might wrongly conclude that 'not necessarily the presence' suggests some phenomenological distance between full presence (the dream of metaphysics) and less-than-full-presence ('not necessarily the presence'). But in *Wolf Solent* before-presence is not a lessening of presence. *As affectivity*, fiction here asks us to behold the dream of an atmospherium in which the evaporation of presence is precisely not a loss of presence … but rather an intensification of its materialization. Feelings *materialize*, and they do so precisely as feeling. Such feeling, whenever it brackets presence, is in no way doing what thought does when *it* brackets presence. In thought, the away-from-presence of evaporated presence is a form of distance, absence. In feeling, by contrast, the vaporous away-from-presence of evaporated presence *does nothing to presence*. Least of all does it create a distance in presence between presence and itself.

In this way we may speak of a critical law to be utilized in defiance of the laws forwarded by reason for the purpose of interpretation. This law is *the law of the atmospherium*. The law of the atmospherium cancels the validity of all laws prescribed by reason for the universal reviewing of ontological structure. Contra reason, the law of the atmospherium pays tribute to the forms of presence that are not affected by the withdrawal of presence, to the forms of love that are not uncertainized by the withdrawal of love. The law of the atmospherium distrusts all theories of displacement, difference, and phenomenological distance — viewing these theories precisely as laws of reason *rather* than as laws of feeling. Presence is not displaced by the moving-away of presence into its vapour.

★ ★ ★ ★

To save presence from the laws of reason is not to hold up presence to the stars in the sublime, suprasensory, Platonic manner. It is rather, as in the case of the Powys romance, to retain in affectivity's heart those distilled moments of affective truth in which ... like lovers 'coming along a dark road to where lamps are lit' ... we know the indubitable presence of 'something' or 'someone'.

Curiously, in *Wolf Solent*, the absolute 'someone' who is not necessarily the absolute presence of someone ... is the reader. Moreover, the reader as someone-not-necessarily-present, and therefore as the reader-not-necessarily-present, is the reader-of-*Wolf-Solent*. Ultimately this means that the reader-of-*Wolf-Solent* ... in other words I myself ... is a reader who is not necessarily an absolutely present reader. The reader of *Wolf Solent* is not necessarily present. I am myself ... when reading *Wolf Solent* ... not necessarily present ... in my reading, in *Wolf Solent*, in myself. But this vaporous freedom from the pressing necessity of complete presence and self-presence is by no means a loss of presence, of self-presence ... or indeed of anything else. That the reader is not necessarily present: this in no way means that the reader *fails* to be present, that some species of inadequacy is at hand between presence and itself, between the reader and the reader's presence. Nor is it the case that reading itself is the victim of such a dislocation in the order of things. It is rather the case that in the reader there is a gloriously immature delight in the readerly 'not yet' of reading. This 'not yet' befalls the reader too … this demi-creature being nothing less than the one who 'reads' … *Wolf Solent*. This being is 'someone' *rather than a being.*

Half an hour later they were all four making their way past the last houses of Blacksod.… In one of the smaller houses, where for some reason neither curtain nor blind had been drawn, Wolf could see two candles burning on a small table at which someone was still reading.

He touched Mr Valley's arm, and both the men stood for a time looking at that unconscious reader. It was an elderly woman who read there by those two candles, her chin propped upon one arm, and the other lying extended across the table. The woman's face had nothing remarkable about it. The book she read was obviously, from its shape and appearance, a cheap story; but as Wolf stared in upon her, sitting there in that commonplace room at midnight, an indescribable sense of the drama of human life passed through him. For leagues and leagues in every direction the great pastoral fields lay quiet in their muffled dew-drenched aloofness. But there, by those two pointed flames, one isolated consciousness kept up the old familiar interest, in love, in birth, in death, all the turbulent chances of mortal events. That simple, pallid, spectacled head became for him at that moment a little island of warm human awareness in the midst of the vast non-human night.

He thought to himself how, in some future time, when these formidable scientific inventions would have changed the face of the earth, some wayward philosopher like himself would still perhaps watch through a window a human head *reading by candlelight*, and find such a sight touching beyond words.… [I]n his heart he thought: 'That old woman in there might be reading a story about my own life. She might be reading about Shaftesbury town and yellow bracken and Gerda's whistling! She might be reading about Christie and the Malakite book-shop'. (180–81)

★ ★ ★ ★

It is no doubt already apparent that there is a relationship between the event of *'reading by candlelight'* (181; Powys's emphasis) and the event of 'coming along a dark road to where lamps are lit!' (170). In both cases there is a foregrounding of *'someone'*: 'the existence, but not necessarily the presence, of someone' (169; emphasis added); 'Wolf could see two candles burning on a small table at which *someone* was still reading' (181; emphasis added). In both cases the 'someone' arises as 'someone' *rather* than as presence. In fact the word 'someone' does not merely point to an identity or lack of identity; it points to a *way of arising*, an arising-manner. To say that 'someone' is there at a small table reading by candlelight is to say that the reading-activity occurring by the small table is beforehand penetrated by the special someone-affectivity rather than by the standard presence-affectivity; it is to say that 'someone' arises in the something-manner, in the someone-manner, rather than in the usual manner ... rather than as presence.

In this way the reader 'reading about Christie and the Malakite bookshop' (181) is not one who enters presence according to the protocols of presence. In fact this odd (because vaporized ...) reader — the *strangest possible reader* — does not enter presence in the first place. This reader enters, indeed has entered beforehand, the vapour of reading's originary atmospherium. This reader is not *presenced*. Instead of entering presence, the reader (the vapour) enters 'someoneness', 'somethingness'. 'But whenever he had seen [the imaginary city], it was always associated with the first lighting up of lamps, and with the existence, but not necessarily the presence, of someone ... some girl ... some boy ... some unknown ... whose place in his life would resemble that first lighting of lamps ... that sense of arriving out of the cold darkness of empty fields and lost ways ...' (170–71). We do not first have a world, and then subsequently a local appearing of 'someone' or 'something' in this world. Instead we first of all have no world whatsoever ... but only atmospherium, *atmospherium without world*. This, for the sensitive reader, is actually the affectivity-meaning of the quaintest penumbra of reading-fields, rarest candlelight. Like 'something', 'someone' makes an originary appearing ... not in the world but in 'somethingness', 'someoneness'.

This 'somethingness' or 'someoneness' is not a somewhere, not an anywhere. It is not a place, a locus, a spot, a region-to-be-found-in-the-world. It is to be found only in the atmospheric-affective half-light of the expectant 'coming along' (170). The expectant 'coming along' is not a coming along to a lamplit place, but a coming along 'to where lamps *are lit*' (170; emphasis added). The coming along to the small house with 'two candles burning on a small table' is not a coming along to a lamplit reading place, but a coming along to a 'somethingness' where 'someone *was still reading*' (181; emphasis added). To be reading by candlelight is not the same as to be *still reading* by candlelight. The still of 'still reading' beforehand effectu- ates a distillation of reading as well as a distillation of looking … of observing, of being rather astonished, of being quite mesmerized, tranquillized, and overwhelmed. To be *still reading* by candlelight: this signifies a titanic but inconspicuous uninterruptedness in reading, a without-death in reading which, without exactly being a timelessness or immortality, is an everlastingness … an enduring pain … perhaps life itself as that which cannot be endured by any single human being. … but only by 'someone' … someone still reading in the abode 'where for some reason neither curtain nor blind had been drawn' (180–81).

★ ★ ★ ★

In sum, the dimming of presence in *Wolf Solent*, far from being the Adamic fall-from-presence gloomily posited in our academies by the sombre professors of critical melancholia, is an absolutely undimmed arising of something akin to presence. This kinship is signalled by the words 'something', 'someone'. As atmospherium, the dimming of presence hails the volatilized advent — even in the dead of night — of a photosensitive corona. Within the affective field of the fictional domain that we are asked to imagine, the felt reality of this photosen- sitive corona is the property, indeed the living essence … not of the reader, but of one who happens still to be reading.

Timothy Hyman: Talking with Gerard Casey at Mappowder, *1983–4*

TIMOTHY HYMAN

John Cowper Powys
The Quest for the Pictorial Equivalent

The lecture on which this text was based was presented at the Society's Uppingham Conference in 1996; it was delivered mostly impromptu, cued and structured by some sixty slides — the images perhaps counting for more than the words. What follows is a kind of reconstruction, but without most of the pictures.

The moment of my discovery of John Cowper Powys happened to coincide with the moment of my entering art school; and in England, art school nearly always entails an *induced identity crisis*. Probably the choices faced by a young painting-student are more urgent and fundamental than in — say — an English Literature course; you're not just writing an essay a week, you're having to decide, immediately, what you're going to paint, and in what idiom. From the beginning, my interest in the fiction of Powys was bound up with my trying to find a way forward for myself as a painter.

When I was searching — as every young artist must search — for mentors and exemplars among earlier artists, I had already been affected by my reading of Powys. An elderly London dealer, whenever I mentioned some painter unfamiliar to him, would ask in his heavy German accent, 'Who is the father and who is the mother?' And it was true, it was nearly always possible to conjure the absent artist by summoning two such names. Painting comes out of painting. In my own case, the combination of Beckmann as sire and Bonnard as dam might adequately stake out a tradition and a territory where my art feels at home; and yet, there'd be a lingering unease — a sense that somewhere, somehow, I should be bringing up the name of John Cowper Powys. More than any painter, Powys shaped me; my first apprenticeship as an artist was in his — however unsteady and improbable — hands. And my assumption now, in dragging before you Bonnard and Beckmann and those other painters who were formative for me, is that they might feed back again into our understanding of Powys — might illuminate, or help us to see him differently.

★ ★ ★ ★

When I first read *A Glastonbury Romance* in 1963 as a seventeen-year-old student at the Slade, I'd just spent two months travelling alone in Italy. In Siena, I'd encountered what I would still identify as my favourite painting in the world, Ambrogio Lorenzetti's frescoed wall, forty-four foot long, depicting *The Well-Governed City*. It recreates the Siena of the 1340s as an imagined world, a microcosm. We are above the circuit of the wall, but we see only the right-hand segment. The enclosure must continue far below and to the left of us, just as the vast tract of countryside under the curving horizon implies an even larger, almost cosmic vista. Lorenzetti's panoramic viewpoint gives us access into the heart of the city and its workings: cutaway views, windows and loggias allow us to penetrate into a great range of human activity. Close by the shoe-shop and the bar, someone is giving a lecture; above, they're working on the roof. Beyond the gate, we're invited to make a journey — past the peasants at work in the fields, to where the asses are plunging down into the gully near the mill ... In the sky above the gate floats a winged allegorical figure, labelled SECURITAS; but it has been suggested that this 'Security' may also embody Astraea, the goddess who presides over the Golden Age, and who signposts the millenarian hope of its renewal. While Virgil and most earlier artists located that Golden Age in a remote, pre-urban society, Lorenzetti seems to affirm it as a *possibility* within his own contemporary city. You might say, then, that Lorenzetti prepared me for the cosmology of *A Glastonbury Romance* — and for all those attempts (Geard's, Uryen's, Owen's, Arthur/Myrddin's) to reconstitute the utopian community.

But of course, when I came to the Slade, it was all a terrible shock. Instead of finding myself among the heirs of Lorenzetti, I was confronted with the cult of Barnett Newman. There is a famous photograph of him in 1963, standing in front of an enormous canvas divided into three absolutely flat colour-fields, entitled *Who's Afraid of Red, Yellow and Blue*. Modernism was, in painting, a much tighter construction, more exclusive and more repressive, than it ever became in literature. My generation had to come to terms with a view of twentieth-century painting as a kind of relay-race: Cézanne had passed the baton to Cubism, Cubism to Mondrian, Mondrian to American Abstract Painting ... The feeling was, overwhelmingly, that if you didn't participate in that evolutionary imperative, you were condemning your art to total irrelevance. If I was to dissent from doctrinaire modernism, I needed a weapon; and looking back, I can see it was above all John Cowper Powys who supplied this — who allowed me to be less cowed and intimidated than I would otherwise have been.

★ ★ ★ ★

I chanced to first buy *Weymouth Sands* (in its new and restored edition) on my way to the great Bonnard exhibition held in London in 1966, and during all the weeks that followed the wateriness of Powys merged with the wateriness of Bonnard. It seemed to me both shared a kind of bonelessness, a lack of muscle, so that their sense of things was conveyed by glimmerings and shimmerings, effects of light suddenly making the humdrum splendid and meaningful. Bonnard was born in 1867, John Cowper in 1872; both were really Symbolists, shaped by the aesthetic of the 1890s; and both would appear anachronistic to the successive 'movements' of modernism. Yet after 1920, Bonnard, like Powys, was able to transfer the terms of the Symbolist quest (the storing-up of aesthetic moments) to the harsher world of the interwar years — renewing that quest, and in a sense redeeming it. They join with contemporaries such as Proust, Yeats and Musil in exploring the epiphany, the moment of heightened or visionary perception, through the medium of the self. I would want to place beside such Bonnard pictures as the Tate's *The Bowl of Milk* (1919) (*see* page 11), some lines from Yeats's 'Vacillation' (1932):

> My fiftieth year had come and gone,
> I sat a solitary man,

In a crowded London shop,
An open book and empty cup
On the marble table top.
While on the shop and street I gazed
My body of a sudden blazed;
And twenty minutes more or less
It seemed, so great my happiness,
That I was blessèd and could bless.

In the 1930s and 1940s, Bonnard, like Powys, experienced a late flowering — those ambitious works that have made both so difficult to place ever since. Their art always retains an 1890s elaborateness and sumptuousness of surface, in contrast to the starkness we've come to expect of 'modern' art. I like to think of both, working away in a language fifty years 'out of date' yet creating some of the most *timely* art of those decades. (Whereas their more obviously modernist contemporaries often now appear dated.)

In *Weymouth Sands*, Perdita is bewildered, because unable to place the music Jerry Cobbold is playing:

'Is it,' she thought 'some modern musician imitating the old style? No, no! This is no imitation. This is life itself, life filling out the patterns and rules that it has made, *as if they were sails*, to carry it beyond itself, over unknown seas!' (211)

We share something of that confusion in front of a late Bonnard. As Perdita listens on, she finds herself 'drifting through the liquid ether of a substance that resembled mother-of-pearl': very much how one might describe the nacreous vision of Bonnard's late bathroom reveries.

As young men, both had been permanently marked by anarchism, by the vision of a past and future Golden Age. But Bonnard's *Age d'or* only becomes fully convincing when he renounces any explicitly mythological imagery — when a literally golden light transforms an ordinary domestic interior. Many of his greatest paintings could be described — in the phrase used by John Crow in *A Glastonbury Romance* — as 'domestic vignettes':

He got a sudden delicious feeling of the continuity of these domestic vignettes as they gather themselves together and take varied patterns ... all answering and responding as they reappeared down the ages to some preordained harmony which was forever being just missed or lost as soon as it came together ...

Bonnard's art is concerned with the most evanescent and fugitive experience: to recreate the remembered moment, to monumentalise the glimpse, to make altarpieces out of the ephemeral. Like Proust (and like Powys) he was receptive to Bergson's ideas of 'involuntary memory' — of the moment of perception as a rare grace. He almost never painted from life; starting out from small, very swift drawings (made sometimes months or years earlier) his canvases develop into grandly constructed images, often six foot or more in scale, yet diffuse and almost tentative, tender and vulnerable. He frequently locates himself as a kind of authorial presence — perhaps his own knee jutting into the image, or, more often, a spatial construction that makes explicit his own positioning. 'Let it be felt that the artist was there', he wrote in 1937.

Bonnard's first-person art might be seen as a sustained argument for ecstatic modes of being, very much analogous to Powys's constant defence of the values of 'sensuality'. Thirty years after my initial double-dose, and double identification, the parallels still seem to hold; so that recently, writing a monograph on Bonnard, I've been astonished to recognise how often the terms in which I'd earlier written of the writer, prove to be transferable to the painter also.

★ ★ ★ ★

Throughout my twenties, as I voyaged in search of a useful painting tradition, my main anchor was my conception of an Ideal Picture, based on (of all things) a Powys romance. That ideal picture would need to be large and complex, fluid enough to accommodate 'just everything'. It would have to combine the mythical and allegorical with the most minutely observed depiction of everyday life. It would be panoramic, map-like, yet within this aerial view human figures

Max Beckmann: The Cabins, 1948 (reproduced by kind permission of Kunstsammlung Nordrhein-Westfalen)

would loom large, individuals with their share of the grotesque. The picture would contain within itself a cyclic rhythm ... All this may sound more like cinema than painting and it's true that Fellini's *8½* and Tarkovsky's *Solaris* (with its astonishing homage to Brueghel) became paradigms for me also.

But I did find, in Max Beckmann, one painter whose structures were complex enough to match John Cowper's. Looking at the many compartments of a late picture like *The Cabins* (1950; Düsseldorf) I might think of John Cowper's letter to Littleton of 1951:

> The idea of which William James speaks, of a *multiverse*, or a *Strung-Along Jumble-Chaos* of all sorts of weird and funny worlds and still odder dimensions and 'cosmoses', with cosmographies and cosmographers of their own.

When I first saw Beckmann's work in the 1960s, I was entirely unprepared, and my response was rather like that on first encountering *A Glastonbury Romance*. How could I, brainwashed by modernism, take seriously these fourteen-foot triptychs, with their multiple stages, crowded with figures in mythological fancy-dress, where classical gods, Jungian dream-archetypes, and the home-made avatars of Madame Blavatsky all rubbed shoulders on equal terms? In the 1930s a contemporary called these triptychs 'Post-Christian Altarpieces'; what Beckmann is partly doing, is filling the void. Early on, he'd written: 'Oh, this infinite space, which one must constantly pile with any kind of junk, so that one will not see behind it to the terrible depth.' (*Letters from War*, 1914) His later works were often painted on a black ground, so that one literally glimpses the void through the interstices. And while Beckmann, like Powys, creates mythological figures of apparent solidity, both are careful always to undercut. Illusion and disillusionment are present together; as John Cowper puts it at the end of *A Glastonbury Romance*, 'the Lies of great creative Nature give birth to Truth that is to be' (1174).

For both, it is essential that the crowding be indiscriminate, and all-inclusive. As Beckmann commented to Stefan Lackner in 1938, 'Basically, my thing originates in an almost demented mirth, but then it aims at not leaving anything out.'

In his first triptych, *Departure* (1932; Museum of Modern Art, New York) the general scheme is clear enough: between two panels depicting suffering, the middle opens into a calm sea. Iris Murdoch in *Henry and Cato* (1976) describes the central panel as follows:

> Against an empty blue sky, an empty blue horizon, a masked helmsman takes a fisher king, his queen, his fair-haired child, away to sea, while an old divinity clutches the edge of the boat and an immense wise blue fish lies looking upwards. On either side of this great confident calm are scenes of torture.

The triptych-structure allows Beckmann to present different states of being side by side, in a kind of dialectic; joy *out of* despair, transcendence *from* oppression. And Beckmann was as aware as Powys of the name of the god of such contradictory or cyclic

Timothy Hyman: Wilson Knight — The House of the Interpreter, *1982*

possibilities; the word SATURN is inscribed on several canvases. Beckmann's (more than a hundred) self-portraits are the richest of our century, and usually present the artist in rôle. To quote Iris Murdoch again:

> How wonderful to be able to look at oneself in a mirror and become something so permanent and significant and monumental: a revolutionary leader, an epic hero, a sailor, a *roué*, a clown, a king ...

In the 1920s, the category of Selbst-Kunst was coined by Weimar critics; and 'Self-Art' may be a useful way of looking at a whole range of twentieth-century painters. The narrative of the self has been as much a key theme in modern painting as in modern literature — from Chagall to Guston, from Stanley Spencer to Ken Kiff — even if modernism, with its bias against explicit subjectivity, often seemed to repress this dimension.

★ ★ ★ ★

Probably the most significant artist to have actually visited John Cowper Powys was Sidney Nolan; he seems to have read Powys in Australia, before embarking on his remarkable cycle of paintings about the outlaw Ned Kelly. It was probably Nolan also who introduced Patrick White to Powys's work. I'm not sure exactly when Nolan made his first pilgrimage to see Powys in Wales, nor how often he returned. But certainly in the early 1950s he inscribed a small landscape to John Cowper; and twenty years later, when I visited Phyllis Playter in Blaenau Ffestiniog, it still hung there. I'd like to know what happened to it. I did attempt, about twelve years ago, to question Nolan after a lecture in London, but he was evasive — exclaiming only of John Cowper: 'Great guy! Terrific! Terrific!' He wasn't going to tell me anything. And now he's dead. I wonder if we will ever learn that story in any detail.

★ ★ ★ ★

Among British painters, the deepest Powys affinity may be with Stanley Spencer, and especially with the late work. I was involved in

Ken Kiff: Talking to a Psychoanalyst, 1975–79

the Barbican Art Gallery's 1991 project, to reconstruct Spencer's 'Church/House' — a kind of cathedral to the self, in which, for example the famous 'Leg-of-Mutton' *Double Nude Portrait* (1936–7), now in the Tate, would serve as an altarpiece for the 'Patricia Chapel', one of several dedicated to each of the women in his life. I called my catalogue essay 'The Sacred Self'; in Spencer, the whiff of masochistic self-revelation, and of crazy ritualising behaviour, often brings to mind John Cowper in his Dud No-man aspect. And when God appears, as in *The Scorpion* from the *Christ in the Wilderness* series (1939), the sense is of an outcast divinity somewhat in the Myrddin Wyllt mould, communing with the unregarded, the lowly or mis-shapen.

Who were Spencer's heirs among my contempories? In 1978 I was invited to set up a large touring exhibition under the title *Narrative Paintings*, bringing together work by twenty-one artists (including my own). The catalogue cover would illustrate two recent pictures I particularly admired: on the front, a six-foot square 'altarpiece' by the American-born, but then London-based, R. B. Kitaj — one of several pictures to come out of this painter's passionate interest in Pound and Eliot. Kitaj's relevance to my argument here is that he always declared his bookishness; as he once quipped 'some books have pictures, and some pictures have books'. *If Not, Not* (1976; Scottish National Gallery of Modern Art, Edinburgh) was a complex tangle of imagery based on *The Waste Land*; 'these fragments I have shored against my ruins' could stand for all Kitaj's work. Yet this was essentially a public image, a modern History Painting (and it has now been enlarged to four times the scale, to hang as a tapestry in the entrance to the new British Library).

On the back cover, deliberately contrasted, was a smaller and far more intimate work, Ken Kiff's *Talking to a Psychoanalyst* (1975–79), where the figure seated in the armchair is a self-portrait, confronting the shadowy analyst. Kiff, born in 1935, had only recently emerged from obscurity; he would in the 1980s become probably the most influential painter of his generation in Britain, creating a marvellously compelling archetypal imagery. One of the first topics that came up when we met was our shared interest in the work of John Cowper

Powys. Kiff had read Powys's *Rabelais* at eighteen; then, much later, already in his thirties, he'd come across *Wolf Solent*, and had subsequently read his way through several of the major fictions.

What follows is my transcription from a recent taped conversation. Kiff began by emphasising (what I'd often heard him say before) that Powys was 'enormously talented'.

> You might say, "He's not Tolstoy", but then you'd still have an interesting thought: the skill, the intensity of the writing, sometimes seems of such a high order that one was thinking: "Well, *isn't* this a great writer?" He *is* a great writer! It was especially parts of *A Glastonbury Romance* that convinced me of this (though I felt more at home with *Wolf Solent*). The texture of *A Glastonbury Romance* seemed wonderfully dense, but where exactly the whole thing was going, I wasn't quite sure.... Thinking of Powys in relation to Hardy, or to Lawrence — in some ways I love Powys most. What Powys has got which the others haven't: an imaginative grasp. You know how I care very much about a kind of unity, gradually introducing more and more differentiation. It's as though, with Powys, it's all *moulded together*: and any kind of memories, or real facts, are totally moulded into the stuff. (Even if you move from one key, or one idiom, to another, if your grasp is strong enough, you can still mould it all together ...)

Later we spoke of the mythological element in Powys's work — the way he signals that gods *could* be around. (Not by belief, but by hypothesis.) Somehow Powys has a place for all that. Kiff replied: 'I think the reason that I was so pleased, so *grateful* that *Wolf Solent* had come my way, was very much because of that dimension.'

There are several other British painters that one could bring in. For instance, Cecil and Elisabeth Collins made some kind of Powys pilgrimage in the 1930s. Frank Auerbach once told me he'd read almost all of Powys. And Christopher Lebrun, when we had a recent public dialogue at the Tate, spoke of his admiration for *Wolf Solent*. But of course my subject in this essay is my own quest, and, however reluctantly, I must conclude by talking of my own work.

★ ★ ★ ★

I find it very much harder to speak of my own paintings, but I suppose what they all have in common is a kind of spatial compression, with my own presence as witness of the scene (sometimes in the comic persona of a myopic fool). I will concentrate here on four pictures whose themes are more directly of Powys relevance. About sixteen years ago I made a portrait of Wilson Knight (page 114). I worked mostly from imagination, as an act of affectionate remembrance, though of course he was still alive at this time. I wanted his head to *float up* as it were, through the medium of memory, into consciousness. *Talking to Gerard Casey at Mappowder* (page 120) was completed a few years later; it is more about a relationship, and my cornered presence on the left partly reflects my habitual sense of discomfiture when taking tea with this fierce prophet. (John Cowper looks on, by proxy, in a portrait by his brother Will.)

Parallel to the smaller images, I've always had at least one big 'composition' on the go. This six-foot picture is entitled *"Weymouth Sands": John Cowper Powys Introduces Me to a Circle of his Admirers* (page 6). It was shown at the Royal Academy in 1990; Richard Maxwell chose to feature it (with suitable quotations) on the cover of *Powys Notes* (USA) in 1995. When the image first came to me, its conjunction of 'the spire, the clock, the statue', together with the Powysians hovering above, seemed to encapsulate the experience of twenty years. Wilson Knight who first introduced me to The Powys Society, is the stepping-stone to these various friends. I wanted all these personalities to be suspended in a kind of *affectionate substance* ('Saturnian Gold'?) for which buttery paint might provide some equivalence.

More recently, I've completed a picture called *Mid-River: The Bearer* (page 128). I suppose I've always feared that my 'allegorical' paintings — the vein closest to my Powys roots — might be both ridiculous (corny, archaic) and obscure in meaning. It was therefore an enormous relief to find (when the picture was shown in London) that a reviewer in *The Times*, someone I'd never met, nevertheless understood pretty well what it was about. The picture was identified as

Timothy Hyman: Mid River: The Bearer, *1954–7*

loosely based on the story of St Christopher carrying the infant Christ across a river on his broad shoulders.... The giant figure, satchels flapping from each shoulder, is fording the Thames somewhere near Wapping. He seems to be carrying a second world on his back, as well as a smirking mannikin, while little Bosch-like figures suffer unpleasantly human experiences around his feet.... In depicting the apparent indifference of higher powers to the individual tragedies of everyday life, Hyman has connected with one of our deepest preoccupations. Perhaps this is the painting for the millennium.

I can gloss a bit further. It is one of several images that reflect the problems of mid-life. The figure is a kind of self, but using John Cowper as alter-ego. I see the child as a 'seraphic' or Ariel presence, getting me through the muck ...

★ ★ ★ ★

It becomes part and parcel of reading John Cowper Powys, to learn to defend his integrity and artistry; and thereby, to question and to redefine prevailing criteria. Reading Powys makes one, willy-nilly, a kind of critic. When I started to write on painting, it was easy to transfer the terms of my defence of Powys, to a defence of, say, Bonnard or Beckmann. I think what all Powysians might have in common is a quarrel with the prevailing culture, but a quarrel not easily shaped into an ideology. That quarrel includes an anti-enlightenment bias that leaves us exposed to the charge of being reactionary; and at the same time, an anarchic, anti-authoritarian strain that alienates us from those neo-traditionalists (I'm thinking of Kathleen Raine's *Temenos*, for example) who seek a 'Return to Order'. We are easily dismissed as eccentric, or marginal.

In the late 1960s and the 1970s, as John Cowper's reputation grew, our hope increased; what our enthusiasm partly amounted to, was the perception in each one of us, that if Powys was not a lost cause, then neither was I. The Powys circle, living invisibly in small towns and isolated cottages all over Britain, forced me to jettison assumptions about the superiority of London-based intelligentsia. The archetypal dream of the rebellion of the misfits against the dominion of the 'well-constituted' (the theme of all John Cowper's fiction, from *Wood and Stone* onwards) seemed to gather strength in a new, global and 'green' culture. In London, the Village Bookshop appeared in Regent Street, like a portent of the millennium — presided over, astonishingly, by the bust of John Cowper. As more and more Powys titles appeared each month, one felt linked to a great possibility ...

Fifteen years later, at the end of the Thatcher years, that new culture might seem to have been wiped out as thoroughly as Geard's commune was by the Glastonbury flood. Yet, in parallel, much had occurred in the visual arts that seemed to me hopeful. For example, in the case of Stanley Spencer, his work had been literally marginalised at the Tate throughout the 1970s; they couldn't altogether exclude him, so they confined him to the stairwell leading down to the lavatories. There was no place for him in the internationalist canon; he was listed by the British Council as 'unexportable'. Yet today there is nearly always a Spencer room at the Tate, and a British Council retrospective is planned for 1997 in Washington. Similar upgradings have occurred for all the (previously marginalised) artists mentioned above. And so, despite the grim fact that John Cowper is now mostly out of print, I'm convinced that his work also will eventually be 'rehabilitated' within the new cultural climate of the twenty-first century.

NOTE

The following editions of works by J. C. Powys are used in the text:
   A Glastonbury Romance (London: John Lane The Bodley Head, 1933).
   Weymouth Sands (London: Macdonald, 1963).

PETER J. FOSS

The Proustian Equivalent
A Reading of *Love and Death* *

The remarkable enterprise of Llewelyn Powys's last years — the years between 1933 and 1939 — was one of reclamation. During years of, at worst, illness and at best, seclusion and retirement (first at Chydyok, 1933–36), then in Switzerland (1937–39), Llewelyn composed among other essays the meditative topographical pieces of *Somerset Essays* (1937), the childhood reminiscences of *A Baker's Dozen* (1940), and the posthumously published *Swiss Essays* (1947), with their generous recall of fragments of his earlier life. Above all, he composed the book he considered his culminating work, *Love and Death* (1939).[1]

I have called this period of work an enterprise of reclamation, because it seems to me that one of Llewelyn's chief intentions after his major illness of August 1933 was to review his past life in revivified terms — terms of which, in the words of *Love and Death*, he had since his boyhood been 'storing the experiences of a lifetime' (24). The 'distant purpose' for which this storing of experience was intended is described as the imparting of a 'clue' — and elsewhere that 'clue' is equated (in phraseology characteristic of Llewelyn) with the 'secret' or the 'meaning' of life. What I want to show here is how — by focussing on the 'imaginary autobiography' *Love and Death* — this clue is linked with the reclamation of the significance of past life through creative reordering (what Llewelyn called 'the magical mirror of retrospective memory').

This phrase is interesting for the reasons that it is precise but also deceptively glib. Llewelyn often used formulaic phrases to try to pin

* This paper was given by Dr Peter Foss to The Powys Society Conference at Cirencester, 27 August 1990.

down his particular philosophy of life or to define the nature of the
clue he felt he was destined to impart. The phrase comes from the
essay called 'The Sea! The Sea! The Sea!' in *Dorset Essays* (1934), and
lovingly describes the memory of the time when he and his brother
Littleton walked from Montacute to Seatown one summer in 1899
(Llewelyn was 14 years of age):

> In those days my attention was always so passionately occu-
> pied with its childish interests that I seldom consciously took
> pleasure in the passing of the seasons and yet it appears to me
> now that never since those mornings have I tasted the golden
> wine of April in so pure an essence, with my father on the drive
> before his usual time, his sermon finished out of hand before
> the first swallow flashing past his study window; with the
> daisies and daffodil petals shining bright; and two eggs already
> in the hedge-sparrow's nest by the front gate, and the fugitive
> hours belonging, so it seems in the magical mirror of retro-
> spective memory, not only to the importunate actuality of the
> moment, but to an antiquity lightly confederate with the
> eternal. (50)

Llewelyn's use of vocabulary is characteristic but significant; he
uses terms such as 'essence' in association with the reclaimed recollections of that April morning, they are 'fugitive' hours — both 'fugitive'
and 'actual' — and are said to belong to the 'eternal', they are timeless,
reclaimed from time. The 'mirror' of memory is therefore not simply
a recollection of past experience; it is 'magical' precisely because it re-
vivifies and gives value to fugitive life.

The element of love is important here; the affectionate description
of his father on the Montacute drive; the brotherly comradeship and
protectiveness of Littleton, who was ten years older that Llewelyn; the
memory of the Montacute garden and the hedgerows and lanes of
Somerset and Dorset at the turn of the century. The essay is rich with
the vocabulary of delight. It was, says Llewelyn, 'one of the happiest
days of my life' (53).

The later topographical essays of Llewelyn Powys are characterised
by such experiences — fragments of time (to use Proust's phrase)

isolated 'in the pure state', and these memories are often accompanied by a kind of outpouring of love towards the people and incidents of Llewelyn's childhood. In the essay written in memory of his brother 'Albert Reginald Powys' in *Somerset Essays* (1937), Bertie's death in 1936 occasions a particularly loving and detailed evocation of Llewelyn's childhood at Montacute. Illuminated fragments from their past together stand out 'bold and clear' as Llewelyn says, 'with the abruptness of a lantern slide' (162). Smells are particularly evocative: burning wood, because of its sensory associations with Bertie and Marian in their garden den, would free his spirit 'from ordinary time and space restrictions, to be transported, swift as any Ariel, back to the Mayberlulu' (167).

The detail of the light blue colour of forget-me-nots in the Montacute garden, which the child suddenly encounters when racing round a corner of the kitchen garden, defines the visionary nature of this recollective experience:

> As I came racing round the corner of the kitchen garden, past the July apple tree, and saw these pools of blue, the sodden Somerset soil might have been subjected to some airy transmutation associated with the sky above the outspreading garlands of the milk-white blossoms of the fruit trees. (163)

The apparent 'transmutation' of earth into air (which is also this-world into the other-worldly, earth into heaven — note the alchemical terminology) in a momentary transposition of the blue sky and the blue flowers shows how the value of his childhood life is altered when refracted by the experience of his brother's death and the renewed sense of love occasioned by that death. The conditioning phrase 'might have been' holds the actuality of the remembered experience in balance with its visionary value; just as, later, the vicarage drawing room where the brothers sit listening to the birds in the garden, occupies both the world of a Victorian English childhood and also, via the transforming agency of this vision, the paradise that is Nishapour and its sultan's aviary:

> I was a very small boy, but I remember as I saw the tears suddenly begin to flow from the eyes of my brother, always so

133

proud and reserved, my very marrow bones melted with a longing to be able to comfort him. We sat, I recollect, side by side on the drawing room sofa, with the singing of the birds coming in to us through the wide open sash window so loud that the familiar room might have belonged to a summer bower in a Sultan's aviary at Nishapour rather than to a Victorian vicarage in England. (164)[2]

The conditionals 'would have' and 'might have been' are important for the way they envisage individual moments as representative experience. They serve to confirm that the purport of what is being described is a reclamation of experience, its *essence*. We are of course familiar with the technique from Proust, whose *A la Recherche du Temps Perdu* provides us with a philosophical basis and artistic justification for what we experience when we read Llewelyn Powys. A passage such as the following from Proust's first book, *Du Coté de Chez Swann* (1913), can be put alongside that quoted from Llewelyn Powys's essay on his brother, in the way that Proust's recollection of his childhood tries to understand the hidden significance of objects and events in the context of the totality of his life 'reclaimed' through his book:

And again, after mass, when we looked in to tell Théodore to bring a larger loaf than usual because our cousins had taken advantage of the fine weather to come over from Thiberzy for luncheon, we had in front of us the steeple, which, baked and brown itself like a larger loaf still of 'holy bread', with flakes and sticky drops on it of sunlight, pricked its sharp point into the blue sky. And in the evening as I came in from my walk and thought of the approaching moment when I must say good night to my mother and see her no more, the steeple was by contrast so kindly, there at the close of day, and I would imagine it as being laid, like a brown velvet cushion, against — as being thrust into the pallid sky which had yielded beneath its pressure, had sunk slightly so as to make room for it, and had correspondingly risen on either side; while the cries of the birds wheeling to and fro about it seemed to intensify its silence, to elongate its spire still further, and to invest it with some quality beyond the power of words.[3]

The immediate similarities here with Llewelyn are not only evident in the syntax, the parenthetical richness of the sentences, and the frequent use in Proust of 'And' to open sentences and parentheses (which has the effect of sustaining the momentum of recollected fragments); but also in the extravagance of the similes — the church spire like a loaf of holy bread — and in the imaginary transposition between active steeple and passive sky: the sky cushioning the steeple and making room for it, as though the sky were a substance acted upon. It is this transmutation (like Llewelyn's of the forget-me-nots) that gives the church a 'quality beyond the power of words' (equivalent almost to the disintegration and reformulation of the image in Proust's search for captured significance); and manages also to distil from an unrealised period of happiness deeply felt (and a hurt which has life-long reverberations), an illumination which Proust is not afraid to call visionary.

A la Recherche du Temps Perdu was a favourite work of Llewelyn's wife, Alyse Gregory. It was also much admired by Llewelyn himself, who seems to have first read Proust in about 1924.[4] In a letter of 14 September 1939, during a time when Alyse was re-reading the whole of Proust to Llewelyn, Llewelyn compares the work of this 'greatest writer of our generation' to his own poetic vision.[5] In the first part of *Du Coté de Chez Swann* (the 'Overture'), Proust describes the well-known incident of the madeleine dipped in tea which has triggered the 'vast structure of recollection' which was the truth of himself and his life. Proust uses the significant word 'essence' to characterise the memory liberated from him, and the word 'truth' to define the value of that reclaimed life, a life which of necessity is 'new-create': 'Il est clair que la vérité que je cherche n'est pas en lui, mais en moi ... Chercher? Pas seulement: créer. Il est en face de quelque chose qui n'est pas encore et que seul il peut réaliser, puis faire entrer dans sa lumière.'[6]

In the final book of Proust's novel, called *Le Temps Retrouvé* (1927) Proust distinguishes between ordinary recollection which is governed by the 'ineluctable law ... which ordains that we can only imagine what is absent' and that 'ideal condition of complete coincidence between experience and image' which is occasioned by certain sensory triggers. For Proust, the vision which accompanies his 'recapturing of time' is in effect an experience of timelessness, and is described in terms of ecstasy:

> The being which has been reborn in me ... is nourished only by the essences of things, in these alone does it find its sustenance and delight. In the observation of the present, where the senses cannot feed it with this food, it languishes, as it does in the consideration of a past made arid by the intellect ... But let a noise or a scent, once heard or once smelt, be heard or smelt again in the present and at the same time in the past, real without being actual, ideal without being abstract, and immediately the permanent and habitually concealed essence of things is liberated and our true self which seemed — had perhaps for long years seemed — to be dead but was not altogether dead, is awakened and reanimated as it receives the celestial nourishment that is brought to it. A minute freed from the order of time has re-created in us, to feel it, the man freed from the order of time.[7]

I have said already that Llewelyn Powys's autobiographical essays of the 1930s were not simply a way of recalling, nostalgically, moments in his past life (although reflection and nostalgia are ingredients of Llewelyn's writing all his life), but were, in fact, a way of reclaiming and creatively revivifying the past in precisely the way described by Marcel Proust. The Proustian nature of Llewelyn's topographical writings — in *Somerset Essays* and particularly in *A Baker's Dozen* — gives them, through their highly-charged vocabulary, rich imagery and oracular phraseology — an incandescence which is distinctive and extraordinary. Their evocation of the West Country landscape as paradisal is distinguished by a blessedness which in a sense redeems the fragmentary and fugitive nature of actual life. This was the objective of the Proustian method: to redeem through imaginative art one's 'true life — notre vraie vie, la réalité telle que nous l'avons sentie — the reality we have felt it to be'.[8]

The objective is also Llewelyn's — and nowhere is this more explicit than in the 'imaginary autobiography' itself, *Love and Death*. Without this key, *Love and Death* is bound to be a profoundly misunderstood work. This is clear not only in the light of the reaction to its publication, but also in many of the subsequent comments on the book, for example Michael Roulstone's 1973 article read as a paper at the Powys Society that year. When Llewelyn wrote in a letter of 1938, that *Love and Death* was his 'most important book', he was conscious that it was a consummate work. One of the few contemporary reviewers who recognised this was George Painter — interestingly the critic and biographer of Proust — whose review of the second edition in *The Listener* (21 September 1950) described the book, wittily and perceptively, as 'a self-given gift in the last hour … of a debt that even his youth had never paid'. What Painter realised was that *Love and Death*, like *Remembrance of Things Past*, was a work of reclamation, of discovering truth: *notre vraie vie*. As Painter was to say of Proust, *A la Recherche du Temps Perdu* was 'the symbolic story of his life … [designed] not to falsify reality, but, on the contrary, to induce it to reveal the truths it so successfully hides in this world".[9] Accomplished though the insights of maturity and love were, Llewelyn's book was a debt paid to himself, a gift his youth was never able to formulate, the gift of the significance of his own life — and this at the time when he stood, literally, on the verge of death, during the crisis of his haemorrhage beginning on 3 August 1933.

The tripartite time-sequence of *Love and Death* should be understood aright. There seem to me to be two precise periods of time, and one imprecise one; the 'present time' is 1933, beginning on 1 May and ending with his anticipated death on 13 August 1933, Llewelyn's birthday. Then there is the period of his childhood in Montacute — anywhere between his earliest memories of 1887 and his fourteenth year. Lastly, there is the 'unreal' time of the summer of his twenty-third year — which is 1907, but not 1907. To all intents and purposes, the 'summer of his 23rd year' is an amalgam of the summers spent fragmentarily at Montacute between leaving Cambridge in July 1906 and the first appearance of his tuberculosis in the Autumn of 1909. The fact that many of these summers were as painful, worrying and depressing as they were 'happy' — for example, working for his Cambridge pass degree in the summer of 1906, schoolmastering at Calne until August 1908, nursing John during his illness of 1909 — illustrates to what extent *Love and Death*'s 'summer of his 23rd year' was imaginary.

But this 'middle period' as we may call it, is the core of *Love and Death*'s story, a story which is so simple as to be negligible, so unreal as to be (purposely) illusory. There is no excuse made for the unreal nature of the beloved, Dittany Stone.[10] She is, like the stylised beloveds of medieval romance, a *typos*. That her literary unreality happens to coincide with the ethereal nature of the woman herself is of course apt, but that this also happens to coincide with very real aspects of the character of Gamel Woolsey, on whom, to a large extent, the figure of Dittany Stone is based, opens up biographical cross-currents which are not wholly irrelevant. Why? Because it was Llewelyn's real-life love-affair with Gamel Woolsey that provided the motivation for reclaiming that fragmentary and fugitive period of his life before the onset of his tuberculosis in terms of the affection and happiness which rightly belonged to it. Proust saw clearly that living life in the throes of the moment is never commensurate with the longing we have to grasp its significance. The temporary reality of one's actual life — in Llewelyn's case that group of summers from 1906 to 1909 — was so flawed and incoherent as to make it, in the throes of living it, misunderstood and therefore inaccessible to meaning. In retrospect, the realisation that it was impossible fully to appreciate the house and garden at Montacute, and his life there, at the same time as living it, necessitated the reconstitution of that life and its context as a gift of love. To render that love, Llewelyn had to perform an act of renuncia-tion — renunciation of one kind of reality for another (biographical reality for symbolic reality). Dittany is the agent, the sensation Dittany arouses, the means. When Llewelyn says that he felt the same kind of 'mystical ecstasy' in the presence of Dittany Stone as Christian mystics say they experience in connection with the figure of Christ (93), he is affirming to what extent Dittany is an incarnational touchstone, enabling the eternal to be revealed through the temporal.

This 'middle period' of *Love and Death* re-envisages the landscape of Montacute as a type of 'earthly paradise' and also reclaims a lost and flawed period of Llewelyn's life. The affectionate descriptions of the environs of the village — familiar haunts visited in the company of Dittany — Bagnel, Hedgecock, Norton Covert, Tinker's Bubble, Ilchester and the Tintinhull lanes — have this quality of richness and delight which we associate with Llewelyn's later autobiographical writing, a richness Alyse Gregory recognised in the Introduction to *Love and Death* was overburdened with imagery 'as fruit too heavy on the bough may bear it down' (xi). Most of the walks and explorations described were certainly part of Llewelyn's life between 1906 and 1909. The long description of boating down the river Yeo in Chapters 15–17, for example, is based upon an adventure with John, when Llewelyn quoted poetry to him as he does to Dittany.[11] What is noticeable, however, in the light of our acquired knowledge of Llewelyn's biographical history (augmented by his own earlier auto-biographical writings such as *Skin for Skin* (1926)) is the shift of perspective which we recognise towards this landscape and this period evident in the subject himself. This is clearly not the Llewelyn of 1906–1909, the man whom Elwin describes as 'tireless', but at the same time 'haunted', 'worried' and 'depressed', with reserves of intolerance, petulance and revolt.[12] On the contrary, the Llewelyn of *Love and Death* is a projection of his 1930s self, matured as we might say, in the Epicurean vision, mellowed through his 'struggle for life', and recon-ciled to the divisive elements of his Christian upbringing (against which his whole life had been a revolt) and the stifling aspects of his Montacute family background which had emerged, covertly, in earlier stories such as 'The Necrophilias' and 'Threnody'. These negative reactions are clearly present in the Montacute section sof the Diaries of 1908 to 1914, and form part of the relationship with his mother and father in *Skin for Skin*. Such a revaluation (one might almost say atonement) is partly responsible for the loving account of Llewelyn's father in *Love and Death*, and for the feeling of remorse in relation to his mother that we also find in the book.[13]

None of this re-imagining of a period of Llewelyn's past life makes any sense without the framing device of *Love and Death*'s other chronological sequences: the carefree happy childhood at Montacute and the dying man at Chydyok in 1933. The timeless days of the imaginary 'summer of his twenty-third year' are sandwiched between a chronological account of terminal illness and an unspecific chronology of boyhood memories. The latter, which recur spasmodically, are many of them familiar to us from Llewelyn's earlier writings; and, to some extent, it is Llewelyn's intention that they should be so. The reason is that *Love and Death* deals both with the reclaimed whole of Llewelyn's life, Proust's 'vast structure of recollection', and its mythicised portrayal; the 'true life' is the 'reality we have felt it to be'. In addition to this, it is Llewelyn's intention to show the happy garden life at Montacute in all its fugitive moments, to use his words in *Dorset Essays*, 'confederate with eternity'. Fleeting and purposeless they may be, these days are lived by a being which 'even as a very infant' is 'aware of eternity', as Llewelyn says of himself in Chapter 19. This awareness is implied in several passages in *Love and Death*. One particularly significant passage explicitly connects the 'timelessness' of childhood with the 'timelessness' of Llewelyn's recollections of past time on his Chydyok death-bed in Chapter 25. He describes how, when a very small boy, collecting up the garden chairs from the Montacute lawn, he experienced 'an awareness of our earth existence that stirred me from crown to heel':

> A mood was upon me which I knew of old, a mood wherein I became suddenly aware of time as if it actually were static, as if the swift flaming of the immortal moments had been suddenly arrested in the cold hand of eternity, and I awake to know it ... I was still a child, but I had become suddenly possessed by the liveliest realization of birth and death and the dream nature of the hours that lay before me to spend as I liked. (238–9)

The passage is cryptic but important. The realization which is described is a recognition of finite and mortal life, but that finite and mortal life — in the living of it by the child — has a character of unending richness — 'the swift flaming of the immortal moments'. The child, however, in his moment of vision, suddenly finds himself outside it; his *aperçu* recognises its fugitive nature, but the *aperçu* itself occupies the dimension of timelessness — 'the cold hand of eternity'

— cold because the boy has momentarily been taken out of the dimension in which he can enjoy, unthinkingly, the richness and delight of his childhood life. Obviously, the *aperçu* is only understood in retrospect, by the mature man, as being 'confederate with eternity'; to the boy, it is only disturbing — indeed revelatory. A passage in the early pages of *Apples Be Ripe* (1930) which describes the same experience, and which, in comparison, helps to clarify the idea, shows the effect on the child to be one of 'infinite sadness' as well as 'infinite peace':

> There would come over his spirit a sensation of deep and infinite peace, mingled with a sense of infinite sadness, as though for a moment his immature intelligence had under-stood without further demonstration that the insistent beauty of the visible world was in actual fact but a dream without punishment or purpose.[14]

The moment of vision has had the startling effect of questioning the illusory 'timelessness' of childhood's fugitive life — 'the insistent beauty of the visible world'. To the mature man, the moment of vision enables the opposite to be achieved: to reclaim through moments of ecstasy (what Llewelyn always preferred to call moments of 'height-ened awareness' or 'heightened consciousness') the pristine quality of that life 'like a lantern slide'. The 'ecstasy' of the visionary moment is no longer 'cold' as it was to the child (because the child contrasts such detachment with the heat of the living moment of happiness), but is, on the contrary, warm with meaning, indeed with love, with insight. This accounts for the extraordinarily exhilarant opening of *Love and Death*, where Llewelyn describes his acts of worship at Chydyok, and how he would voluntarily detach himself from routine actuality and see things 'with the frenzied eye of a poet'.

These ecstasies — Llewelyn uses the term 'tercel flights' — reproduce a spiritually appropriate mode in which captured time can be experienced. They are, of course, closely connected with the illness which the subject suffers; the consumption produces moments of 'heightening' — *Steigerung* as Thomas Mann called it[15] — and, in the intensity with which they evoke life, throw into deeper contrast the absoluteness of extinction. Like Proust in his cork-lined room, inducing through the savouring of 'essences' the 'vast structure of recollection' — shutting out extraneous sights and sounds and training himself to summon forth the 'real state — *la réalité* — in whose presence other states of consciousness melted and vanished',[16] Llewelyn's illness is an agent which will enable him to call forth his past life 'like a lantern-slide':

> It had been my custom, whenever my pulse-beats were being counted, to think myself back to the quiet of our garden playhouse at Montacute. I would concentrate my mind on an imagined piece of clay far beneath the roots of the Mayberlulu pear trees ... Glimpses of my life passed by me in rapid succession. Once more, as a four-years-old child, I stood in the 'little-room', ready to be measured for my velvet suit by Ellen Greenham, so excited at being alive that my mother had to be called to stop me jumping up and down and repeating over and over, 'Happy Me! Happy Me!' (298)

The juxtapositions in this last chapter of *Love and Death* are, of course, artistically apt: the spontaneous, innocent happiness of childhood and the apprehensive 'wisdom' of the dying man; but for Llewelyn's task of re-evaluating his life *sub specie aeternitatis*, the nearer the abyss, the wilder the dance. It is a component part of Llewelyn's 'clue' to life, which this book has been an attempt to bring to light, that the 'insistent beauty of the visible world' and his love of earthly life which he declares on the last page of *Love and Death*, should become more real the more urgently our mortality presses upon us. In support of this truth, the American essayist and reviewer Stuart Sherman, produced a startling image of a dance (echoing perhaps 'the frenzied eyes of poets' down the ages) in a perceptive comment on Llewelyn's creative mission as early as 1926:

> His contention is that he, by a slight excess in the malignity of nature towards him, has attained an intenser sense than most men of the conditions which nevertheless confront and encompass us all. We — the rest of us — dance before a pictured

curtain masking a bottomless pit. For him, the veil has been rent — he dances with a wilder elation because he sees where the last figure ends.[17]

NOTES

[1] L. Wilkinson, ed., *The Letters of Llewelyn Powys* (London: John Lane The Bodley Head, 1946), 268

[2] 'Nishapour', interestingly, was a type of 'enclosed paradise'. See *Rats in the Sacristy* (Watts, 1937), 127. It was Omar Khayyam's city.

[3] M. Proust, *Swann's Way* (London: Chatto and Windus, 1966), 85–6.

[4] Alyse Gregory in her journal recorded reading Proust to Llewelyn (on, for example, 19 November 1937). There is a reference to Proust in Llewelyn Powys's review of Elie Fauré in *Nation* (30 June 1926). Amongst Alyse Gregory's papers, formerly in the hands of Rosemary Manning, was an unpublished letter which, though undated, was sent by Llewelyn from Montana in 1924 to Alyse when she was working in New York, in which he mentions that he was reading Proust in his spare time.

[5] *Letters*, 305 ('except the last two volumes').

[6] M. Proust, *A la Recherche du Temps Perdu* (Paris: Gallimard, 1954) Vol I, 45.

[7] M. Proust, *Remembrance of Things Past* III (Harmondsworth: Penguin Books, 1983), 906.

[8] Ibid., 915; Proust (Gallimard, 1954), 881.

[9] George Painter *Marcel Proust* 2 Vols (Harmondsworth: Penguin Books, 1977), xiii.

[10] Indeed her reality is continually being challenged. See *Love and Death* (John Lane The Bodley Head, 1939), 35, 48, 57.

[11] R. P. Graves, *The Brother Powys* (London: Routledge Kegan Paul, 1982), 58.

[12] M. Elwin, *The Life of Llewelyn Powys* (London: John Lane The Bodley Head, 1946), 51–2.

[13] There are two passages in *Love and Death* — one describing him 'making a fig' at his mother (174), and the other describing the affectionate concern he has for his father after his mother's death (257), which can be compared with the following passages (unpublished) from his diaries of 1911 and 1914:

> After the prayer bell rung I still walked on the lawn, between the bright flower beds. Mother's tired beckoning figure at the dining room window filled me with vague feelings of mistrust and revolt. That dark, dusty cavernous room so filled with Bibles and Christian resolution, with what vividness, with what reality it seemed to represent all that I hate most in the world, all that is diseased and anti-pagan. (30 May 1911)
>
> At the front door Gertrude spoke to him, but he merely turned his back on her. I saw him standing on the drive and glared at him. So it is

that a week after mother is buried we are quarrelling about who should take the wreaths off her grave ... (10 August 1914)

Gertrude and Katie were late for prayers. Father in his worst Sunday mood began to sigh and groan. I was furious and as I poured out the tea glared at him. 'Why do you look so stern?' 'Gertrude was very tired yesterday and it is obvious Katie wants as much sleep as possible.' 'Don't say any more, don't say any more ... My God! My God! I have always done what I could for you and will continue to do so.' 'You expect too much.' 'Will you be silent and not be impertinent!' — and rushing behind my chair with clenched fist. (16 August 1914) (Elwin evades this scene on pages 115–16).

14 *Apples Be Ripe* (London, New York, Toronto: Longmans, Green & Co., 1930),6.
15 T Mann 'The Making of the Magic Mountain' *Atlantic Monthly* (January 1953).
16 M. Proust, *Swanns Way*, 56–60.
17 Stuart Sherman, *Critical Woodcuts* (New York: Scribner's 1926), 145–6.

GAMEL WOOLSEY

I hated to leave Earth,
for I was certain that disaster awaited us on
The Star of Double Darkness

There is no use trying to pretend that space travel is ever a pleasure. However often you set out on these expeditions to the farther stars, there are moments when you wish you weren't going; you never get used to it. And yet we've so arranged things that we've got to go. We bring our raw materials — our rare metals — from farther and farther away, and we couldn't do without them now; our whole economy is based on them. So there's a constant coming and going. Its like a hive. We fly off to distant stars the way bees fly off to flowers.

Still, being a metallurgist, I should get used to space travelling, because I'm always being sent off somewhere. I've visited planets where there were crimson tress with green flowers and no living creature larger than a fly; and I've landed on asteroids where there was nothing at all but brick-red stone. I should be used to space travelling by now. The trouble is that I'm not, and I never shall be.

And I minded going on this expedition I was about to start on even more than usual because I was leaving Earth, and I love Earth. I am of Earth stock, but I was brought up on Mars, and perhaps that's why I like Earth so much. Mars is beautiful in a way, I suppose, but it's a barren, frightening way. What with its dry red and yellow bushes, and its perpetual dust storms, and its queer, superintelligent worms and beetles, I've never liked Mars much. But I love Earth. It's so green and so fresh, and so safe — anyway, compared to most of the places I go to on my travels. And then it's so beautiful — I can never get used to that — it's so beautiful. Besides, I didn't like the idea of this trip I was going on at all, because we were going to a place that had never been visited before — and with good reason! We were being sent to explore one of the dark double stars that can't be seen in any telescope. Only radar tells us that they are there.

However, all the time that I was wishing that I could stay happily on Earth and didn't have to go on this trip at all, the space ship was preparing to blast off, and I was getting into my armor and strapping myself down and trying to be ready for that awful acceleration I can never get used to. And there it was, worse than ever! After a while I lost consciousness, and when I came to, it was all over and the second mate was bathing my face with cold water.

'It sure takes you badly,' he said.

'It sure does,' I managed to whisper.

But I felt better, and before long I was able to get up and have a drink and even play poker with some of the officers afterward. By that time we were through the space barrier and I was all right again.

There is nothing much to say about space travelling when all goes well, and even less when it doesn't, so I'll go on to our landing, which was the nearer face of Syncroses, the dark double star in Ostricias. No one has ever seen Syncroses — we know it is there only because we can hear it — so this voyage of ours was something in the nature of an experiment. I can see that if we are to learn anything about these dark stars, we shall probably have to go and visit them. But I couldn't help feeling that, in view of our lack of knowledge, our expedition was rather a desperate venture. I suppose we were expendable. The crew were all volunteers and had been carefully picked for their skill and courage. I hadn't volunteered, and had been sent along only because I was the most experienced metallurgist available at the moment. My heroism had still to be tried out.

Even when we got close to Syncroses, we still couldn't see it; we could only tell that we were getting nearer by means of radar and by the tremendous drag of gravity we began to feel.

'Either these stars are bigger than we thought,' the captain said to me, 'or else they are extremely dense. Which do you think it is?'

'I wish I knew,' was all that I could contribute to the discussion. By that time we were using jet propulsion in reverse to keep us from crashing, but even so we landed with a terrific jarring jolt which threw us all in different directions and covered us with bruises. As soon as the ship stopped rocking, we crowded to the portholes, but we could see nothing. Our powerful searchlights had absolutely no effect on the darkness outside. Their light stopped short, as if there were a black wall in front of them; they were useless. And we tried infrared rays, ultraviolet rays, X rays and the new Katchinkin rays — all with the same result. The blackness was impenetrable. And there was absolute silence too.

While we'd been coming down, however, we'd realised, to our surprise, that Syncroses must have some kind of atmosphere. There was a resistance to our passage that could only be atmospherical. But what kind of atmosphere? There are all sorts. Almost as soon as we'd stopped rocking, the chemists got to work on a sample of it, and the strange thing is that it turned out to be a good deal like Earth's, only much thinner. As to how that could be true, your guess is as good as mine. It was while we were sitting round waiting for the chemists to finish their tests, idle and keyed up at the same time, that there was a knock on the hull of the ship.

Then a low intermittent tapping began, like someone knocking on a door that doesn't open. Someone — something — but what? I confess I was frightened; I hadn't been chosen for my heroism after all. Fortunately, the captain had. He was the pilot who had once landed a space ship on an unknown planet in Leda, and got it up again with the assistance of the six-eyed, prong-horned inhabitants. He seemed pleased that we had visitors.

'What do you suppose they are like?' he asked with interest. I didn't even want to think.

The captain began trying to talk to them through the radio loud-speaker, and it was then that we discovered the second snag. All our radio and radar equipment had ceased to function. When we turned on our walkie-talkie sets to test them, we found that they were completely dead too. Radio evidently didn't work on Syncroses either. This was a nasty shock, because we had expected to use our walkie-talkie sets to give us our bearings and to keep us in touch with the ship. It was going to be extremely difficult to do any exploring in that darkness without them.

By the time we'd discovered all the things that were wrong, the chemists had finished their report on Syncroses' atmosphere — quite like Earth's, except for thinness; quite breathable, with sufficient added oxygen; no noxious elements, as far as could be discovered in the short time available.

'What are we waiting for?' said the captain gaily. He was longing to get out and make contact with the denizens of darkness. I was far from feeling the same way, but, after all, I hadn't been brought along just for the ride; so, when he began to put on his space suit, I began to put mine on too. We had meant to go out in some force — the captain and I, a sergeant and four space ratings. There was an assistant metallurgist, but we were going to leave him behind, in case anything happened to me. But now that we'd found that we'd get no help from lights or radio, the captain changed his plans. He decided that only three of us would go out the first time, discover what outside was like, and try to make contact with whatever was knocking. The three he selected for this small party were himself, a tough space sergeant called James, and again me.

How do we get ourselves into these things? At that moment I'd have given anything I had to be safe at home on Earth, with dawn always coming tomorrow. Instead I found myself following the captain into the space lock, my legs moving forward without any instructions from me, as if they were caught in a current. Then the last door of the lock slid open and we stepped out into the darkness. And, if anything, it was worse than I'd expected.

The immense gravity of the star gripped us and seemed to be pulling us into the ground, so that when we tried to walk, we staggered and almost fell. But it was the blackness that was so appalling. It wasn't negative — just the absence of light. It was positive — the presence of darkness. It was truly a darkness that could be felt. And there was a stagnant silence; the only sound we could hear was the captain's voice calling to our visitor in the faint hope that it might still be around and would answer. But the knocking had ceased as soon as we had started opening the space lock, and whatever it was was probably far away by that time.

When we'd secured our communications with the rear as well as we could by making sure that the crew inside could hear us through the air-conditioning vent they'd opened, we began to edge our way out from the ship, a few feet at a time. I've forgotten to say that we were roped together like Alpine climbers, for fear of losing one another in the darkness or falling over unseen precipices. The captain went first, of course, and I followed a few yards behind him, while James stayed beside the ship paying out the rope to us. It was the captain's plan, and seemed rather amateurish to me, but I couldn't think of anything better.

When we'd got a dozen or so yards from the ship, the captain stopped and called again, 'Who's there? Where are you?' It didn't seem likely to me that English was the native language on Syncroses, but the captain was known for getting on with the inhuman inhabitants of remote stars, so I left it to him and stood waiting while he shouted. Just then something put a furry hand on my wrist. I gurgled with surprise.

'What is it? Who's there?' cried the captain; thinking, I suppose, that my gurgling was the reply of some mysterious dweller in darkness.

'Something touched me!' I babbled. 'Something like a small furry hand!'

'Take hold of it! Pat it! Try to make friends with it!' the captain ordered peremptorily.

I tried to catch the hand, but it was gone. And though I searched all around me in the darkness, I couldn't find anything. I told the captain so, and could hear him searching too. At that moment, for some reason, I suddenly remembered that I was a metallurgist, and leaned down to examine the ground. I seemed to be all bare rock, and I picked up a few loose bits I found and stuffed them in my pockets. Just then the man who was holding the rope screamed.

I almost screamed, too; it was such a shocking surprise.

'What is it? What's the matter?' I could hear the captain saying as he hurried back, brushing against me as he felt his way along the line. Then, after a minute or two, he said flatly, 'Why, he isn't here! ... James!' he called. 'James!'

And I could hear him scrabbling around for what seemed like a long time.

'Then he said quietly, 'He's gone, and I can't find the ship either.' He made a funnel of his hands — or so I imagined by the sound — and shouted, 'Ship ahoy! Ship ahoy!'

But no one answered. It was so black at that moment that I couldn't even imagine light, and when the captain's voice died away, it was so silent that I couldn't imagine sound.

'Come up to me,' the captain said quietly. And I felt my way along the rope until I touched him. It was wonderful to touch a fellow human being in that dead darkness. I had to fight against a desire to grab him and hold on.

'I think we ought to stick together,' he said. 'And at the same time I think we'll have to separate if we're ever to find the ship again. I believe that what's happened is that James has been carried off by something and that the rope was dragged some distance before it was cut or broken, and that that's why we can't find the ship. But I don't understand why they can't hear us.'

'I can't imagine,' I said miserably.

'I think the best thing that we can do,' he went on, 'is for you to stand still here while I circle round you with the rope as radius. We can't be very far from the ship after all, and that way I'll probably stumble over it. I'll keep calling to you as I go round,' he added reassuringly. His voice still sounded perfectly cheerful and as if he were in complete control of the situation.

He moved off at once, and I could feel the tension in the cord round my waist, increasing as he drew it out until it was taut, and then began to walk slowly in a circle round me.

'All right, Collier?' he called after a few minutes.

'All right, Captain!' I answered.

A few minutes later he called again and I answered, and this happened several times. But the last call seemed to me to sound much farther away than it should.

'Are you all right, Captain?' I shouted. And no one answered.

I had to find him. I knew that it might be forfeiting my last chance of finding the ship if I looked for him. But I had to do it; it was more for my sake than his. I just couldn't be lost alone in that darkness; I had to find him. So I followed up the cord to its end. There was nothing there;

it simply stopped. It had been cut or broken as before. And though I shouted over and over — first to the captain and then to the ship — no one answered.

I knew that when you're lost its fatal to start looking for something without fixing your direction first. I'd heard how men go round and round in the desert and die of thirst only a short distance from where they started. But I could think of no way to tell north from south on Syncroses. In the blackness there was a mortal chill of utter loneliness, and suddenly I felt so weak and exhausted that I had to sit down, I couldn't stand up any longer. Cold ripples of fear kept breaking over me. *I must do something*, I thought; *I must do something.* But I couldn't think of anything to do. I was afraid to move for fear of getting more and more hopelessly lost.

I'll wait for morning, I thought crazily. I had some mad hope that there would be a morning after all. I would wait for it. As I sat there in the black silence, the blackness and the deadly gravity seemed to be sucking me down as if I were being engulfed in a black quagmire. I began to breath with anxiety, afraid with every breath I drew that I would find I couldn't breath any longer. That there was no air to breathe. *I shall go mad*, I thought. *I can't stand it. I shall go mad.*

Some lines of verse began to run through my head. It was a passage that had frightened me as a child when I'd happened on it in an old Bible in my grandfather's house: *For they were all bound with one chain of darkness. . . . For they were all bound with one chain of darkness.* I kept foolishly repeating it over and over. And I wanted desperately to remember the rest, because it seemed to have been written especially for us. It might even tell me something I needed to know, I felt. But I could remember only a few lines more, and I wasn't even sure that I had those right.

Only over them was spread the darkness, an image of that darkness which is to come. Oh, yes, it was to come. This was eternal darkness, and I was going to be part of it. Because there was no use thinking of being rescued — no one could rescue me. *I must do something. I must do something*, I thought, with a sudden stab of agonising fear. But I couldn't think what to do. I was afraid to move.

I'll wait for morning, I thought crazily again. Perhaps the captain would stumble over me in the darkness. I'd trusted him and he'd failed me, I thought bitterly, wanting to whimper; he let himself be carried off or killed.

I suppose it was the exhaustion — the gravity seemed literally to be dragging my heavy bones into the earth — combined with shock, but at that point of my despair I simply collapsed full length upon the ground and, strange to say, immediately fell asleep or perhaps only fell into a coma.

I don't know how long I was unconscious, but when I woke, it wasn't because morning had come. The blackness was like blindness. Opening my eyes on that blackness frightened me so much that I could have screamed and sobbed.

Instead, I scrambled to my feet and shouted over and over, 'Captain! Ship ahoy! Captain!' But no one answered — always that dead, dark silence.

Just then a furry hand was laid upon my wrist. And then I did scream. I didn't even try to keep it in. I shrieked. And at the same time I tried frantically to seize the hand — at least it was alive! But it was gone. Still I went on searching round me and calling uselessly, 'Who's there? Where are you?' over and over. But nothing answered, and after a while I stopped calling and began trying to pull myself together. I was shivering all over and drenched in cold sweat, and the blackness seemed to have got thicker and to be pressing against my eyeballs like black felt. I had to sit down again. I began trying to breath more slowly and persuade my heart to quiet down.

And it was just then — perhaps because I was quiet and at the lowest point of weakness — that I began to be aware of something, something new inside me, some difference in my relation to things outside me. I could see nothing, less than nothing — it was as if I were blind — and I could hear nothing; there wasn't the faintest whisper of leaves or the slightest stirring in the air. But what I gradually began to realize was that I could feel. I mean that I could feel things that I hadn't been able to feel before. I could feel the relation of my body to the huge mass of the planet, as if gravity were a sense like sight. And I could feel the things around me — I mean I could feel things at a distance. I was aware, for instance, that there were several small creatures moving about not very far away. The furry hands? And then suddenly, with a great shock of joy, I felt the space ship.

There she was, lying straight ahead of me, a little off to the right. I could feel her mass and shape. I can't explain how. I can only say that I possessed a sense I had never had before. It was as if the weight of the ship affected something inside me, as waves of sound affect the sounding boxes in our ears. I felt the ship there — I can't describe it in any other way — I felt her there. And I got up and started to walk toward her. I walked quite slowly and calmly; I wasn't frightened any longer; I was all right. After a while I even remembered that I was a metallurgist again, and leaned down from time to time to pick up pieces of broken rock and stuff them in my bulging pockets.

And then, farther off to the left, I began to feel a moving form, the form of a man. The captain, I thought happily, hardly at all surprised; he was safe too. I could feel him moving toward the ship, but he had felt me, too, I suppose, because he was veering a little in my direction. Then still farther away, I began to be faintly aware of the form of another man. It must be James, and he was moving toward the ship, too, I thought. But I didn't stop or call to them. I suppose I wanted to make sure that it wasn't a mirage or a dream.

I went on steadily until I felt the great ship bulking huge in front of me, and then, with a thrill of delight, actually touched her hard, invisible hull. I stopped then because I could feel the captain getting close to me.

'Hello, Captain,' I said, trying to keep my voice from shaking.

'Hello Collier,' he answered, as cheerful and calm as ever. 'We'd better wait for James; he'll be along in a minute.'

He was, and when he came, we knocked and shouted, and the crew hurried to let us in. Just before the lock opened, I felt something moving toward me, and again felt a soft furry hand laid on my wrist. I tried again to catch it, but it was whisked away, and I could feel something retreating in the darkness — something quick and small.

When we were safe inside the ship, I more or less collapsed and had to be put to bed. But no one held it against me. James was pretty worn out too. The captain, however, was as cheerful and competent as ever; he apparently hadn't turned a hair.

And that was all we saw, or rather felt, of Syncroses. The ship's instruments were being so affected by the gravity — and by some other unknown factor — that the captain had to agree with the other officers, who had been observing them, when they suggested that we had better leave Syncroses while we were still able to. So, within an hour of our safe return, the ship was blasting off. And leaving was almost more difficult than landing had been, but somehow the captain and crew managed it.

As soon as we were out in space our new radio sense deserted us completely, and afterward we could hardly even remember what it had been like to feel things at a distance. We only knew that we had, and our behaviour proved it. But the strangest thing was our confusion over what had happened to us out there in the darkness. We all disagreed. Each of us thought that he had kept on holding the rope and that the others had been lost. And when we tried to work out what had really happened we sounded like characters in Midsummer Night's Dream describing how they were bewitched and lost in the woods. In the end, the captain laughed and gave it up; he was as confused as James and I were. He made a short noncommittal entry in the ship's log; it erred on the side of brevity and of leaving a good deal out, but it was the best he could do.

Back home they gave the captain another star, and James and I got decorations too. I felt that James deserved his for having volunteered to go to Syncroses at all. But I wasn't really happy about mine, because I didn't feel that it corresponded to what you might call the inner facts. I couldn't have felt less heroic than I did on Syncroses; I was frightened to death the whole time. However, I got a lot of credit for those specimens of rock I finally remembered to pick up. I think the scientists imagined me climbing bravely from peak to peak, chipping off bits in the darkness, my collection was so extraordinarily varied. It turned out that it contained some of the strangest minerals ever found anywhere, as well as some new elements.

So I am afraid that I am slated for another trip to Syncroses. The captain will certainly head the expedition, and I'm sure that he can hardly wait to be off. But I don't feel like that at all; I only wish that I could decently get out of going. I shall never learn to like space travelling; I seem to mind it more every time. And then I never want to leave Earth again. It's so beautiful. After Syncroses, it looks more beautiful to me than ever, with its sunlight and its moonlight and starlight, and its electric lights that darkness into day, even on the blackest night.

The Saturday Evening Post, June 18th, 1955.

MICHAEL ALSFORD

'The Star of Double Darkness' by Gamel Woolsey

The 1950s were a time of fascinating contradictions for science fiction. The raging xenophobia of the cold war resonated throughout the cinema in films such as 'Invaders from Mars' and the classic 'Invasion of the Body Snatchers' while at the same time humanity was looking beyond itself to the stars in the wake of the first sputnik. The destructive capacity of human technology recently witnessed at Hiroshima and Nagasaki, juxtaposed with the hope that such power would put us amongst the gods, brought to full focus the ambivalence towards natural science first suggested in Mary Shelley's proto-science fiction novel *Frankenstein*.

Brian Aldiss, commenting on the genre's premier short story magazine *Astounding*, observes the overwhelming bleakness of its content in the light of the atomic age:

> Its writers and readers ... were digesting the implications behind the nuclear bomb, its unlimited power for greatness or destruction. It was a painful process: the old power fantasies were rising to the surface of reality. Many stories were of Earth destroyed, culture doomed, humanity dying, and of the horrific effects of radiation, which brought mutation or insidious

death. Nor were things depicted as much cheerier beyond the solar system. (*Billion Year Spree*, Corgi, 1975, 280)

Hugo Gernsback (1884–1967) is commonly attributed with first using the term 'science fiction'. Editor of a number of pulp magazines during the 1920s & 1930s, the term he used was *Scientifiction*. Gernsback was interested in the idea of science fiction as a didactic tool, a map of technological advances founded upon current scientific developments. For that reason he roundly rejected any notion of science fiction as an exercise in the fantastic or the speculative. The emphasis was on the science rather than on the fiction:

> If an author ... made a statement as to certain future instrumentalities, he usually found it advisable to adhere closely to the possibilities of science as it was then known. Many modern science fiction authors have no such scruples. They do not hesitate to throw scientific plausibility overboard, and embark upon a policy of what I call scientific magic, in other words, science that is neither plausible nor possible. Indeed it overlaps the fairy tale, and often goes one better than the fairy tale. (*Wonder Stories*, 1932)

The science fiction of the 50s in many respects — and in spite of its ideological biddability at times — saw the genre increasing in sophistication and maturity. In moving away from the conventions set by the Gernsback model a bolder and more imaginative fiction began to emerge. Many of the concerns of science fiction authors and film makers of the time revolved around issues relating to the human condition in general and human identity in particular.

This rather unassuming short story by Gamel Woolsey deploys many of the trappings typical of the science fiction of this period while at the same time presenting us with ideas and images that are only now beginning to achieve their full potential within the genre. As is the case with much of her work this story is principally concerned with loneliness and nostalgia and is, in this respect, emotionally autobiographical. Illness, a failed marriage, a painful love affair with Llewelyn Powys and a number of miscarriages — twice while carrying Llewelyn's children — established a deep melancholy in Gamel

Woolsey. Her fear of loneliness and her wistful longing for the past golden age of her youth occur frequently within her work.

In her semi-autobiographical novel *One Way of Love*, completed in 1930 but not published until 1987, Gamel Woolsey has her central character express the fear that 'if she were not to find a lover she would be lonely in another world as well as in this'. One could idly speculate whether she had this in mind when she turned to science fiction to tell a story about loneliness on another world. Remarkably, Woolsey's foray into science fiction — while clearly owing a great deal to her own introspection — manages, serendipitously perhaps, to contribute to developments occurring within the mainstream of the genre.

'The Star of Double Darkness' takes the form of a first person account of a mineralogical expedition to Syncroses, a mysterious planet beyond our own solar system. The title of the piece refers to the absolute and impenetrable darkness the members of the expedition encounter on arrival at Syncroses, a darkness that isolates them from each other and from their ship, their one link with home.

As is often the case with science fiction the technological backdrop, while plausible, is nothing more than window dressing to help establish a context — in this case travel to another world. Woolsey seems quite at home in the deployment of the necessary technological props as is witnessed to in her understated use of the paraphernalia associated with space flight. Never for a moment does her focus dwell upon exotic machinery and instrumentalities nor for that matter does the extra-terrestrial context detain her overly long — the impenetrable darkness denying any possibility of description:

> As soon as the ship stopped rocking, we crowded to the portholes, but could see nothing. Our powerful searchlights had absolutely no effect on the darkness outside. Their light stopped short, as if there were a black wall in front of them; they were useless. And we tried infrared rays, ultraviolet rays, X rays and the new Katchinkin rays — all with the same result. The blackness was impenetrable. And there was absolute silence too.

Woolsey's concern is clearly with the human condition, more

precisely with her condition, her sense of a lost past and her fear of a lonely future. In this respect, coincidentally perhaps, 'The Star of Double Darkness' is perfectly in tune with developments occurring within the science fiction of the 1950s as we shall see.

The twin themes of nostalgia and loneliness are expressed right at the very outset of the story in a sentiment that might have be considered heretical to many science fiction writers of the period entranced as they were with the possibilities of space travel;

> There is no use trying to pretend that space travel is ever a pleasure. However often you set out on these expeditions to the farthest stars, there are moments when you wish you weren't going; you never get used to it.

By the time we reach the end of the story this attitude has not changed, but rather has intensified: 'I shall never learn to like space travel; I seem to mind it more every time. And I never want to leave Earth again. It is so beautiful.'

However, even though leaving the safety and beauty of earth is considered so distasteful there is an imperative laid upon humanity, a need to strike out into the unknown in search of the resources that sustain us: 'we've so arranged things that we've got to go ... It's like a hive. We fly off to distant stars the way bees fly off to flowers.'

For some, like the heroic captain of the expedition, the unknown and its possibilities are to be embraced. In spite of all that occurred on the planet of Syncroses the captain is, in the author's view, likely to head-up a second expedition and will no doubt be looking forward to it. For the writer, while it is clear that leaving the safety of Earth is still a necessity it is something that should be avoided if at all possible.

In the planet of Syncroses Woolsey paints a picture of supreme isolation and loneliness. Nothing can penetrate the darkness; communication, even between crew members physically connected by a length of rope, finally breaks down. The only evidence that one is not alone is the fleeting touch of an alien hand which never remains long enough to be grasped or to give comfort. Is this really a glimpse of the world that Gamel Woolsey saw herself being forced to return to again and again? a world that drives its inhabitants to the brink of madness and despair? a world where any intimacy is ultimately withdrawn and leaves one alone and comfortless? This would certainly fit with what we know of the author. The eulogising over the beauty and safety of Earth parallels Woolsey's idealisation of her past. As Shena Mackay tells us in the introduction to *One Way of Love*,

> In later life Gamel Woolsey was to look back on her Southern childhood as on a paradise lost; her poem 'Carolina Low Country' paints the landscape of her youth in the regretful blue of Houseman's remembered hills, and her land 'Where yesterdays are better than today' is his 'land of lost content'. (*One Way of Love*, Virago 1987, vii)

Compare this to the account of Earth given in the 'The Star of Double Darkness':

> I love Earth. It's so green and fresh, and so safe — anyway, compared to most of the places I go to on my travels. And then it's so beautiful — I can never get used to that — it's so beautiful.

While the introspective focus of the story is undeniable there is, I believe, another aspect to it and one that is perhaps more optimistic than the elements so far discussed.

Although the physical terrain of Syncroses defies description Woolsey provides us with a very detailed account of the emotional terrain of the terrified explorer once even his ship mates had been swallowed up into the darkness:

> In the blackness there was a mortal chill of utter loneliness, and suddenly I felt so weak and exhausted that I had to sit down, I couldn't stand any longer. Cold ripples of fear kept breaking over me ...
>
> I was afraid to move, for fear of getting more and more hopelessly lost ... As I sat there in the black silence, the blackness and the deadly gravity seemed to be sucking me down as if I were being engulfed in a black quagmire ... *I shall go mad*, I thought. *I can't stand it. I shall go mad.*

It is at this point of deepest despair that Woolsey introduces the one note of hope, the one possibility for a return to safety. A seemingly miraculous transformation is experienced by the lost explorer: while Syncroses itself remains unchanged, he now is able to perceive this strange world with a new sense. Suddenly the planet and its inhabitants were making themselves felt, the external world was coming into a new focus. Even the ship could now be felt and returned to.

> And it was just then — perhaps because I was quiet and at the lowest point of weakness — that I began to be aware of something, something new inside me, something different in my relation to things outside me. I could see nothing, less than nothing — it was as if I were blind — and I could hear nothing; there wasn't the faintest whisper of leaves or the slightest stirring in the air. But what I gradually began to realize was that I could feel. I mean I could feel things that I hadn't been able to feel before. I could feel the relation of my body to the huge mass of the planet, as if gravity were a sense like sight. And I could feel the things around me — I mean I could feel things at a distance.

Human adaptability to an alien context and environment is here seen as the only hope of salvation once human ingenuity has failed. We may, as a matter of necessity, find ourselves again and again thrust into impenetrable alien contexts which defy our best attempts at mastery and yet there is hope that while the context may be intractable, we are not. Our ability to be transformed by our environment is our strength, indeed I believe Woolsey to be saying that nothing is ultimately alien to us, no matter how much it may seem to be so. It is this ability to adapt to the unknown that makes it possible to enter the dark and mysterious places despite our reluctance to do so.

While the science fiction of the 1950s was replete with stories concerned with alien beings either taking control of our world or our bodies or both, the notion of an alien environment affecting and even transforming our humanity was less well known although no less significant. It is only since the 1960s, when environmental issues began to receive serious attention, that the significance of place and context upon human identity has been given serious treatment within the genre. There have been notable exceptions of course. One of the most well known instances in which context begins to define identity is within Ray Bradbury's *Martian Chronicles* written during the early 1950s. In this sequence of stories the human beings who colonise Mars eventually begin to regard themselves as Martians while the original indigenous Martians are constantly, and rather tragically, transformed by the increasingly human context of Mars.

Indeed Woolsey's short story has much in common with Bradbury's brand of science fiction which is wont to dwell on themes such as loneliness, nostalgia and the loss of youthful innocence. It is interesting to note that Bradbury's entry in *The Encyclopedia of Science Fiction* (edited by P. Nicholls) speaks of 'an altogether too cosy and comfortable heartland sentiment, of the kind generally associated with *Saturday Evening Post* fiction'. It was of course the *Post* that published Woolsey's short story.

In the short story 'The Enchanted Village' published in 1950 A. E. Von Vogt tells of a man who, having crashed on Mars, finds himself alone in a totally alien environment. Near to death the man discovers a village that seems able to provide for all his needs only to find that its provisions are also totally alien — the food makes him sick, the music hurts his ears and the climate is unbearably hot. Having concluded that the village is actually alive the man sets about trying to teach it to serve his need rather than that of its long dead alien inhabitants. However, ultimately it is the man who adapts to his new environment;

> 'I've won!' thought Jenner, 'the village has found a way!' After a while, he remembered something and crawled to the bathroom. Cautiously, watching the ceiling, he eased himself backward into the shower stall. The yellowish spray came down, cool and delightful. Ecstatically, Jenner wriggled his four-foot tail, and, lifted his long snout to let the thin streams of liquid wash away the food impurities that clung to his sharp teeth. Then he waddled out to bask in the sun, and listen to the timeless music.

It was in the early 1960s with Frank Herbert's *Dune* and its sequels that issues relating to human identity and context were to receive their classic treatment within the genre. In this epic science fiction story the planet Arrakis exerts an overwhelming influence not only upon both the psyche and physicality of the indigenous population but even more so upon alien colonisers. To live on Arrakis is to become part of Arrakis.

Robert Holdstock has explored similar themes in his novel *Earthwind* published in 1977 and the whole cyberpunk sub-genre of the 1990s, fronted by writers such as William Gibson, Bruce Sterling and Ruddy Rucker, gives considerable attention to the humanity / environment interface. Indeed, the preoccupation amongst many modern science fiction writers with virtual reality and its variants can be seen as an aspect of a larger concern with human transformation stimulated by contextual variation.

With this in mind Gamel Woolsey — hardly a name one would usually link with science fiction — can be seen as contributing to one of the most important and abiding themes within the genre. While 'The Star of Double Darkness' at first sight appears to be a deeply melancholy tale, what Woolsey gives us, in a snapshot of her own life, is cause for hope in the face of impenetrable alienation. Not only are we fated always to strike out into the dark unknown to seek that which sustains us (much as we would rather remain with the safe and familiar) but also we have it within ourselves to adapt to each new context and to become part of it so that we might find our way in it again.

> And it was just then — perhaps because I was quiet and at the lowest point of weakness — that I began to be aware of something, something new inside me, some difference in my relation to things outside me.

ROBERT KUNKEL

John Cowper Powys's *Porius*:
A Partial Glossary of Proper Names

This Glossary includes many, but far from all, of the proper names in John Cowper Powys's 'Romance of the Dark Ages', *Porius*. I daresay that anyone even casually acquainted with *Porius* will recognize that a glossary of this sort could be helpful; how well this one fills the bill is for the reader to judge.*

Many proper names occur in variant forms in both published versions of the novel (i.e., the Colgate University Press edition of 1994 and the shortened version originally published by Macdonald in 1951 and later reissued by the Village Press). Some of these variants are presumably inadvertent (e.g., 'Caer Dathyl' and 'Caer-Dathyl'), while others are clearly intentional, not to say wilful (e.g., 'Little Mound' and 'Mound of y Bychan'). For the present purpose it has seemed best to record all such variants, cross-referencing where necessary.

Appended to the glossary is a list of proper names that occur in the novel but aren't in the body of the Glossary. Some of these will be familiar to everyone; some can easily be looked up in dictionaries or other reference works by curious readers; some are explained in the contexts in which they occur; and others, although obscure, occur but once or twice and are not material to an understanding of the text. From the list, in conjunction with the Glossary, it is apparent that the proliferation of proper names in the novel is neither fortuitous nor unavoidable, but deliberate. However, this is not the place to consider

*   An earlier, briefer, version of the Glossary appeared in *The Powys Society Newsletter* 27 (April 1996).
    We are very sorry to report that Robert Kunkel died on April 29th 1998 before this volume appeared, but he saw final proofs and continued to correspond up to a month before his death.

Powys's artistic aims, or whether the novel's profusion of proper names truly furthers their attainment.

Also appended are some useful notes on Welsh names and forms by Stephen Powys Marks. Stephen's sharp eyes and well-stocked mind have also spared me the embarrassment, and the reader the inconvenience, of numerous errors in the Glossary itself. I trust that whatever slips survive are few in comparison to the many that have been eliminated. In his notes, Stephen points out that some of the Welsh forms used by Powys are not authentic; those shown below are exactly as Powys gives them.

THE GLOSSARY

Aberffraw	Town on Mona, for a time (after the period of the novel) the capital of Gwynedd.
Acheron	In Greek mythology, river connected with, or in, the underworld.
Afagddu	('Utter Darkness') An old retainer of the princes of the Gaer, tentatively identified with Pendaran Dyfed. He is nicknamed for Afagddu, son of Ceridwen, a famous swineherd and the ugliest man in the world. *See* Camlan.
Agenor	(1) Greek slave, freed at Uriconium; father of Gwrnach and grandfather of Rhun. (2) In the *Iliad*, one of the Trojan heroes.
Alarch the Fair	Deceased sister of Einion and Brochvael; m. Gwrnach; mother of Rhun and foster-mother of Porius.
Alban	(= Yr Alban) Scotland.
Amaethon	A son of Don and Beli Mawr.
Amherawdr	*See* Arthur.
Amreu ap Ganion	Steward of the Modrybedd; m. Lela/ Lelo.
Anastasius	Byzantine emperor (reigned A.D. 491–518) who championed Pelagius in opposition to the Pope.
Andromache	In the *Iliad*, the wife of Hector, the chief hero of the Trojans.
Annwn/ Annwfyn	Celtic 'Otherworld' to which the souls of the dead are borne and from which they emerge to renewed life. *See* Pwyll, Arawn, Caer Sidi, Eryri.
Apollinaris Sidonius	= Sidonius.

Arans	Twin mountains S.W. of Lake (Llyn) Tegid.
Arawn	King of Annwn, who exchanged shapes and places with Pwyll for a year.
Ardudwy	Province near Harlech, ruled by Einion.
Arenigs	Mountain range W. of Lake Tegid.
Arglwydd/ Arglwyddes	'Lord'/ 'Lady' (a title).
Arianrod	Daughter of Don, sister of Gwydion, and mother of Llew and Dylan.
Artemis	Proud virgin-goddess of the hunt, armed with a bow and arrows.
Arthur	Romanized Brythonic Emperor ('Amherawdr') of Britain (the 'King Arthur' of medieval legend), who staves off the 'Anglo-Saxon' conquest of Britain.
Arverne/ Arverna/Averne/ Averna	*See* Sidonius.
Arvon/ Arfon	Region of N.W. Wales opposite Mona, where Math kept court at Caer Dathyl.
Arwystli	(1) Mountain (E. of Aberystwyth), in (2) district ruled by Einion in E. Central Wales.
Atlantis	The lost island 'utopia' described in Plato's *Critias*. According to legend the Druidic religion was first brought to Britain by refugees from Atlantis.
Aulus	Roman ex-centurion and servant to Porius Manlius; father of Nesta.
Avalon	Arthur's last dwelling-place, to which he was taken after the battle of Camlan. Often identified with modern Glastonbury.
Avanc	('Beaver') Reptilian monster said to have first emerged from Saint Julian's Fount, to have been pulled out of Lake Tegid by Huw Gadarn's oxen, and to have had a lair in the Avanc's Cave.
Avanc's Cave	Cave occupied by Cadawg ab Idris. *See* Avanc.
Avenue of the Dead	= Path of the Dead.
Avernus	Lake near Naples, regarded by the Romans as an entry to the underworld. Its name (= Gk. a-ornos) signifies the absence of birds.
Badon/ Badon Hill/ Bryn Badon	*See* Mount Badon, Caer Badon.
Baldulf	Saxon chieftain, brother of Colgrim. *See* Mount Badon.
Beli Mawr	Ancestral death-god of the forest-people; m. Don; father of many children including Lludd and Caswallawn;

grandfather of Bran Bendigeit.

Bendigeit Bran/ Bendigeit Vran/ Bendigeitvran   = Bran Bendigeit.

Berbers   *See* Forest-people.

Bishop of Arverne/ Arverna/ Averne/ Averna   *See* Sidonius.

Bleiddyn   ('Young Wolf') Name of image of wolf cub belonging to
                 the 'magic child' y Bychan. (In the *Mabinogion*, Bleiddyn
                 is the incestuous wolf-child of Gwydion ap Don and his
                 brother Gilfaethy, produced while they were transformed
                 into wolves by Math.)

Blessed One   Gorthevyr Bendigeit.

Blodeuwedd   ('Flower Form' or 'Flower Face,' and by extension, 'owl')
                 Maiden created from flowers by Math and Gwydion as a
                 wife for Llew Llaw Gyffes. After she betrayed Llew for
                 her lover Gronwy, Gwydion changed her into an owl.
                 See Maenor Penardd.

Boethius   (Anicius Manlius Boethius) Roman philosopher and
                 inventor of the water clock, *c.* A.D. 480–524; executed on a
                 charge of conspiring with Byzantium against Theodoric.
                 In the novel, an 'Aristotelian young friend' of
                 Brochvael's.

Bontdu   Town near modern Dolgellau, S.W. of Corwen.

Bran   ('Crow' or 'raven') (1) Epithet of heroes.
                 (2) Bran Bendigeit. *See* Dinas Bran.

Bran Bendigeit   ('Bran the Blessed') A Brythonic hero-god, son of Llyr
                 and grandson of Beli Mawr, who fought the Gwyddylaid
                 in Ireland. His decapitated head lived on at Harlech and,
                 later, London. *See* also Caswallawn, Cradawc ap Bran,
                 Manawydon fab Llyr.

Briareus/ Briaraeus   With his brothers Gyes (or 'Gyges') and Cottus (or
                 'Cottes'), one of the 'Hundred-handed', monstrous sons
                 of Uranus and Ge (sky and earth). Imprisoned by Cronos
                 in Tartarus, they were freed by Zeus and helped him to
                 defeat Cronos and the Titans. Zeus then made them
                 guardians of Cronos and the Titans when they in turn
                 were imprisoned in Tartarus. (At one point Briareus is
                 identified by JCP as a Titan, according to the tradition
                 reported by Statius.)

Brochvael   Son of Iddawc and Indeg, brother of Einion and Alarch;
                 m. Kymeinvoll; father of Morfydd and Morvran; uncle of
                 Porius.

166

Brother John   Aged Pelagian hermit-monk, mentor of Porius. *See* Pelagius.

Bryn Badon   = Mount Badon.

Brythons/ Brythonaid   (= Britons) A Celtic people who inhabited much of pre-Roman Britain, descended, according to legend, from the Trojans. By the 5th cent. A.D. most upper-class Brythons living in the area ruled by the Roman Empire were Christians and Roman citizens.

y Bychan   ('The Little One') (1) Iscovan.
(2) The mysterious child of Chap. 31, apparently the son of the Derwydd and his brother Llew.

Cadawg ab Idris   'The Disinherited'; son of Gorthevyr Bendigeit; lover of Tonwen.

Cad Goddeu   ('Army' [or 'Battle'] of the Trees') The name is that of a poem attributed to the historical Taliessin.

Cader Idris/ The Cader   ('Chair of Idris') A mountain on the coast S.W. of Corwen. ('Idris' may have been the name of a legendary giant.) *See* Cewri.

Caer   (= Gaer) 'Fort', or by extension, 'palace', 'town', or 'city.'

Caer Badon   Either Bath (the city) or, possibly, Mount Badon.

Caer Cystennin/ Gystennin   ('Fort of Constantine') Constantinople.

Caer Dathyl/ Caer-Dathyl   The home of Math (at Pen y Gaer in Carnarvonshire in modern Wales).

Caer Drewyn   Mynydd-y-Gaer.

Caer-Einion   Birthplace of Taliessin.

Caer Efrog   York.

Caer Gwydion   ('Palace of Gwydion') The Milky Way.

Caergwynt/ Caer Gwynt   = Caerwynt.

Caerleon/ Caer-Lleon/ Caer-Leon/ Caer Leon/ Caerlleon
('Fort of the Legions') Roman legionary fortress (Caerleon-on-Usk) near Newport in S.E. Wales, where Arthur has a palace.

Caerloyw   (1) Gloucestershire.
(2) (= Caer Lloy or Loyw) Otherworld palace in which Mabon ab Modron was imprisoned.

Caer Llyr/ Caerlyr   Leicester.

Caer Myrddin/ Caer-Myrddin   (= modern Carmarthen, in Dyfed) Childhood home of Myrddin Wyllt.

167

Caer Sidi   A castle in Annwn, where Pryderi and Rhiannon were
                   held prisoner by Llwyd until rescued by Manawydon.
                   ('Complete is my chair in Caer Sidi' is a recurrent line in
                   a poem by Taliessin which depicts Caer Sidi as a land in
                   which no one grows old.) *See* Gwair, Caer Vanddwy.

Caer Vanddwy   In the *Spoils of Annwn*, an early Welsh poem attributed to
                   Taliessin, a place visited by Arthur on his voyage to
                   Annwn, along with Caer Sidi, Caer Veddwit, and Caer
                   Pedryvan.

Caer Veddwit   ('Fortress of Carousal') *See* Caer Vanddwy.

Caerwynt/ Caergwynt/ Caer-Gwynt/ Caer Gwynt   A place where Arthur
                   holds court; probably Winchester (*see* p.188 below).

Caius Sollius Modestus   *See* Sidonius.

Camel   *See* Camlan.

Camlan   ('Ferocious battle') The battle in which Arthur killed
                   Medrawd and was himself fatally wounded. Traditionally
                   held to have taken place by the Camel River in Cornwall.
                   In Welsh myth, Afagddu son of Ceridwen was a partici-
                   pant in the battle. *See* Avalon.

Canna ferch Glam   Servant of Brochvael; Morfydd's old nurse; m. Gwrgi.

Cantref   ('Hundred') As in English, a district originally compris-
                   ing a hundred dwellings or farmsteads.

Carbonek   (= Corbenic) In Arthurian legend, the castle of the Holy
                   Grail.

Castrum   Fortified Roman camp.

Caswallawn   (= Caswallon) A son of Beli Mawr who succeeded Bran
                   Bendigeit as ruler of Britain. *See* Cradawc ap Bran.

Caswellen Llawhir ('Caswellen with the long hand') A deceased grand-
                   son of Cunedda, and Einion's cousin; ruler of Deganwy
                   in Gwynedd. Historically, he completed the expulsion of
                   the Gwyddylaid from what is now Wales. *See*
                   Maglocunus.

Cave of the Dog of Mithras   Cave where Rhun has a shrine to Mithras.

Cawr/ Cawres   = Gawr, Gawres.

Ceredigion   = Cardiganshire in modern Wales.

Ceridwen   An earth-goddess worshipped by the forest-people and
                   Cadawg. Wife of Tegid Foel (*see* Lake Tegid). She pre-
                   pared a magic potion in a cauldron to make her son
                   Afagddu all-wise. The potion, however, was consumed by

the shape-changing Gwion Bach, who eventually became a grain of wheat which she, in the shape of a hen, consumed. Subsequently, Ceridwen gave birth to Taliessin, who is a reincarnation of Gwion Bach.

Cernyw Cornwall.

Cewri ('Giants') Aboriginal race of giants lingering in the mountains of Eryri and Cader Idris. *See* Rhitta Gawr, the Gawr, and Creiddylad.

Cheldric/ Childric Saxon chieftain.

Clud Goddess; mother of Gwawl.

Coed Sarn Elen Forest in the vicinity of Sarn Elen.

Coelbren-y-Beirdd Bardic alphabet.

Colgrim Saxon chieftain who sets out from York to invade Edeyrnion; brother of Baldulf.

Coranians Race of ancient invaders from the continent, whose preternatural hearing enabled them to hear news borne on the wind. *See* Lludd ap Beli.

Corwen ('White Circle', 'White Choir' or 'Dwarf-Mound') Town across the Dyfrdwy from Mynydd-y-Gaer, formerly known as Llan-Mithras ('Shrine of Mithras'), Mithras-Market, or Rhyd-Mithras ('Ford of Mithras').

Cradawc ap Bran (= Caradawg) Son of Bran Bendigeit, enveloped by Caswallawn in a veil of illusion.

Craig Hen ('Old Stone') 'Haunted' rocky eminence near Saint Julian's Fount, associated with Gwydion and Llew.

Creiddylad (= Cordelia) (1) Cewri wife of Edeyrn; Porius's great-grandmother.
(2) The Gawres.

Cretinloy of Gaul Chronicler associated with Galahaut.

Cronos In Greek mythology, the ruler of the Titans, who were the children of father heaven (Uranus) and mother earth (Ge). Cronos overthrew his father and emasculated him with an adamantine sickle, but was in turn overthrown by his own son Zeus, who imprisoned him in Tartarus. According to one tradition, Cronos (Roman Saturn) ruled over a golden ('Saturnian') age and will eventually rule over another. In the novel, Cronos is the all-begetting, all-devouring god of time, and is identified with Myrddin Wyllt. *See* Briareus, Cytherean, Eryri, Othrys, Rhea, Tartarus.

Cunedda (= Kenneth) Historically, a Romanized Brython who defeated pagan Gwyddyl invaders from Ireland and founded the Brythonic kingdoms of N. Wales. *See* Edeyrn, Stilicho.

Cymraeg/ Cymreig/ Cymric The emerging Welsh language, as distinguished from earlier Brythonic. ('Cymreig' is strictly the *adjective* 'Welsh'.)

Cymry The common people of Britain, as distinguished from their Romanized rulers and the English (Saxons). Still the national name of the Welsh.

Cynan ap Clydno Arthurian knight and patron of Taliessin.

Cystennin Constantine the Great (A.D. 272–337), Roman emperor. *See* Caer Cystennin.

The Cytherean Aphrodite (Venus), who, according to Hesiod, sprang from the foam that gathered about the severed testicles of Uranus when Cronos flung them into the sea.

Dee *See* Dyfrdwy.

Deganwy Cunedda's capital on the Conwy estuary in N. Wales, ruled by princes descended from his eldest son. *See* Caswellen Llawhir, Maglocunus.

Democritus Greek philosopher (460–361 B.C.); a proponent of the theory that everything is composed of atoms 'hooked together.'

Derwydd (*pl.* Derwyddon) ('Druid') Usually refers to Gogfran ap Greidawl, the last of the Druids of the forest-people. *See* Atlantis, y Bychan, Little Mound, Mona.

Deva Roman name (derived from that of the Celtic goddess of the River Dyfrdwy or Dee) of what is now Chester. *See* Dyfrdwy.

Dinas 'Fort', 'refuge', or 'city.' In place names, sometimes interchangeable with 'Caer.'

Dinas Arianrod Arianrod's palace on an island near Mona.

Dinas Bran ('Fort of the Crow') Ancient hill fort by the Dyfrdwy E. of Corwen (near modern Llangollen).

Dinas Cystennin/ Efrog/ Llyr = Caer Cystennin, Caer Efrog, Caer Llyr.

Diomed (= Diomedes) In Greek myth, one of the Epigoni who conquered Thebes, and later one of the principal Greek heroes of the Trojan War.

Dion Dionides Greek merchant, owner and master of the trading vessel

	Calypso, docked at London.
Divine River	*See* Dyfrdwy.
Dodona	Ancient oracle, located in a grove of oak or beech trees in N.W. Greece.
Don	Sister of Math, wife of Beli, and mother of Gwydion, Lludd, Arianrod and others.
Drom	('Glimpse') Servant of the Derwydd, and later of Brochvael; half-brother of Morgant.
Drudwyn	Rhun's dog (the name is also that of a dog who figures in the *Mabinogion*).
Dulyn	Dublin.
Dyfed	Area in S.W. Wales (county name). *See* Henog, Pryderi, Pwyll.
Dyfnwal Moelmud	Legendary pre-Gwyddyl-Ffichti king of Britain.
Dyfrdwy	('Divine Water') River (the Dee) flowing from Lake Tegid N.W. through Corwen towards its estuary N.W. of Chester; worshipped as a goddess by the Modrybedd (especially Tonwen) and Indeg. *See* Deva, Dinas Bran.
Dylan	Son of Arianrod; a sea-god.
Ecclesiazusae	A comedy by Aristophanes, in which the government of Athens is turned over to women. *See* Praxagora.
yr Echwyd	The castle or district of which Uryen was lord.
Edeyrn	(= Latin 'Eternus') (1) Son of Cunedda; m. Creiddylad; father of Iddawc and grandfather of Einion. (2) = Edeyrnion.
Edeyrnion	The province ruled by Edeyrn and princes descended from him, including Einion and Porius (the 'Princes of the Gaer').
Eigr Mallt	Myrddin Wyllt's cow.
Einion	Throughout most of the novel, the reigning Prince of the Gaer; son of Iddawc, grandson of Edeyrn, and great grandson (erroneously called great-great-grandson in JCP's 'Characters of the Novel') of Cunedda; m. Euronwy; father of Porius.
Eleusinian Mysteries	Secret religious rites of spring celebrated at Eleusis, N.W. of Athens.
yr Ellylles	('The She-Devil') = Rhelemon.
Empedocles	Greek poet-philosopher (5th cent. B.C.).

Endymion   A beautiful youth beloved by the goddess of the moon
                  and allowed by Zeus to sleep forever without growing
                  old.
Erddud   Second of the Three Aunties, long infatuated with her
                  nephew Brochvael. *See* Modrybedd.
Erebus   Cavernous subterranean pathway to Hades.
Erim ab Uchtryd   The Silentiary, adviser to the Modrybedd.
Eryri   Mount Snowdon, on whose highest peak, y Wyddfa ('the
                  tomb'), is an entrance to Tartarus or 'road to Annwyn'
                  and the tomb of Cronos. *See* Cewri.
Euronwy   Wife of Einion and mother of Porius; first cousin once
                  removed of Arthur; daughter of Porius Manlius.
Ffichti/ Ffichtiaid   (= Picts) An aboriginal people antedating the forest-
                  people and at one time slaves of the Cewri; at the time of
                  the novel, mostly intermarried with the Gwyddyl. *See*
                  Gwyddl, Gwyddyl-Ffichti, Ynys Prydein.
The Ffichtiad   Nineue. *See* Ffichti.
Fflam   Boy page to Gwendydd.
Fisher King   In Arthurian legend, a wounded king pending whose
                  recovery the land lies waste. In the novel, 'the Mystery of
                  the Fisher King' is an ancient erotic ritual of the forest-
                  people that originated in N. Africa.
Fisher King's Fount   Saint Julian's Fountain.
Ford of Mithras   (1) Paved Roman ford across the Dyfrdwy at Corwen.
                  (2) by extension, the town of Corwen.
Forest-people   Non-Aryan, pre-Brythonic matriarchal inhabitants of
                  (what is now) Wales, whose ancestors were North
                  Africans (Berbers) who had first migrated to Iberia. The
                  surviving forest-people cleave to their Druidic religion.
                  See Ceridwen, Derwydd, Modrybedd, Iscovan,
                  Ordovices, Venedotians.
Fors Fortuna   The Goddess Chance. *Cf.* Tyche Soteer.
Gaer   (= Caer) (1) Mynydd-y-Gaer.
                  (2) The people of Mynydd-y-Gaer, i.e., the tribe of
                  Einion and Porius. *See* Edeyrnion.
Galahaut   (= Galahad) Arthurian knight; Prince of Far Isles of
                  Surluse (possibly the Scilly Isles).
Galen   Widely travelled Greek physician and philosopher of the
                  2nd cent. A.D.

The Gawr/ Cawr ('Giant') The last of the male Cewri.

The Gawres ('Giantess') The Gawr's daughter Creiddylad.

Gens Manlius *See* House of Manlius.

Germania Roman name (*cf.* 'Britannia') for Germanic-speaking area of the continent.

Geryones Triple-bodied monster slain by Hercules.

Giant's Cave = Ogof-y-Gawr.

Glam Canna's mother.

Gog and Magog Sons of Lot-el-Azziz and Zora (see Ezekiel 38–39 and Revelation 20:8).

Gogfran *See* Derwydd.

Gorsedd Bardic gathering.

Gorthevyr Bendigeit/ Vendigeit ('Gorthevyr the Blessed') Son of Gortheyrn Gorthenau; father of Cadawg. He sought to expel the Saxons from Britain but was betrayed and poisoned by his Saxon step-mother Ronwen.

Gortheyrn Gorthenau/ Gortheneu (= Vortigern) Brythonic king, son-in-law of Maxen-Wledig, who recruited Saxon mercenaries under Hengest to fight the Ffichti and Gwyddyl, thereby laying the groundwork for the 'Anglo-Saxon' conquest of Britain resisted by Arthur. Consequently, in Celtic tradition Gortheyrn Gorthenau is the arch-traitor. In Welsh myth, the young Merlin (Myrddin) helped him build a castle. *See* Ronwen.

Gosgordd Brythonic chieftain's bodyguard of 300 warriors.

Greidawl Deceased Druid; father of Gogfran.

Gronwy Blodeuwedd's lover, slain by Llew-Llaw-Gyffes.

y Grug ('The Mound') *See* Mound of the Dead.

Gunhorst Sibylla's Saxon lover and father of Gunta; a soldier and emissary of Colgrim.

Gunta Daughter of Sibylla and Gunhorst.

Gwair Youth held prisoner in Caer Sidi in the 'The Spoils of Annwn' (poem attributed to Taliessin). *See* Caer Vanddwy.

Gware Gwallt Euryn = Gwri Wallt Euryn.

Gwawl ap Clud ('Light') Unsuccessful suitor of Rhiannon. *See* Llwyd.

Gwendydd Sister of Myrddin Wyllt.

Gwenhyver/ Gwenhyvar (= Guenivere) Arthur's queen.

Gwent   Region, once a principality, in S. E. Wales.

Gwent-Is-Coed   Region of S.E. Wales ruled by Teirnyon Twyrf Vliant.

Gwern   Alder-swamp. *See* Swamp of the Gwyddyl-Ffichti.

Gwlad-yr-haf   ('Land of summer')   Somerset.

Gwrgi ap Cyngar   Servant of Brochvael; m. Canna.

Gwri Wallt/ Gware Gwallt Euryn   ('Golden Hair') The name given to the infant Pryderi by Teirnyon Twryf Vliant.

Gwrnach   Father of Rhun; son of Agenor; m. Alarch. A worshipper of Mithras.

Gwyddyl/ Gwyddylaid   (= Goidel) Gaelic (non-Brythonic) Celts of Ireland or of Irish origin, correctly if confusingly identified by JCP as 'Scots'. *See* Caswellen Llawhir.

Gwyddyles   Female Gwyddyl. 'The Gwyddyles' = Kymeinvoll.

Gwyddyl-Ffichti   Tribe of intermarried Gwyddyl and Ffichti.

Gwyddylgwern/ Gwyddylwern/ Gwyddyl-Gwern = Swamp of the Gwyddyl-Ffichti.

Gwydion ap Don   Son of Don and Beli, nephew of Math, and brother of Arianrod and Lludd. A shape-changing magician who stole Pryderi's swine and later killed him by trickery. Gwydion created Blodeuwedd as a wife for his nephew (and per JCP, son) Llew Llaw Gyffes. In *Porius*, he is sometimes identified with Myrddin Wyllt. *See* Caer Gwydion. For 'Gwydion's sow', *see* Maenor Penardd.

Gwyn ap Nudd   A warrior of Annwn.

Gwynedd   Region of N.W. Wales that includes Mona (Anglesey). *See* Aberffraw, Caswellen Llawhir, Math.

Gwythyr   The Gaer Messenger; m. Nesta ferch Aulus.

Gyges   *See* Briareus.

Harpies   Winged monsters of Greek and Roman myth.

Helen's Causeway   = Sarn Elen.

Hengest/ Hengist/ Hengyst/ Heyngyst   Leader of Saxon mercenaries invited *c.* A.D. 430 by Vortigern (Gortheyrn) to help fight Ffichti and Gwyddyl; father of Ronwen.

The Henog   ('Chief Narrator') Sylvanus ap Bleheris/ Sylvanus-is-Coed, a Silurian chronicler from Dyfed employed by Arthur to write a biography of Myrddin Wyllt. *See* Pryderi, Hesiod, *Mabinogion*.

Hesiod   Greek poet (8th cent. B.C.), referred to in the novel as 'the Henog of Aeolia'.

House of Stone	= Ty Cerrig.
Huw Gadarn	Mythical first Brython, from 'Taprobani, the Summer-country, where Constantinople now stands'. *See* Avanc.
House of Manlius	One of the oldest of the Roman *gentes* (patrilinear clans embracing families who claimed descent from a common ancestor and bore a common name). Porius Manlius is a member of the House of Manlius.
Iberians	*See* Forest-people.
Iddawc ap Edeyrn	'The Apostate'; grandson of Cunedda; m. Indeg; father of Einion, Brochvael, and Alarch the Fair.
Ignatius	Saint and Bishop of Antioch; died *c.* A.D.110.
Indeg	A deceased princess of the forest-people and elder sister of the Modrybedd; m. Iddawc; mother of Einion, Brochvael, and Alarch the Fair.
Iona	Small island in Inner Hebrides, where (*c.* A.D.565) St Colomba founded a monastery and commenced to convert the inhabitants of what is now Scotland to Christianity.
Iscovan ap Serigi	Outlaw-hero of the forest people; son of Serigi (Gwyddyl-Ffichti chieftain) and of woman of the forest-people. *See* y Bychan, Little Mound.
Iwerdon/ Iwerddon	Ireland.
Ixion	In Greek mythology, a king deceived by Zeus into making love to a cloud shaped like Zeus's wife Hera.
Japhet	Third son of Noah; ancestor of the Indo-Europeans.
Jasion	(= Iasion, Iasius, Iasus) Son of Zeus and lover of Demeter. Slain by a lightning-bolt hurled by Zeus.
Kai	(= Kay, Kei, Cai, Cei) As JCP states, Arthur's 'bosom-friend and chief seneschal'.
Kessar	Caesar. Iwl or Ul = Julius; Gloyw = Claudius.
Kraken	Sea-monster dwelling in Norwegian waters.
Kymeinvoll	('The Gwyddyles') Deceased Irish Gwyddyl-Ffichti wife of Brochvael; once lover of Einion.
Lela/ Lelo	Wife of Amreu and maid to Erddud; variously described as an Egyptian and an Iberian.
Little Mound	Burial place of Iscovan and home of Gogfran Derwydd.
Llan-Mithras	('Church/ Shrine of Mithras') *See* Corwen.
Llan-Tysilio-Sant	*See* Tysilio-Sant.

Llew   (1) Llew ap Greidawl, brother of Gogfran Derwydd
            (*see* y Bychan).
            (2) Llew Llaw Gyffes/ Cyffes, son of Arianrod (and per
            JCP, her brother Gwydion ap Don) and the cuckolded
            husband of Blodeuwedd (*see* Maenor Penardd).
            (3) Llew ap Cynvarch/ Kynfarch, husband of Arthur's
            sister Anna and putative father of Medrawd.

Lludd ap Beli   Son of Beli Mawr and destroyer of the Coranians, from
            whose name 'London' and 'Ludgate' were thought to
            have been derived.

Llwyd ap Cilcoed   Friend of Gwawl, who avenged him by placing a curse
            on Dyfed and holding Rhiannon and Pryderi prisoner.
            See Caer Sidi.

Llychlvaid   Norsemen.

Llychlyn   Scandinavia.

Llyn Tegid   *See* Tegid.

Llys   ('Place' or 'court') A palace-fortress.

Lot-el-Azziz   A wandering Jewish doctor; m. Zora; father of Gog and
            Magog.

Ludd's Town/ City of Ludd   London. *See* Lludd ap Beli.

Lysistrata   A comedy by Aristophanes in which the women of
            Athens and Sparta refuse to sleep with their husbands
            until the Peloponnesian War is ended.

Mabinogion   A medieval collection of Welsh folk tales. The novel
            suggests that the tales concerning Pryderi were first
            redacted by the Henog.

Mabon ab Modron   In the *Mabinogion*, Mabon is rescued from captivity
            in Caerloyw by Culwch.

Mabsant ap Kaw   Youthful noble horseman of Arthur.

Maelgwyn   = Maglocunus.

Maenor/ awr-Coed-Alun   Site of the first engagement between the
            armies of Dyfed, led by Pryderi, and those of Gwynedd,
            led by Gwydion ap Don, when Pryderi invaded Gwynedd.

Maenor Penardd   A place in Arvon visited by Gwydion ap Don in his
            search for his nephew Llew, who has escaped from
            Blodeuwedd and Gronwy in the form of an eagle.
            Gwydion finds Llew, perched in an oak, with the aid of a
            sow who eats the lice and rotten flesh that fall from
            Llew's wasted body.

Maglocunus/ Maelgwyn/ Malcunus	Son of Caswallen Llawhir; at the time of the novel, the boy-king of Gwynedd.
Manawydon/ Manawyddan fab Llyr	In the *Mabinogion*, a brother of Bendigeit Bran and second husband of Rhiannon. *See* Caer Sidi.
Mari Llyd	Merlin's mare.
Math	Mythical Lord of Gwynedd and magician uncle of Gwydion ap Don.
Mawddwy	A district ruled by Einion, W. of Corwen.
Maxen-Wledig	(= Macsen Wledig, Magnus Maximus) Roman general declared emperor by legions in Britain in A.D. 368. Defeated by Theodosius and executed in A.D. 388.
Mecaenas	(= Maecenas) Roman statesman; for a time friend and minister of Augustus Caesar, from whom he was eventually estranged.
Medrawd	(= Modred or Mordred) Arthur's nephew and heir-apparent to his throne; the son of Arthur's sister Anna and either Llew ap Cynvarch or possibly Arthur himself.
Meirion	A district ruled by Einion, on west coast of N. Wales.
Melenryd	*See* Pryderi.
Memnon	In the *Odyssey*, the son of the goddess Dawn and the handsomest of men.
Metamorphoses	*See* Ovid.
Minnawc Gorsant	Christian priest, mentor of Euronwy. *See* Morvan ap Brochvael and Saint Julian's.
Mithras	Sun god, originally Persian, whose worship (Mithraism) was widespread in the Roman empire, especially among the legionnaires. Rhun is a worshipper of Mithras.
Mitylene	Chief city of the island of Lesbos.
Moab/ Moabitess	A Semitic tribe said in the Bible to be descended from Moab, an incestuous son of Lot. 'The Moabitess' is Lot-el Azziz's wife Zora.
Modrybedd	('Aunts') The 'Three Aunties' of Einion, Brochvael and Alarch; princesses of the forest-people; individually, Yssylt, Erddud and Tonwen. *See* Inweg.
Moel y Famau/ Fammau/ Faman	('Mountain of the Mothers') A ridge in Edeyrnion, visible from Mynydd-y-Gaer.
Moly	Herb given by Hermes to Odysseus to counteract Circe's power to turn men into animals.

Mona   Ancient name of Anglesey (Welsh 'Ynys Môn'), island off coast of N. Wales. A centre of Druidic worship, which the Romans first attacked in A.D. 60 and conquered in A.D. 79.

Monophysite heresy   The doctrine that the incarnate Christ had but one nature, rather than two (human and divine).

Mons Badonicus = Mount Badon.

Mons Castrum = Mynydd-y-Gaer.

Mor Hafren   The Bristol Channel.

Morfydd ferch Brochvael   Porius's cousin and, later, wife. Daughter of Brochvael (or possibly Einion) and Kymeinvoll.

Morgant   Servant to Derwydd and Llew; half-brother of Drom.

Morvran ap Brochvael   Son of Brochvael and brother of Morfydd. Murdered by fanatical Brythonic Christians incited by Minnawc Gorsant.

The Mound   ('y Grug') = Mound of the Dead.

Mound/ Mount of the Dead   Prehistoric earthwork between Mynydd-y-Gaer and Saint Julian's Fount, reached by the Path of the Dead.

Mound/ Mount of the Little one/ y Bychan/ the Outlaw   = Little Mound.

Mount Badon   Near Bath, where Baldulf has his camp. The site of Arthur's last victory (not recounted in *Porius*) over the Saxons.

Mountain of the Mothers   = Moel y Famau.

Mur-y-Castell/ Mur Castell   ('Castle Wall') In the *Mabinogion*, the locus of the court of Llew and Blodeuwedd, by Lake Tegid.

Mynydd-y-Gaer   ('Mountain of the Fort') The palace-fortress of the Princes of Edeyrnion, overlooking the Dyfrdwy at Corwen. Built by Rhitta Gawr, who is said to be buried in it. (= Caer Drewyn)

Myrddin Ambrosius/ ap Morfryn/ ap Morvran/ ap Morvyrn/ Emrys/ Wyllt   (Myrddin Wyllt = 'Merlin the Wild') Arthur's counsellor, identified with Cronos, Gwydion ap Don, and Ambrosius Aurelianus (Emrys Wledig), a magician who assisted Gortheyrn Gorthenau.

Nantcoll   (Nant = 'brook' or 'stream') A stream near which Pryderi's army, retreating from Gwynedd, was badly defeated by the forces of Gwydion ap Don.

Neb ap Digon   Boy page in Arthur's service, and acolyte of Myrddin Wyllt.

Nereus   In Greek myth, the Old Man of the Sea, father of the
                     Nereids (sea-nymphs).

Nesta ferch Aulus   Daughter of Aulus and handmaid to Euronwy;
                     m. Gwythyr.

Nineue ferch Avellach   (= Tennyson's Vivien) Ffichti enchantress who
                     holds sway over Myrddin Wyllt; handmaid to Gwendydd.

Oceanus/ Ocean   Name of a river issuing from the underworld and
                     encircling the earth, and of its Titan god. In the *Odyssey*,
                     Odysseus visits the shore of Oceanus and there calls up
                     the spirits of the dead. *See* Styx.

Ogam   Early form of Celtic writing found in Wales, Ireland and
                     Scotland (*adj.*, 'ogamic').

Ogof-y-Gawr   ('Giant's Cave') House of the Modrybedd.

Ogof-yr-Avanc   = Avanc's Cave.

Old Man of the Sea   *See* Nereus.

Old Stone   = Craig Hen.

Ordovices   Tribe of N.W. Wales subjugated by the Romans in the 1st
                     cent. A.D.; one of the names of the forest-people.

Orthus   Many-headed dog, son of the monster Echidna.

Othrys   Mountain in Greece occupied by Cronos and the other
                     Titans during their strugle with Zeus and the other gods
                     of Olympus.

Ovid/ Ovidius Naso   Roman poet, 43 B.C.– A.D.18, author of *Metamor-
                     phoses*, *Amores*, *Ars Amatoris*, etc.

Owen ab Uryen   Arthurian knight. *See* Uryen.

Owen-Pen-Uchel   ('Owen of the High Peak') A famous horse breeder
                     and trainer of hunting dogs.

Pair Dadeni   ('Cauldron of Rebirth') A magic cauldron in which
                     a slain person could be restored to life. According to the
                     Henog, there are seven such cauldrons in the world.

Path of the Dead   Avenue through the forest leading from
                     Mynydd-y-Gaer to the Mound of the Dead, Saint Julian's
                     Fountain, and, ultimately, Moel y Famau.

Paun Bach   ('Little Peacock') A dwarf of the household of Ogof-y-
                     Gaer.

Pedryvan   (= Caer Pedryvan, 'Four-Cornered Fortress')
                     See Caer Vanddwy.

Pelagius   British monk declared a heretic by the Western Church
                     A.D. 416; mentor of Brother John. Pelagius and his

179

followers denied original sin, rejected infant baptism, and affirmed the natural goodness of man.

Peleus — Father of Achilles.

Pen Beirdd — *See* Taliessin.

Pendaran Dyfed — Legendary swineherd who gave Pryderi his name and to whose care the youthful Pryderi was entrusted by Pwyll.

Pengwern — Abandoned ancient fortress at Shrewsbury.

Penlyn — Ancient district that included Lake Tegid.

Peredur/ Peredwr — (= Percival, Parsifal) Arthurian knight.

Piraeus — The seaport of Athens.

Porius — The hero of the novel, son of Einion and Euronwy.

Porius Manlius — Roman patrician; retired commander of the Roman legion formerly stationed at Uriconium; Euronwy's father; a Christian. *See* House of Manlius, Villa Nova Praeneste.

Praxagora — Heroine of Aristophanes' *Ecclesiazusae.*

Pryderi — ('Care' or 'Sorrow') Lord of Dyfed and benign hero-god of S. Wales worshipped by Brother John and the Henog; son of Pwyll and Rhiannon; introduced swine to Britain; duped by Gwydion ap Don and killed by him at Melenryd after he had unsuccessfully invaded Gwynedd. *See* Caer Sidi, Gwri Wallt Euryn, Maenor-Coed-Alun, Nantcoll, Pendaren Dyfed, Teirnyon Twryf Vliant.

Pwyll — ('Thought' or 'Wisdom') Lord of Dyfed; husband of Rhiannon and father of Pryderi. *See* Annwn, Arawn.

Pythagoras — Greek philosopher, mathematician, and astronomer of the 6th cent. B.C., who claimed prophetic powers and believed in the transmigration of souls.

Rhea — Sister and wife of Cronos, who conspired with their son Zeus to overthrow him.

Rhelemon — Mother of the Derwydd.

Rhiannon — Wife of Pwyll and, after Pwyll's death, Manawydon fab Llyr; mother of Pryderi.

Rhitta Gawr — Last king of the Cewri; buried in Mynydd-y-Gaer.

Rhuddlan Teivi — Site of Pwyll's and Pryderi's palace in Ceredigion, on the River Teifi.

Rhufein/ Rhufeinaid/ Rufeinwyr — ('Rhufein' = 'Rhufain') Rome/ Romans.

Rhun ap Gwrnach   Son of Gwrnach and Alarch the Fair; cousin and
foster-brother of Porius.

Rhyd Mithras   = Ford of Mithras.

Ronwen/ Rowena   Saxon woman, daughter of Hengest and second wife
of Gortheyrn Gorthenau; poisoned her stepson
Gorthevyr.

Saint Julian's   (1) Christian church being built in Corwen by Minnawc
Gorsant.
(2) ('Ffynnon Julien Sant') 'Fountain,' 'Fount,' 'Lake' or
'Water.' A large pond, by which Brother John lives. *See*
Avanc, Path of the Dead.

Sais/ Saesnes/ Saeson/ Seisnig   Saxon (*m./ f./ pl./ adj.*).

Sarn Elen   (= Sarn Helen) Roman road in W. Wales. ('Sarn' =
causeway).

Scaean Gate   In the *Iliad*, one of the gates of Troy, from which the
elders and the women of Troy view the fray.

Serigi   Gwyddyl-Ffichti chieftain whom Cunedda drove to
Mona and killed there; father of Iscovan.

Sibylla   Gwyddyl-Ffichti woman; mother of Gunta and former
mistress of Einion.

Sidonius   Apollinaris Sidonius Modestus (*c.* A.D. 430–484); Roman
patrician, Bishop of Arverne (i.e., Auvergne, a central
region, formerly a province, of modern France); man of
letters and former correspondent of Brochvael.

The Silentiary   Erim.

Silures   Tribe of Iberian origin in S.E. Wales, subjugated by
Romans in 1st cent. A.D.

Stilicho   Roman general executed A.D. 408. In the novel, it was
Stilicho who authorized Cunedda to take control of
N. Wales.

Stone House   = Ty Cerrig.

Styx   Name of chief river of Hades and of its goddess, a
daughter of Oceanus who aided Zeus in his war against
the Titans. Zeus decreed that the most inviolable oath a
god could swear should be by the waters of Styx.

Surluse, Isles of   *See* Galahaut.

Swamp of the Gwyddyl/ Gwyddyl-Ffichti/ Irish   Area N. of Corwen
occupied by Gwyddyl invaders and their Gwyddyl-Ffichti
descendants; home of Sibylla and Gunta.

Sylvanus ap Bleheris/ Sylvanus-Is-Coed   *See* Henog.

Taliessin   ('Radiant Forehead') Poet spoken of as 'Pen Beirdd, Ynys Prydein' (Head Bard of the Isle of Britain). *See* Ceridwen, Cad Goddeu, Caer Einion, Caer Sidi, Caer Vanddwy, Cynan ap Clydno, Gwair, and Uryen.

Tartarus   In Greek mythology, an underworld below Hades, where Cronos and the Titans were imprisoned after being deposed by Zeus. *See* Briareus, Cronos, and Eryri.

Lake/ Llyn Tegid   (Lake Bala) Lake from which the Dyfrdwy flows east and north towards Corwen and Chester. Named after Tegid Foel, Lord of Penlyn, husband of Ceridwen and father of Afagddu. *See* Avanc.

Tegvan   Boy page attending Nineue.

Teirnyon Twryf Vliant   In the *Mabinogion*, Lord of Gwent-is-Coed and foster-father of Pryderi.

Teleri   ('Little Ghost') Half-witted girl coming under Medrawd's influence.

Theodoric   Ostrogoth King of Italy, A.D. 493–526.

Thesmophoriazusae   A comedy, by Aristophanes, lampooning the tragic playwright Euripides.

Thorson   Saxon captain.

Three Aunties   *See* Modrybedd.

Timaeus   Platonic dialogue containing an account of the creation of the universe.

Tiresias/ Teresias   Theban seer whose spirit, summoned by Odysseus, cannot prophesy until he has drunk the blood of sacrificed sheep. *See* Oceanus.

Titans   *See* Briareus, Cronos, Oceanus, Othrys, Tartarus.

Tithonus   Lover of the Goddess of the Dawn, who made him immortal but, having neglected to make him ageless, eventually turned him into a grasshopper.

Tonwen   Youngest of the three Aunties, lover of Cadawg. *See* Modrybedd.

Ty Cerrig   ('The House of Stone') Residence of Brochvael and Morfydd.

Tyche Soteer   (= Chance the Saviour) Goddess of good fortune. *Cf.* Fors Fortuna.

Typhaeus/ Typhoeus   Hundred-headed monster.

Tysilio Sant   ('Saint Tysilio') A hamlet also referred to as Llan-Tysilio-

	Sant ('Saint Tysilio's shrine'), located E. of Corwen near Llangollen.
Ultima Thule	('End of the World') A mythical island believed to be the northernmost land in the world, six days' sail from Britain.
Uranus	Sky-god; *see* Cronos.
Uriconium	(= Viriconium, Uriconio) Former Roman camp S.E. of Corwen at Wroxeter (near Shrewsbury); childhood home of Euronwy. *See* Agenor, Pengwern, Porius Manlius, Villa Nova Praeneste.
Uryen	King of Rhegid, a Brythonic-speaking kingdom of northern Britain. Father of Owen. He is celebrated in the poems of Taliessin. *See* yr Echwyd.
Usk	River in S.E. Wales. *See* Caerleon.
Uthyr/ Uther Pendragon	Father of King Arthur and great-uncle of Euronwy.
Venedotians	Latin name of the forest-people of Edeyrnion and Ardudwy.
Villa Nova Praeneste	Former home of Porius Manlius and Euronwy at Uriconium.
Vreichvras Llaw-goch	Progenitor of the Gwyddyl-Ffichti.
Ynys Prydein	(Ynys, 'island', + Prydein, possibly ultimately deriving from Pretani or Preteni, Brythonic Celtic for 'Picts') The Isle of Britain.
yr Wyddfa	*See* Eryri.
Yssylt	Eldest of the Three Aunties. *See* Modrybedd.
Zora	Wife of Lot-el-Azziz, mother of Gog and Magog.

APPENDIX OF PROPER NAMES OMITTED FROM THE GLOSSARY

Abraham
Acharnian
Achren
Adam
Adda
Aegean Sea
Aegisthus
Aeolia
Africa
Agave
Agenorides
Age of Gold
Amazon
Amos, Book of
Amphitrite
Anakim
Aphrodite
Apollo
Aporia
Appenines
Appian Way
Aquarius
Arddun
Ares
Argos
Aristophanes
Aristotle
Artemis
Asia, Asia Minor
Assyria
Athene [sic]
Athenians
Atlas
Avallach

Baal
Babylon
Bashan
Beelzebub
Behemoth
Bethlehem
Bishop's School
Blackie
Bosphorus

Britain
Brithlas
Brutium
Byzantium

Cabbala
Cadmus
Caer-y-Gawr
Caesar
Calcoed
Caledvwlch
Calvary
Calypso
Carnwenhau
Carthage
Cassiodorus
Catgor
Cerrig-Gwynt
Charon
Charybdis
Chimaera
Christ
Christmas
Cimmerian
Circe
Circus of Dagon
Claudian, -anus
Clio
Clydno
Coed Gwyllt
Collen Sant
Constantinople
Conway
Cottus
Crete, Cretan
Crocaw
Cymothe
Cyngar
Cynvarch

Damascius
Damascus
David
Dead Sea

Death-Mound,
   The
Democritus
Demogorgon
Dewi Sant
Digon
Dinodig
Dionysian
Dol-Pen-Maen
Doris
Druid

Easter
Echidna
Efiliau
Eirene
Eivionydd
Elijah
Eliseg
Elysium
Emerchred
Empedocles
Endymion
Epops
Erb
Erinyes
Eros
Etruria
Etruscan
Eudora
Euripides
Eve

Falernian
Father of the Gods
Feast/ Festival of
   the Sowing

Gabriel
Gaer Keint
Gaia Peloria
Galene
Galilee
Ganion

Garauwyn
Gaul, Gallic
Glauce
Golden Age, The
Goliath
Goths
Great King, The
Greece
Gwerin
Gwrgwst
Gwydr Drwm
Gwylan
Gwyr-yr-Avanc

Hades
Hadrian
Hagfan
Harlech
Hebron, Mount
Hecate
Hector
Helen of Troy
Helena
Hephaestus
Heracles
Heraclitus
Hercules, -ean
Hermes
Herodotus
Heveydd Hen
Hill of Seven
   Horsemen
Homer
Horace
Horeb
Hydra
Hylas
Hyperborean
Hypericinae

Iceni
Ida (Vales of)
Idris
Ilium

Impetrum Nigrum
Infernal City
Iris
Isaac
Italy

Jacob
Japhet
Jehovah
Jehovahtimamlu
Jericho
Jerusalem
Jesus
John, Saint
John the Baptist
Jordan
Jorwerth
Jotunheim
Jove's Day
Judah
Judas

Kynon

Lamia
Lemnos
Lesbos
Lethe, -ean
Leviathan
Little Peacock
Llamrei
London
Lord of Hosts
Lord of Summer
Lucretius, -ian
Lynnette

Mabinog
Mabon ab
   Dewein-Hen
Macedonius
Macedon, -onian
Maen Tyriac/ -awg
Maenad
Manichean
Manlius, House of
Mantuan Cloak

Marinus
Marmora (Sea of)
Mary
Mar(r)akesh
Mazdean god
Melian nymphs
Melita
Memnon
Menelaus
Mercury
Mercury's Day
Mesopotamia
Metamorphoseon
Metamorphoses
Minoan
Mithras-Market
Mnemosyne
Moch Annwyn
Moch Nant
Moel Gamlin
Morddyd
   Twyllyon
Morfrin
Morgan Tud
Moses
Mother of Earth
Mother of God
Mother of Heaven
Mother of the
   Muses
Mount of Olives
Muse of Chance
Mycenae of
   Argolis

Nestor
Non Hen
Numidia
Numina

Olivet
Olympian, The
Olympus
Ostro-Goths, -ic

Patrician, The
Paul, Saint

Peloponese [sic]
Pen Annwn
Peneius
Pentecost
Pen-y-Gewri
Persephonean
Persepolis
Persia
Peter, Saint
Pharis
Philistines
Philoctetes
Phoenician
Phrygian cap
Pilate
Pillars of Hercules
Pisces
Plato, -onic
Plutarch
Pluto, -onian
Proclus
Prometheus, -ian
Propontic waters
Psalmist, The

Rabbi Penuel
   Zodotokos
Ravenna
Red Sea
Rhegid
Rhitta-Trefnant
Rhongomyant
Rhydderch
Rhyd-y-Gaer
Rhysiart
Rome
Rubicon
Ruth

Sacred Fount
Samothrace
Samson
Satan
Saturn (god), -ian
Saturnalia
Saturn's Day
Scylla

Scythian
Sicily
Sieffre
Sybylline
Syria

Talmud
Taprobani
Telemachus
Tenebrions
Thessaly
Thor
Thor's Day
Thucydides
Thunderer, the
Titaressus
Tref-y-Glawdd
Troy
Tudor
Twryf Mawr
Twysogian
Ty-Llys-Sulian
Tyriawc, -awg

Ul-Kessar
Ulric Wolfson
Ultima Thule
Usk

Vales of Ida
Valhalla
Valkyrie
Via Perdita
Virgil/ Vergil, -ian

Wales
White Tower
Woden
Woden's Day

Zeno
Zerviah
Zeus
Zodiac, The

SOME NOTES ON WELSH AND THE NAMES IN *PORIUS*

These notes will, I hope, make clear some of the apparent oddities of Welsh as it occurs in the names of places and people in John Cowper Powys's *Porius*. In my notes I touch on spelling, including the confusing impact of initial mutation and vowel affection, pronunciation, some Latin origins, and a few pronunciations. It should be noted, however, that some of the varied forms listed above may not (a few certainly do not) represent authentic Welsh spellings, since J.C.P. himself seems not to have been unduly concerned to be consistent; I suspect, too, that some of the variations listed may not emanate from his pen at all (see the review of the Colgate *Porius* (1994) in *The Powys Society Newsletter* 28 (July 1996)).

First, **mutation**. Mutation is the phenomenon, common to Welsh and some other Celtic languages, by which the initial letter of a word or component of a word is changed. Its origin is related to the final sound of the preceding closely connected word or component during the period within the first millenium AD when the variations occurred. In the spoken and written language of today, these variations reflect the compromises. In effect, it seems to me, it formalises in written form the compromises which the mouth makes in moving quickly from one word to another. The Welsh system of mutation now follows complex rules by which certain initial letters might have one, two, or even three, forms of mutation depending on the kind of preceding letter, but there are then other factors which inhibit mutation.

Thus, to take examples found in *Porius*, **caer** ('fort') becomes after **y** ('the') **gaer**, as in 'Mynydd-y-Gaer'; **cawr** ('giant') becomes **gawr** (this is an incorrect formation used by Powys, though the feminine **gawres** is correct); **merch** ('daughter') becomes **ferch**, as in 'Canna ferch Glam'; **Gwyddyl** ('Irish') with **gwern** ('swamp') gives **Gwyddylwern**, dropping (though not consistently in *Porius*) the **g** in the combination.*

Sometimes the mutation is retained where the word has become a name (or perhaps the preceding word is implicit, like **y**), so we have **the Gaer** and **the Gawres**. Another interesting example is **Moel y Famau**; in fact, this is incorrect Welsh again, because, under the rules of mutation, 'Mamau' ('Mothers') would not, as a plural, suffer mutation after 'y'. The traditional form is 'Moel Famau' with mutation but no 'y'.

Vowel affection (or vowel mutation) is another important feature of Welsh. This is the change of an internal vowel under the influence, most often, of plural formation; a very good example is in the plural of **cawr**:

---

* Another possible derivation is from **Gwydd**, meaning 'wood' or 'trees'.

Cewri, where the plural termination has affected the preceding vowel **a**. Of course it happens in other languages, as in German **mann, männer**, and, as pronounced but not spelt, in the English pair **woman, women**. There is a considerable range and variety of plural formations: examples in *Porius* are: **modryb, modrybedd; Derwydd, Derwyddon; Cewri** already quoted. Feminine forms are often formed with **-es**, pronounced just like English **-ess**: **arglwyddes, cawres (gawres), Saesnes**.

As for **pronunciation**, Welsh, though unfamiliar, is at least consistent. Words are normally accented on the penultimate syllable, with final vowel groups such as **-ion** or **-iau** treated as one syllable. There are no silent letters.

Of the consonants, **c** and **g** are always hard; **dd** is a separate letter of the alphabet, like **th** in English **this** (Welsh **th** is always as in **thin**); **f** is always like **v**; **ll** is a very distinctive sound (try saying **l** and **h** with your tongue against the palate); **r** is rolled, and always aspirated with an **h** at the beginning of a word; **s** always like **ss**, but **si** as **sh. w** is sometimes a vowel and sometimes a semi-consonant; as a vowel it is pronounced just like English **oo** (long or short), while as a consonant it also retains something of its quality as a vowel. **ff** is a separate letter, pronounced like English **f**, hence **ff** at the beginning of some Anglo-Welsh family names (if in doubt about the Welsh pronunciation, think of **f** and **ff** as in English **of** and **off**). **q, x**, and **z** are not used in Welsh. **k** and **v** were common in medieval and early modern Welsh, and **j** is used in a few words borrowed from English, but these three are not properly part of the Welsh alphabet, though of course Evans is a good Welsh name! **ch** is similar to German or Scottish **ch**.

There is a degree of ambivalence about some spellings in *Porius*; for example Arfon is also spelled Arvon, but the pronunciation is the same (**v**).

Of the simple vowels, **a, e, i,** and **o** are consistent and pose no surprises; they may be long or short. **u** is roughly **ee**; **y** is like **ee**, short in final syllables, short or long in monosyllables, but usually an indeterminate sound in earlier syllables, like a short **uh**; the words 'y' and 'yr' and some unaccented monosyllables are indeterminate . Diphthongs follow reasonably logically the sounds of the component vowels. There are noticeable differences in Welsh as spoken in different parts of the country, but in reading *Porius* you might not be too far out with these notes. Generally **ae, ai, au, ei** and **eu** are all like 'eye', except that as a plural ending **au**, as in 'Blaenau' [Ffestiniog], is short **a** or short **e**.

Here are a few names. 'Porius' has a short **o** as in 'pot'. 'Brochvael' rhymes with 'vile'. 'Morfydd', with **v** in the middle, rhymes with 'breathe'. 'Arawn' rhymes with 'down', 'Afagddu' with 'thee'. 'Blodeuwedd' is pronounced, roughly, 'blod-eye-(oo)weth', accented on 'eye' (th = 'th' as in 'this'). 'Rhyn' is pronounced 'rheen', 'Yssylt' 'ússeelt', and 'Myrddin Wyllt' 'murthin weelht' (u=uh, not er).

Welsh, along with Cornish, Breton and Gaulish, belongs to the Brythonic branch of the Celtic language. It has, however, a significant input of **Latin**; much of this can be traced to the strong Roman presence throughout Wales, to keep the wild tribes under control, and its aftermath. Many of the changes in letters follow recognised patterns, such as **g** for **c** and **d** for **t** and various vowel shifts and also conflations. So, here in *Porius* there are Lake 'Tegid' from 'Tacitus', 'Edeyrn' from 'Eternus' (as Powys points out at the outset).

Another recognised change is also of interest: many words beginning with Latin **v** (i.e. sound of **w**), acquire a **g**, then can drop it again as required by mutation (simple examples of acquired **g** are 'vinum'/ 'gwin' ['wine'], 'vitrum'/ 'gwydr' ['glass']). So, we have Venta Belgarum (Winchester) becoming, as Robert Kunkel pointed out in our correspondence, 'Kaerguenit' and kaer wynt', and the present Welsh for Winchester is Caerwynt. We discussed at some length whether this was Powys's 'Caerwynt/ Caergwynt'; another candidate is present-day Caerwent in south Wales, Venta Silurum of the Romans, becoming 'Caer Gwent' with added **g** and then losing it again by mutation (with 'Gwent' surviving as a regional name). He favoured Winchester (and I agree now) mainly because there would be little point in Arthur having important palaces only eight miles apart at Caerleon and Caerwent; they are often mentioned in *Porius* in the same breath. There is yet another Roman 'Venta', Venta Icenorum (near Norwich). The meaning of 'Venta' is not known, but it may be a Celtic word meaning something like a settlement or market or central place of a tribe.

Other derivations from Latin are 'Emrys' from 'Ambrosius', 'Cystennin' from 'Constantinus', 'Bendigeit' from 'benedictus', and 'lleon' from 'legionis', as in 'Caerleon'. Powys's 'Amherawdr' comes from the Latin 'imperator'.

I am grateful to my Welsh-speaking friend Geraint Rees of Menai Bridge for his most helpful observations on my Notes.

Stephen Powys Marks

RODNEY AITCHTEY

Humanity : Inanity
Two Giants and the Poor Fish

Robinson Jeffers and John Cowper Powys were contemporaries

The seed of greatness and calling for the artist — that is, writer, composer, painter — is sown in the first seven years of life. The child, on first emerging into life, absorbs without ceasing, to create a sensibility rarely whole, normally bruised, which may come to be healed by a nurturing partner. John Cowper Powys and Robinson Jeffers (1887–1962) were two such writers who achieved greatness in their lifetimes, following that schema.

Robinson Jeffers was the great American cosmic poet who explored mankind's alienation from Nature. A very rare phenomenon for California occurred at his death: when people woke in the morning they were amazed to find that it had snowed. The fall of snow seems to have been a synochronicitous happening, to be compared to the events which accompanied C. G. Jung's death, when his favourite tree was struck by lightning. Jung treated the effects of people's divorce from nature successfully; he found correspondence in his findings with Chinese and Tibetan texts. Most people have become distanced from their natures, so much so as to believe that the planet and Cosmos are inert and unfeeling; this has been a tendency since the Renaissance. Now, in ways inimical to man there have been reactive warnings which have been ignored, or at most cosmetically addressed; and are referred to loosely as 'global warming', as though people and their farmed animals have nothing to do with it. Jeffers' verse tries to make people return to their senses, speaking for the planet and Cosmos, whereas Powys, in his philosophical works, tries to help people come to terms with their alienated selves.

T. S. Eliot considered Robinson Jeffers to be 'a first-rate poet',[1] and

New York critics eulogised him with superlative praise, such as James Rorty in the *New York Herald and Tribune*: 'California has another great writer to place beside John Muir. America has a new poet of genius.' Mark Van Doren in *The Nation* said, 'Few [works] are as rich with the beauty and strength which belong to genius alone.' And Babette Deutsch said, in *The New Republic*, 'This reviewer felt somewhat as Keats professed to feel on looking into Chapman's Homer.' Jeffers was compared with Whitman, without his sentimentality, and given equal standing with Aeschylus, Euripides, Shakespeare, Blake, Coleridge, Marlowe, Dostoevsky, Dante, et al. But also, he was regarded with contumely, and that has had the most lasting effect. Yvor Winters was the most vitriolic: ' ... for brute clumsiness and emptiness such writing can hardly be equalled.... The book is composed almost wholly of trash.' And, ' ... lines ... heavy with dross'.[2]

Unfortunately the latter criticisms have contributed to Jeffers' decline and neglect in the USA. Richard Hughes attributed his unpopularity to the bad taste of the American public.[3] What *has* caused the decline of appreciation of Jeffers' work? I'd suggest that it is the same prevalent evil force which is chasing the quality out of life. But with the increasing concern for the deterioration of the planet caused by incorrigible man, Jeffers' verse has been returning to favour among the ecological philosophers in the train of Arne Naess of Oslo University, with his ecosophy of 'Total View'.

Jeffers' mythic and cosmic Californian-rooted verse drew its inspiration largely from the Old Testament and dramas of ancient Greece, his treatment of which in the long narrative works provoked consistently adverse criticism. The short poems which follow the narrative verse are not mythic but philosophical explorations which serve to amplify ideas in the main works. In fact, his short poems may come to be the preferred choice, along with passages extracted from the long works which can function as short organically whole poems. For example, from *The Answer*:

> Integrity is wholeness,
> the greatest beauty is

Organic wholeness, the wholeness of life and things, the divine
    beauty of the universe. Love that, not man
Apart from that, or else you will share man's pitiful confusions,
    or drown in despair when his days darken.

Even aphorisms may be formed from such works, as here from *The Double Axe*: 'The beauty of things —/ Is in the beholder's brain — the human mind's translation/ of their transhuman/ intrinsic value.'

The reason why Jeffers found inspiration in ancient sources is, I believe, because he used his recall of dreams as cathartic material, which he transformed into profound verse. Greek had been instilled into him when he was seven, if not earlier, by 'slapping' from his determined theological father, who also moved him from one school to another to ensure his isolation from his peers.[4] In his lisping loneliness he grew bookish and turned in on himself; and came out of himself under the healing and lasting influence of Nature.[5]

Jeffers was influenced by Schopenhauer, and his philosophy is in accord with Schopenhauer's definitive volume, *The World as Will and Representation* (*Die Welt als Wille und Vorstellung*, 1819), published as *On the Will in Nature* in 1992. There, Schopenhauer says, 'Sensibility, objectified in the nerve, is the chief characteristic of human beings, and the truly human element.' He believed the will to be metaphysical; to have nothing to do with intellect, and to be distinct from any guidance or interference from an outside 'God'. Of the will he says:

> As the one and only thing-in-itself, that which alone is truly real, the only original and metaphysical thing in a world in which everything else is only appearance, in other words, mere representation, this will endows all things, whatever they be, with the power of virtue whereof they are able to exist and act.

Stones and boulders, he maintained, contained 'the first step toward consciousness'.[6]

Schopenhauer's 'thing-in-itself' equates with the Taoist *tzu-jan*, self-so, natural and spontaneous. Arising from his reading of Schopenhauer, later corroborated and enhanced by Powys's *Philosophy of Solitude*, Jeffers, in his mind, went east of Ancient Greece to the ancient China of Lau Tzu and Chuag Tzu.[7] He had set the Taoist yin-yang symbol in the masonry of the parapet wall at the top of the tower which he had himself built between 1920 and 1925. He had collected the large stones from the sea shore, and put them one upon another to become the tower he built for his wife, Una.

As early as 1922, Jeffers had addressed criticism that the content of his 'stories' was 'unpleasant'. His response was that '... the stories speak of things not commonly spoken of in poetry, unpleasant things because unaccustomed', and that general 'poetry flinched from expressing the whole of humanity and occupied itself with refinement and tenuous emotions, and lost its soul for having lost its body.' And he described his own practice: 'The poet is not to make beauty but to herald beauty; and beauty is everywhere; it needs only senses and intelligence to perceive it.'[8] In his Foreword to *The Selected Poetry* in 1938 he reiterated what he had said in 1922.

Robinson Jeffers was first published in Britain on November 11th 1928, by Virginia and Leonard Woolf at their Hogarth Press. Their selection was considered by American literati and favourable critics to be Jeffers' finest works. The first volume was *Roan Stallion, Tamar, and Other Poems*. It was an 'English Export Edition', which meant that the sheets had been printed in the USA to be trimmed and bound in England; it cost 7/6d. 'Roan Stallion' and 'Tamar' are situated on that part of the California coast which has become known as 'Jeffers Country'. 'Roan Stallion' introduced what would be described as Jeffers' 'inhumanism': 'Humanity is the start of the race ... the mould to break away from.' In 1935, in a short poem, 'Sign-Post', his 'inhumanism' is explicit: ' ... free, even to become human,/ But born of the rock and the air, not of a woman.' This recalls Taliesin's self-proclaimed origin!

'Tamar' is considered to be Jeffers' first mature verse, even his masterpiece. Extracts given are good demonstrations of his great poetic art. 'Tamar' is also a good example of Jeffers putting his Classical dreaming into a modern context. '... Only because I was to be named Tamar and to love my/ brother and my father./ I am the fountain.' Incest, jealousy and violence are featured in a contemporary setting:

O swiftness of the swallow and strength
Of the stone shore, brave beauty of falcons,
Beauty of the blue heron that flies
Opposite the color of evening
From the Carmel River's reed-grown mouth
To her nest in the deep wood of the deer
Cliffs of peninsula granite engirdle,
O beauty of the fountains of the sun
I pray you enter a little chamber,
I have given you bodies, I have made you puppets,
I have made idols for God to enter
And tiny cells to hold your honey.
I have given you a dotard and an idiot,
An old woman puffed with vanity, youth but botched with
    incest,
O blower of music through the crooked bugles,
You that make signs of sins and choose the lame for angels,
Enter and possess. Being light you have chosen the dark
    lamps,
A hawk the sluggish bodies: therefore God you chose
Me, and therefore I have made you idols like these idols
To enter and possess.

Tamar's miscarriage prompts this vision:

              About the hour of sundown
Tamar was dreaming trivially — an axman chopping down
    a tree and
        field—mice scampering
Out of the roots — when suddenly like a shaft of wind the
    dream
Changed and grew awful, she watched dark horsemen
    coming out of
        the south, squadrons of hurrying horsemen
Between the hills and the dark sea, helmeted like the
    soldiers of the
        war in France.

Carrying torches. When they passed Mal Passo Creek the
columns
Veered, one of the riders said, 'Here it began,' but another
answered,
    'No. Before the granite
Was bedded to build the world on.' So they formed and
galloped
    north again, hurrying squadrons,
And Tamar thought, 'When they come to the Carmel
River then it will
    happen. They have passed Mal Passo.

In *Criterion*, December 1928, F. S. Flint in reviewing the volume said that he considered Jeffers to be a tragic poet, and that his 'poems gripped me from the start, and, at times, I had to read them aloud. Their imagery, their movement, their pathos gave me intense pleasure.'[9] And a penetrating review in the *TLS*, March 29th 1929, said, 'It is certainly an interesting experiment to go directly, and apparently quite consciously, to the unconscious for the material of poetry.'[10]

In 1929, the Jeffers family visited Kelmscott Manor. And it seems probable that a meeting occurred in Rodmell in Sussex with Virginia and Leonard Woolf, Jeffers' publishers, to make their acquaintance and discuss *Cawdor*, and their next choice, *Dear Judas and Other Poems*. On October 10th 1929, Hogarth Press published *Cawdor*, which cost 6/–. In *Cawdor* Jeffers forsook his source of dreams for contemporary reality, what he knew to be accurate about the lives of people living on the California coast. In a review in *Criterion* (January 1930) Peter Quennell compared *Cawdor* with *Roan Stallion*: '*Cawdor* is as disturbing and impassioned; Mr. Jeffers' verse is consistently vigorous and has occasional flashes of real beauty; but its beauties seem to me primarily the beauties which should belong to prose.'[11]

On November 13th 1930, there came *Dear Judas and Other Poems*, costing 5/–. Jeffers described Dear Judas as 'a species of passion play', and said, 'It seems to me to present in a somewhat new dramatic form, new and probable explanations of the mythical characters and acts of its protagonists.'[12] *Dear Judas* is accompanied by an extraordinarily sensitive long poem, 'The Loving Shepherdess', which suggests that the cruelty inherited from parents makes the world into what it is. I believe that both poems were the result of Jeffers finally wrenching himself away from a deeply paternally imbued and prescribed Christianity in favour of the deeper espousement of the Earth and her wondrous mysteries; he had in fact reached Heraclitan understanding. Jeffers wrote an explanation in the *New York Times* for the opening performance of his dramatised *Dear Judas*. He said, 'The thoughts and attitudes it presents are not those that would be expected by any probable audience and people are bewildered or repelled by what is strange to them.'[13]

In *Criterion*, January 1932, F. S. Flint said of the volume, 'Robinson Jeffers stands on a rock looking out over the ocean; and, in the grand manner of the prophets, tells us sad stories of the death of Gods, Kings and Shepherdesses. He is a lonely figure, chanting the ancient heroic virtues and pities in sweeping measures.'[14] And on August 23rd 1948, Jeffers' adaptation of *Medea* for the stage opened at the Edinburgh Festival.

In America, at the end of 1928, Anne Singleton reviewed *Cawdor* perceptively in the *New York Herald Tribune*, and said, 'From first to last Robinson Jeffers turns up with his verse the fresh earth of experienced tragedy, the stuff of reality the Oedipus Rex must have had in it when the material it was made of was still alive and compelling in men's minds.'[15] Her review caused Joseph Campbell, when staying with John Steinbeck in Monterey, to visit Carmel to meet Robinson Jeffers. James Karman in the *Robinson Jeffers Newsletter* 85 describes 'Campbell's discovery of Jeffers at this formative moment in his life ... he himself says it was a revelation — it put him into immediate contact with the mythic imagination — and he paid his debt to Jeffers by referring to him in almost all of the books he wrote thereafter.'

Another person impressed by Jeffers was Krishnamurti. He was staying in Carmel during the Autumn of 1934. Una Jeffers said in a letter, 'He says he feels Robin's tremendous power and nobility!' And of Krishnamurti and Jeffers walking together in the hills she wrote, 'They seem not to talk, — just to <u>walk</u> at lightning speed.' (*Robinson Jeffers Newsletter* 84)

Jeffers was a voracious reader, and Una used to review new books, and propose new titles to him; among them were works by Llewelyn Powys and John Cowper Powys.[16] Jeffers said of *A Glastonbury Romance* (published in the USA in 1932) that 'parts gave me great pleasure.' And of *A Philosophy of Solitude* (published in the USA in 1933) he said 'A fine thing, I think.'[17] And he said he looked forward to Powys's *Autobiography*. It is *A Philosophy of Solitude* that appealed most to Jeffers' Capricorn nature, and which, I suggest, became a seminal influence on him in forming his philosophy of life, his 'reasonable detachment as a rule of conduct' which was regarded as 'inhumanism', but which was actually 'transhumanism'.

In *A Philosophy of Solitude* John Cowper Powys describes the roots of what he calls his 'ironic detachment' which 'remains inviolate'. This would have rung bells in Jeffers' mind. The particular passage reads:

> ... it would seem that from Laotze we learn to flow impercep-tibly through life like running water, while like water we seek our own level in spite of every obstacle; from Kwang-Tze we learn to preserve an ironic detachment from all conceit of place, from all pride of system, from all pretence of moral superiority, while we learn from useless trees, from simple persons, from chance-omens of the way, the Protean art of retaining our identity by losing it; from Heraclitus we learn to keep our inmost being in a fighting mood of tension between opposites, and to despise the idols of the marketplace; from Epictetus we learn to simplify our life to the extreme limit and to preserve an equable temper; from Marcus Aurelius to dig down deep into our profoundest souls and to think constantly of the annihilation of all save 'the God' in us; from Rousseau to make it our dominant life-illusion to enjoy the voluptuousness of a sensuous communion with Nature; and finally from Wordsworth to isolate ourselves austerely and grimly from the levities and banalities of society and to concentrate upon establishing a mystical relation with the primordial elements, until we get into touch with a Mystery 'that disturbs us with the joy of elevated thoughts ... a sense sublime of Something far more deeply interfused ...'.

I imagined that the two would have met, but my enquiries in the USA were abortive. When it was pointed out what John Cowper Powys had written about Jeffers I could understand why he had not made the small effort to go to Carmel (near San Francisco where he met George Sterling) to meet 'that mad savage elementalist', as he described Jeffers.[18] Although he had said in 1935 in his essay 'Farewell to America', 'Robinson Jeffers though dwelling so far from the South and dealing with the elemental powers in a manner much more congenial to the stronger side of my nature than anything I could ever get from the South, remains, in his way, a temptation too! In plain words I have more than enough of non-humanity, anti-humanism, or elemental lust in my nature to need any stimulus along those lines!'

In the Foreword to *The Selected Poetry* (1938) Jeffers said that 'the principles that conditioned the verse' had been effected by two accidents which he enunciated as a lady and the land; the land recalling Homer's Ithaka, and 'the woman to whom this book is dedicated, and her influence constant since that time'. In fact, he said of Una, his wife: 'My nature is cold and undiscriminating; she excited and focused it, gave it eyes and nerves and sympathies. She never saw any of my poems until they were finished and typed, yet by her presence and conversation she has co-authored every one of them. Sometimes I think there must be some value in them, if only for that reason. She is more like a woman in a Scotch ballad, passionate, untamed and rather heroic — or like a falcon — than like an ordinary person.'[19]

The Second World War came with its intolerable strain for Jeffers, who was drawn unwillingly into the vortex of its evil. (He had previously denounced America's interference in the First War.) His great book written during the war, *The Double Axe*, was published in the USA in 1948, but carried an unprecedented publisher's disclaimer. There is in it a short poem, the name of which, 'Cassandra', has significance:

The mad girl with the staring eyes and long white
    fingers
Hooked in the stones of the wall,
The storm-wrack hair and the screeching mouth: does it
    matter, Cassandra,

Whether the people believe
Your bitter fountain? Truly men hate the truth; they'd
  liefer
Meet a tiger on the road.
Therefore the poets honey their truth with lying; but
  religion —
Venders and political men
Pour from the barrel, new lies on the old, and are praised
  for kindly
Wisdom. Poor bitch, be wise.
No: you'll still mumble in a corner a crust of truth, to men
And gods disgusting. — You and I, Cassandra.

In the Preface of the disclaimed edition Jeffers was able only briefly
to define his 'inhumanism' as:

> ... a certain philosophical attitude, which might be called
> Inhumanism, a shifting of emphasis and significance from man
> to not-man; the rejection of human solipsism and recognition
> of the transhuman magnificence. It seems time that our race
> began to think as an adult does, rather than like an egocentric
> baby or insane person.... It offers a reasonable detachment as
> a rule of conduct, instead of love, hate and envy.[20]

The original disallowed Preface was published in 1977, and elucidates
his attitude:

> the devaluation of human-centred illusions, the turning out-
> ward from man to what is boundlessly greater — is a next step
> in human development; and an essential condition of freedom,
> and of spiritual (i.e. moral and vital) sanity; clearly somewhat
> lacking in the present world.[21]

John Cowper Powys puts it beautifully in a letter to his brother
Llewelyn: '... For myself it is enough for me, as I thought within
myself rowing upon the lake surrounded by the mighty mountains, to
feel below my human will and below all material forms of Nature one
great Eternal Spirit in whom we live and move and have our being —
God is everything and everything is God and true worship is that

ecstasy wherein we forget ourselves and are able to live in the great tides of feeling which roll through all animate and inanimate nature.'

Jeffers' opinion of people is suggested in the Preface: '... nine-tenths of its energy is devoted to self-interference, self-frustration, self-incitement, self-tickling, self-worship ... . The rest we discharge onto each other — in conflict and charity, love, jealousy, hatred, competition, government, vanity and cruelty, and that puerile passion the will to power.'[22] In his poem 'Carmel Point' he says:

> We must unhumanise our views a little
>   and become confident
> As the rock and ocean that we were made from.

The need to break out of our western cultural mindframe, to widen oneself to embrace the Earth, which is Our-self, has become the paramount need, and the first step is expressed explicitly by John Cowper Powys in his *A Philosophy of Solitude*: 'Our common Western Civilisation has to be *mentally destroyed* by the individual before any subtle imaginative life becomes possible.'[23] In *Porius* Medrawd says: 'In life there's more pain than pleasure, more ugliness than beauty, more lies than truth, more misery than happiness, more cruelty than pity, more illusion than reality.'

Powys arrived in the USA in 1905, when Jeffers was eighteen and graduating from Occidental College in California. Jeffers' first book of poems (privately published), *Flagons and Apples*, appeared in 1912. Powys's first publication in the USA was in 1914 with *The War and Culture*, which declared the two concepts to be incompatible. But in 1916 when Jeffers published his first long narrative work, *Californians*, John Cowper Powys had already published five books, and his *Wood and Stone* had set the precedent for his voluminous prose, with its 722 pages displaying his strength for idiosyncratic use of language within the framework of the Victorian novel. Jeremy Hooker says of *Wood and Stone*, 'as in all the novels, location in a geographical borderland symbolises the meeting-place of male and female, nature and the supernatural, the human and the non-human, life and death, and this area defines the novels' complex but unified themes.'[24] This would also describe Jeffers' work; as Jeffers' dreaming provided inspiration, so Powys peopled his books with characters from his own 'fragmented self'.

Both men had shown an affinity for Pan in their early works, both in verse, which was to lead to their later mature pantheistic appreciation of the Earth and life, with detachment from humanity's inanities. George Sterling, in his study, *Robinson Jeffers, The Man and the Artist* (1926) says, 'He does not believe in punishment, nor in the taking of life, human or animal. Indeed, he has never killed an animal, and is tender toward such creatures.'[25] In the following lines from 'The King of Beasts', Jeffers ascribes savagery to man as the king of beasts:

> It is quite natural the two-footed beast
> That inflicts terror, the cage, enslavement, torment and
> death on other animals
> Should eat the dough that he mixes and drink the death-
> cup. It is just and decent. And it will increase, I
> think.[26]

Powys was as virulent against vivisection, and in fact became a vegetarian. He believed implicitly in a power within each of us which can refuse to practise cruelty. That power (compassionate love?) is, he says with reference to the Bible at the very end of the *Autobiography*, 'capable of inspiring the individual soul with the wisdom of the serpent and the harmlessness of the dove'. It is a beautiful and quite realisable thought.

Both Powys and Jeffers received very high praise in their lifetimes, and acknowledgement of their 'genius'. But without the effect of the companionship of the two women who shared their lives, each would have been a very different writer. For Jeffers, his statement in the Foreword to *The Selected Poems* given above, explains what he felt he owed to Una; but Powys made no such public acknowledgement in his lifetime of Phyllis Playter's absolute importance to him, even to his being dependent on her. But Powys did dedicate *A Philosophy of Solitude* to Phyllis's father.

An act of Phyllis Playter actually changed Powys's Western cultural mindframe; and we should remember that his muse for poetry deserted him on meeting her in 1921. In 1922 she gave him the two volumes in the *Sacred Books of the East, the Texts of Taoism*, translated by James Legge, a gift he declared he remained indebted to her for until his death. Similarly, an act of Una's had affected Jeffers ever after, in a very revealing way. Because their home building was not advancing as quickly as they hoped, Una pushed Jeffers into helping, and he led the laggard builders. Quite unexpectedly he found the physical building work conducive to his muse; so much so, that on completion of their home, he spent several more years building a stone tower for Una, stone by stone.[27] It was Tolstoy's conviction (discussed in his essay 'Manual Labour and Intellectual Activity') that a balance of cerebral and manual labour was necessary for the spiritually renewing power it gave. The difference in attitude between the two men toward their women may be summarised thus: for Jeffers, gratitude for Una, and for Powys, exultation that he had the power to hold onto Phyllis.

Finally, both writers with their muses settled to live simply out of the public eye. As Powys wrote so appositely: 'Humanity has reached a point in the evolution of our race when we know for certain that it is a simple life and a simple life alone that brings to human beings that desirable condition known as happiness.'[28] And neither writer sought fame. Both were disquieted by the waywardness of Western civilisation, and saw its end approaching. Signs now more pronounced than ever before can be discerned every day, almost everywhere, yet people seem to be unaware, or not to care. Never in the known world has there been such disregard — suggesting that people have become dehumanised and are dead in spirit. Jeffers talks so appropriately of the 'dream-led masses', and here they are to be caught like fish, in these lines from 'The Purse-Seine' in his *Selected Poetry* (1938):

> Lately I was looking from a night mountain-top
> On a wide city, the colored splendor, galaxies of light: how could
> I help but recall the seine-net
> Gathering the luminous fish? I cannot tell you how beautiful the city appeared, and a little terrible.
> I thought, We have geared the machines and locked all together

into interdependence; we have built the great cities; now
There is no escape. We have gathered vast populations in-
capable
of free survival, insulated
From the strong earth, each person in himself helpless, on all
dependent. The circle is closed, and the net
Is being hauled in. They hardly feel the cords drawing, yet they
shine already.

NOTES

[1] Letter to Lawrence Clark Powell, in *An Introduction to Robinson Jeffers*, L. C. Powell (Imprimerie Bernigaud et Privat, 1932), 21.

[2] See Alex A. Verdamis, *The Critical Reputation of Robinson Jeffers* (Archon Books, 1972).

[3] 'But This Is Poetry', in *Forum* lxxxiii, January 1930.

[4] James Karman, *Robinson Jeffers: Poet of California* (Storyline Press, 1995), 11.

[5] George Sterling, *Robinson Jeffers: The Man and the Artist* (Boni & Liveright, 1926), 8.

[6] Arthur Schopenhauer, *On the Will in Nature*, trans. E. F. J. Payne (Oxford, 1992), 20, 45.

[7] See Robinson Jeffers, *The Double Axe and Other Poems* (Liveright, 1977), 173.

[8] S. S. Alberts, *A Bibliography of the Works of Robinson Jeffers* (Burt Franklin, 1968), 110–14.

[9] Verdamis, op. cit., 57.

[10] Ibid., 56.

[11] Ibid., 71.

[12] Alberts, op. cit., 57.

[13] Robinson Jeffers, *Dear Judas and Other Poems*, with an Afterword by Robert Brophy (Liveright, 1977), 133.

[14] Verdamis, op. cit., 79.

[15] Quoted in the *Robinson Jeffers Newsletter* 85 (1993), 9.

[16] Lawrence Clark Powell, *Robinson Jeffers: The Man and His Work* (San Pasqual Press, 1940), 19.

[17] Ibid., 19.

[18] *John Cowper Powys: Letters to Nicholas Ross*, ed. Arthur Uphill (London: Bertram Rota, 1971), 94.

[19] *The Selected Poetry of Robinson Jeffers* (Random House, 1938), 588.

[20] Jeffers, *The Double Axe*, xxi.

[21] Ibid., 171.

[22] Ibid., 172–3.

[23] John Cowper Powys, *A Philosophy of Solitude* (London: Jonathan Cape, 1933), 9.

24 Jeremy Hooker, *John Cowper Powys and David Jones* (London: Enitharmon Press, 1979), 59.
25 Powell, op. cit., 14.
26 Jeffers, *The Double Axe*, 136.
27 Karman, op. cit., 48.
28 Powys, *A Philosophy of Solitude*, 79.

The Powys Bookshop, Hastings
Glory of Life *by Llewelyn Powys can
just be made out behind the cross-bar
of the window (see p. 14)*

REVIEWS

Night Horizons

GERARD CASEY

edited by JAMES WETMORE, with a foreword by JEREMY HOOKER

Ghent, NY: Phudd Bottom Press, 1997. 258 pp., £14.95, ISBN 0 900588 44 6

UK Distributor: Words Etcetera, 2 Cornhill, Dorchester, Dorset DT1 1BA

The two words of the title, *Night Horizons*, form not an oxymoron or a contradiction but an unusual collocation, describing what may be possible but is not normal, a near-paradox. Not only is it an exceptional quality of luminescence that is to be supposed. The horizon gives us the horizontal, solicits the ranging sweep of our eyes. The night, conversely and cross-wise, invites our gaze upwards, affirms us as *anthropos*, upright and considering. The title is not a quotation, nor is it cited within the volume it names. What we find in the Postscript is this: 'Prayer as free response by man to the infinitude of God remains the only horizon not lost in the night of John 13.30.' (228) That verse tells of Judas Iscariot: 'He then having received the sop went immediately out; and it was night.' In one respect, then, night horizons represent the condition or the faith that lost horizons — dreams and aspirations swallowed up in blackness — might be redeemed, of seeing again, renewing vision, re-vision.

The book contains two illustrations, paintings by Timothy Hyman, one a most distinguished and ingeniously-enspaced portrait, 'Talking with Gerard Casey at Mappowder 1983–84' (page 114). The other, 'Night Flight', illuminates the book's title: illuminates, as it were, by reciprocal tenebration. The darkened interior of an aeroplane, whose encircling furnishings are of an organic, Marvellian green shade, leads our eye deep into the front of the fuselage, where two tiny figures, clearly male and female, stand in silhouette. The focal point is thus shadow against light. And one may, seeing this experiment in linear (and 'aerial') perspective, hear in 'Night Flight' a play on the French for 'vanishing-point', *point de fuite*: point of flight/point of escape.

On the back of the book we read these words by Isaac Pennington, an associate of George Fox and one of the founders of The Society of Friends:

> All Truth is a Shadow except the last. But every Truth is Substance in its own place, though it be but a Shadow in another place. And the Shadow is a true Shadow, as the Substance is a true Substance.

What we are to read is thus challengingly framed and illustrated,

Gerard Casey (80 in March this year)
(photo copyright: R. Diender)

presented as a unity. The contents are far from unified in the circumstances and purposes of their composition — letters to his brother
and to his wife, and miscellaneous essays, all but one reprinted — and
it is a tribute to the consistency of Gerard Casey's thinking that
writings over a period of more than forty years should strike the same
notes, should weave a coherence of concern.

Gerard Casey, born in 1918, worked as a young man in Kenya on the
farm of Will Powys, and in 1945 married Will Powys's niece, Mary, the
daughter of Lucy Penny, youngest of 'the Montacute generation' of
the Powys family. The first half of the book, some eighty pages, is
taken up with letters written by Gerard Casey to his younger brother
Patrick in 1953–4. There are only five of these letters, each one an
essay, a polemic: together they form a sustained and fluent argument.
Both brothers were brought up as Roman Catholics, and Patrick has
found a renewed enthusiasm for that faith. Gerard absorbed the
publications of the Rationalist Press Association in his adolescence
(187), but had long since become disillusioned with rationalism. In his
response to Patrick, Gerard finds an energy of dissent which does not
stale, about the church as institution, the compulsory adherence of
Catholics to dogma, especially the requisite belief in eternal damnation, and, in an impressive display of learning, the contempt shown by
the church towards responsible scholarship and free thought.

In his foreword Jeremy Hooker writes that 'Experience of darkness
pervades Gerard Casey's poem *South Wales Echo* as well as his letters.
It is, as it were, the medium of his vision.' One of these letters ends
with lines from the early poem of Gerard Manley Hopkins, 'The Habit
of Perfection':

> Be shellèd, eyes, with double dark
> And find the uncreated Light.

Darkness in these letters has a double sense, to stand for the
suffering of the world, and to be always the condition of our faith, even
of our consciousness. Again and again Gerard Casey honours the
darkness and affirms his loyalty to the dark of ignorance — the cloud
of unknowing — as that which saves one from the superficial certainties of both modern rationalism and Roman dogma. There is a platonic

and neoplatonic recourse to shadows as all of light that we might see; yet as we learn from the citation of Isaac Pennington, in a revision of the platonistic equation of shadows with falsehood, there can be 'true shadows'. In asserting the claims of reason on a Christian, Casey cites 'one of the heinous Saracens': 'Reason is the shadow cast by God: God is the Sun. This Shadow is the Light of God in the Heart.' (29)

There is no clear division between light and dark, wrong and right, good and evil. We move among shadows, and even when we find shadows to be true, we should not count on the authority of a mere shadow to denounce and condemn others. Casey declares that most of those modern thinkers who have influenced him deeply have been Christians: Kierkegaard, Berdyaev, Schweitzer, Niebuhr. At the end of 1953 Casey discovers Simone Weil, *Waiting on God* having been sent as a gift from Lucy Penny: Weil 'is a prophet ... of a Christianity refreshed and cleansed from the accumulated rubbish of centuries.' (70) To this roster of 'Christians' he adds the name of Nietzsche. Casey describes Kierkegaard as 'one of the finest minds and saintliest characters modern Europe has produced'. (31) John Cowper Powys likewise sanctified Nietzsche: 'a timid quiet nervous & saintly man' (Letter to Katie Powys, 6 May 1933). Saintliness enjoyed a certain status through inverted or deviant usage in these years: Camus had meditated on secular or godless sainthood in *La Peste* (1947), and in 1952 Sartre published *Saint Genet*. One might suppose Casey's constellation of modern thinkers to exclude existentialists, and in fact they are hardly mentioned by him. But the emancipation of saintliness from the order and institution of canonization was evidently a power-ful rhetorical instrument in those years, one with a capacity to shock and offend. And, more positively, to redeem those cast out by canonical norms.

While Casey depends on modern thinkers to articulate the claims of both reason and faith, claims which meet or cross or perhaps pass by each other unheeding in the shadows, he is already by this date a devotee of two of the greatest of Christian mystics, Meister Eckhart and Jakob Boehme. It is these rather than the moderns who show us the darkness, and who find in Christianity a way into the darkness, that it should not be avoided or escaped, but redeemed: 'It is', he writes, 'in its insight into the horror of the world's suffering that Christianity has penetrated deeper than all other religions.' (33) That this is no mere abstract generalization is tested by the political actualities of Gerard Casey's experiences as a farmer in Kenya. This passage takes us through the concatenation of suffering, as both cause and effect, of unending consequences, a suffering which does not belong to one side or the other. Suffering rather is that which knows no sides, takes no side:

> God suffers in the heretic burnt three or four hundred years ago, in the slave flogged to death crossing the Sahara a hundred years ago, in the spiritual degradation of the inquisitor, and of the slave owner. He suffers in the suffering of the child chopped up 'like a lemon' by the Mau-Mau, in the suffering of the child's mother as she was slowly strangled, watching her children being chopped up. In the suffering of the women who were strangling her. In the suffering of the men who will have to shoot or hang those women. In the suffering of the women as they are being hung, the suffering of the priest as he administers extreme unction to the broken-necked dying man or woman in the hanging-pit. In the suffering of the woman's husband as he revenges his wife and children. In all the endless intertangled sufferings.... Where track the beginning or end in the agonies of the sideless world? (32–3)

This grim vision, this refusal to 'relapse into comfort and ease' (89), is not entirely without humour, nor without an appreciation of humour as liberation: 'When my African workers had taken the Mau-Mau oath they could not laugh, as long as they were under its power. To get them to laugh, or smile ruefully, was to rescue them from the power of the spirit of gravity.' (90: 'gravity' alludes here to Simone Weil's polarity of gravity and grace.) Casey implies a stark analogy when he then suggests that 'a large infusion of humour — that is, of the eternal perspective — is now needed' in Roman Catholicism.

The last of the letters to Patrick dwells much on the example of Nietzsche, honouring his suffering, his refusal of consolations: 'this spiritual and intellectual crucifixion of perhaps the noblest man of modern times'. (101) In the same letter, somewhat surprisingly, Casey confesses: 'Although I have read with pleasure and respect the works of Kierkegaard and Nietzsche, they have failed to touch me in the depths because they are fundamentally unreasonable.' (100)

This marks a turn in thinking, away from modern concerns with faith and reason, scepticism and commitment, towards both 'traditional wisdom' and a theological understanding in which suffering is less prominent because taken up, assumed in eschatology. The letters to his wife Mary date from 1969 to 1974. Not occasioned by fraternal concern and correction, these letters are circumstanced by absences, when Mary would return to England to visit her mother and other relatives. Of these it should be said that there are many incidental mentions: we are offered a number of oblique and unusual angles for observation of John Cowper and Theodore Powys. And the public status of the Powys family is such that we already have in print Mary's response on receiving Gerard's letters: 'A noble letter came to me today, six pages of foolscap writ neat and small on both sides, from Gerard, a triumph of a letter full of thought, philosophy, adventure, of birds and landscape and W.E.P. and affection for me'. (Mary Casey, *A Net in Water* (Kilmersdon, Somerset: The Powys Press, 1994), 121.) For this particular letter of February 1971 we have to thank the striking workers of the GPO: the thoughts accumulate, the speculations unfold, day after day, until the postal strike is lifted.

'Traditional wisdom' is the favoured term used to hold together Mary's devotion to Plotinus — realized most impressively in her fictional meditation *The Kingfisher's Wing* (1987), and evident throughout the poems collected in *The Clear Shadow* (1992) — and Gerard's more diverse enthusiasms and filiations: 'tradition' is that idea of the perennial truth of religions expressed with particular force for Gerard by René Guénon. Within this context modern thinkers loom less — though Martin Buber is encountered — and the argument turns on the unity of thought in Boehme, Eckhart, Spinoza, Plotinus, and in the 'Tradition' manifest in Hinduism, Buddhism and Sufism. As, in the letters to Patrick, Christianity had been proclaimed more profound than other religions in its apprehensions of suffering, so in these letters it is 'personality' that is presented as uniquely understood by Christianity as a saving mystery: 'I find no truly profound and living and urgent sense of this mystery anywhere outside of the Christian Tradition.' (215) It is a point that certainly needs to be taken up with a follower of Plotinus.

And in defence of the value and mystery of the person Gerard Casey remains implacably opposed to Catholic doctrines concerning judgement, hell and damnation. He holds fast to the concept of *apokatastasis panton* (spoken by St Peter, Acts 3.21: 'restitution of all things'), a phrase developed into an eschatology by Origen, a Christian close in thought to Plotinus. According to Origen, in the end-time all will be redeemed, all will be forgiven, even the devil. The Church found this line to be unacceptable, but it endures in 'the Tradition'. The concept is beautifully elucidated in the one piece specially written for this volume, the Postscript, in which Spinoza is given a place of high honour: 'one of the most searching metaphysical intelligences to appear in the West since Plotinus'. (223) Spinoza's monism is here enlisted in the refusal of eschatological dualism: 'We are under no duress to take the eschatological nightmare of Augustine and Calvin over-seriously, rooted as they are in Manichaean dualism rather than in the Gospels. With Peter and Paul we endure in hope, in eternal hope for all in the Christian vision that shaped the insights of Gregory of Nyssa, of Origen, of Julian of Norwich ... the ultimate hope of the restitution of all things in God.' (230)

Apokatastasis makes sense of suffering for it makes wholeness out of fracture. We are returned to that striking phrase at the end of our citation of the catena of suffering: 'Where track the beginning or end in the agonies of the sideless world?' Sideless as limitless, unbounded, yes. But also, more startlingly, sideless in the sense that one cannot take sides because there are ultimately no sides to be taken. And here we find a clinching eschatological notion, prophetic, apocalyptic, by which we can comprehend — both to include and to understand — the inseparability of light and dark, the dependence of one on the other. *Apokatastasis* is an answer — an answer that opens up new perplexities, horizons in the night — to these eloquent musings and searchings:

I have often been struck by the prevalence in our tradition of symbols of darkness, darkness impenetrable to intellect; and in this ultimate darkness the only light for us is Christ. Abraham fell into a horror of great darkness.... God mediates His Presence through darkness, suffering and death. (118)

A subsequent letter ends in what might be thought a contradictory, even a contrary spirit, a statement of what, from the writings collected herein, seems very far from obvious:

I am not one who is in truth much given to exploring the dark; one rather who rejoices, in his mild unheroic way, in the light; and it is with relief that I return to Heraclitus (dry light), and Herodotus (dry stick), and Hesiod (dryer still), and that supreme poet Homer (bright light of a sun that sees all and shines on all, the just and the unjust: light seekers and dark explorers, the puzzled and the wise ...) (135)

This is no ironic or litotic disclaimer; rather, it is almost a lament that such dark searchings have been necessary, that consciousness of suffering has interrupted attendance on the meridional light. For Homer, and Greek poetry both classical and modern, are Gerard Casey's elected medium, as is manifest in his own poetry and translations (collected in *Echoes*, 1990). But there is, finally, no contradiction between Homer and, say, Jakob Boehme — the subject of a deeply sympathetic essay, reprinted here — when light and dark glint off each other, when substance can turn to shadow, and shadows can be true.

Gerard Casey's writings are, regrettably, to be looked for in obscure corners. As a writer and thinker he has dwelt in the shadows. This is certainly not just. But it may be there that one sees light most clearly, as a horizon of the night. In discerning the ways of this sideless world, Gerard Casey has been both a seeker of the light and an explorer of the dark. The puzzled and the wise are one: this too is a near-paradox, embodied, with dignity and defiance, in *Night Horizons*.

Charles Lock

John Cowper Powys
HERBERT WILLIAMS
Bridgend: Seren, 1997, Border Lines Series
Hardback, £14.95, ISBN 1 85411 196 5
Paperback, £7.95, ISBN 1 85411 197 3

One of the remarkable things about this book (but only one) is that, in an age besotted with literary biographies, this is the first to be devoted exclusively to John Cowper Powys. Louis Marlow, Kenneth Hopkins and Richard Perceval Graves have all produced books which we can be glad to have read, but each dealt with John Cowper Powys (and Llewelyn and Theodore) as if his defining characteristic was that he was part of an extraordinary family. Yet, surely, the tendency in any such family, and especially in one as large as that of Charles and Mary Powys, must be for the individual to distinguish himself from the group and for differences to be exaggerated rather than subsumed into the 'family personality'. Hardy may have seen the 'family face ... Projecting trait and trace' in his poem 'Heredity', but the creative genius behind the face was undoubtedly his own. In fact, what most clearly distinguishes the members of the Powys family is that they were so utterly different from almost everyone else, including one another. Louis Marlow recognised this since, although he spoke of being faced with 'a wall of Powys solidarity' and of confronting 'one monstrous Powys' when the family sat down at table, he called his chapter 'The One Powys and the Many'. It is understandable that these earlier, and excellent, biographers should wish to introduce the entire Powys family to the reading public, and no less understandable that they should seek to enhance their readership by attracting the devotees of all three author brothers. In their books, therefore, a certain homogenisation takes place: but take a passage at random from Llewelyn, Theodore or John and it could never be mistaken for the work of one of his brother. The Powyses, of course, could never be made bland, but there is a tendency in these earlier works to mould their eccentricities to the same pattern and to stress the importance of their shared heritage, rather than to explore them as unique individuals and important artists. To do so inevitably, if unintentionally, diminishes each of these great writers to the status of part, merely, of a scribbling trio.

It is essential, therefore, that John Cowper, Theodore Francis and Llewelyn (not to mention the less famous siblings) be viewed first as individual artists, and only later as members of the Powys family. Until now, only Llewelyn, whom some would regard as the least of the three, has been granted such treatment.

The second remarkable quality of Herbert Williams' book is that he manages to bring together into a coherent narrative the story of a very long life in the space of only 160 pages of text, making of it not only a worthy chronicle but, what John Cowper himself loved best, *an exciting story*. Not a single important event is left out and, indeed, a quantity of new information is included, particularly in relation to Powys's years in Wales. This considerable feat is effected without any sense of cramming by the use of a style which is swift, economical and graceful, and it will come as no surprise to learn that Herbert Williams is a poet as well as a biographer. What also distinguishes the book is Williams' use of precise dates and places where his predecessors have been content to offer rather vague indications of the decade or year in which an event took place. This is especially frustrating in Richard Graves' book, which gives the impression of providing enormous quantities of information until one actually tries to look up a specific point. Try, for example, finding the exact date and place of Powys's marriage to Margaret Lyon, in either *The Brothers Powys*, or the works of Marlow and Hopkins. To be fair, Williams has had the advantage of access to a great deal of information unavailable even to Graves, his most authoritative predecessor. Since the beginning of the eighties, when Graves was working on his book, a number of important collections of letters and diaries have been published, texts edited and archives explored, and Williams has also been granted access to unpublished materials, especially those now in the National Library of Wales, which were specifically denied to Graves by the Powys estate. A number of other Powys scholars have also pursued their own, often quite specialised, biographical researches and Herbert Williams makes excellent use of these. Graves himself recognised that, in due time, his own book would be superseded, for he wrote in his introduction that it 'must be treated in some respects as a work in progress'. Be that as it may, there were things which Graves could have discovered and didn't and things which he could have made clearer. Williams is far more helpful in this respect and it is also gratifying to find that he has made considerable use of research first published in our own *Newsletter* and *Journal*.

Herbert Williams does more in this short book than merely tell the story of Powys's life, however excitingly, for he also finds the space to discuss all of the major works, as well as several of the minor ones. This he does with astuteness and sensitivity, tackling the works directly, without the armour of theory to bolster and justify his critical reactions. He also avoids the temptation to be over-defensive in championing a neglected author. Where he sees greatness he explores and celebrates it, where the work falls short of greatness he declares the fact without apology. Describing the finale of *Rodmoor*, for example, he writes:

> The melodramatic climax finds the 'brain-sick' Adrian dying at the sea's edge and Philippa tying his corpse to her body before plunging suicidally into the waves. Not for the first or last time in his work, Powys succumbs to absurdity. (62)

A more speculative, and less assured, critic might have been tempted to elide the absurdity and concentrate on possible biographical 'originals' for the situations and characters represented in this scene, and I am certain that these could be found without too much trouble. Yet such an approach would leave the perceptive reader with the sense that some sleight of hand had been perpetrated, that he had been consciously deflected from the absurdity of the passage, and such a reaction would inevitably damage the reader's regard for Powys.

Williams continues his theme in the 'Postcript':

> It is true that there are glaring faults in [Powys's] work. It is verbose, his circumlocutions sometimes touching depths of absurdity. His prose is frequently clumsy, his ear for dialogue so faulty that he allows characters to make long speeches without interruption. He can be embarrassingly whimsical,

and his early novels especially have touches of melodrama which make one cringe. (158)

It is a bold biographer who can write such things of his subject and yet still hope to entice new readers to his works. Yet Williams' honesty is in itself a stout assertion of Powys's greatness, and such honesty is essential if he is ever to be recognised as an author of major importance and cease to be 'the invisible man of English letters' (158). Williams makes it clear that these faults represent the essential underside of Powys's genius, which is intrinsically linked to his conception of the world as place of magic and of himself as a magician. In the Powysian sense this is something quite different from the faery world of wizards and wonders, for it is not wizardry and conjuring which Powys sees as the motive force of daily life, but something altogether more earth-rooted, mud-smirched and bodily. Magic, for Powys, is something less portentous than it is for many other authors, and can dwell in the most common objects and actions of daily life. His Merlin, after all, is not the whimsical, absent-minded, donnish and essentially kindly figure portrayed so brilliantly by T. H. White in *The Once and Future King*, but an altogether more physical and less obviously attractive being, with his cropped black hair, his enormous skull and 'broad, low forehead' (*Porius*, 280). As Williams says, 'a magician creates his own reality' (10) and the 'fictional world Powys created … was not the England that actually existed in the late 1920s and early 1930s, but a strange mixture of the Victorian England of his youth and an imagined present' (53). His 'Wessex' books are, after all, 'romances' rather than novels and are set, therefore, in an imagined and magical version of England. As he established himself in Wales, deliberately distant from his living relatives, in the land of legendary ancestors in whom few of the family believed, Powys's vision expanded into the past, which he saw not as 'impossibly distant but something contemporary, co-existing with present and future in a timeless dimension which could be imaginatively entered.' (124)

Although they came to admire and respect Powys and even feel a reserved affection for him, John Cowper was never regarded by his Welsh contemporaries as anything other than a sympathetic English-man, despite his constant proclamations of Welsh ancestry and his tireless efforts to learn the language, which he could read tolerably, write with care and assistance and speak in a way entirely his own and incomprehensible to any Welsh speaker. Yet he wanted to be Welsh because Wales meant antiquity, myth and magic, and because it was a land on the margin, and marginality, being between the wet sand and the dry sand as he calls it in *Weymouth Sands*, was essential to Powys's sense of himself. Whether Wales actually seems quite so marginal to the Welsh or whether this is a perception only possible to a 'resident alien' are questions which Powys seems not to have asked. However, as Herbert Williams says, 'in shaping himself into a Welshman — or at least a 'Cymric' — as convincingly as he could, Powys showed a creative genius at least as strong as any he brought to his novels.' (10) But although it might be as a 'Cymric' that Powys strove to see himself, and although he was constantly aware of the earth-strong forces of nature around him, it would be wrong to regard him as entirely oblivious of the needs and natures of his Welsh neighbours. In his essay 'My Welsh Home', published in *Obstinate Cymric* in 1947, he writes:

> From Corwen to Rhyl is precisely that leap from the time of Owen Glendower to the time of Radio and Cinema that I feel so conscious of in Wales. These gay crowded busses carry people to Movies and Circuses from where men's broodings for thousands of years are as unchanged as those of the salmon and the owls and the eagles.
> Men and women must feel on all sides here the poetic weight of a hoary antiquity from which it is essential to take a vacation sometimes.' (71)

Wales, then, provided Powys not with a secure bolt-hole into the past, turreted by mountains and moated with valleys, from which he could remain unassailed by the harshness of the modern world, but a starting point from which, unchained by expectations, he could explore time past, present and future, and space from the bottom of a ditch to the furthest reaches of the galaxy and beyond. Wales was not Powys's anchor, but his launching-pad. It is fitting, therefore, that this marvellous book should be part of the Border Lines series, which has explored many other neglected and marginal figures, border-dwellers physically and artistically.

Herbert Williams has done a great deal, with his television and radio programmes, to make the name John Cowper Powys familiar to a new audience, but even these achievements pale into insignificance compared to this book which does exactly what needs to be done for Powys's reputation and does it in a style which is nothing short of masterly.

Paul Roberts

Steeple on the Hill
GLEN CAVALIERO
Tartarus Press, 1997. Hardback, £8.99, ISBN 1 872621 23 6
Lives
PETER FOSS
Headland Publications, 1995. Paperback, £5.95, ISBN 0 903074 68 0
Writers in a Landscape
JEREMY HOOKER
University of Wales Press, 1996. Paperback £12.95, ISBN 0 7083 1391 4

Jeremy Hooker's book *Writers in a Landscape* differs from the other two here for entirely formal reasons. First it is a critical study of prose and novels, whereas Cavaliero and Foss give us collections of poems; but also, I previously reviewed it elsewhere, a fact known to your editor and graciously accepted. Since my view of the book is unchanged, I don't want either to just repeat it or to seek spurious variants for their own sake. More important is how Hooker's vision, here and elsewhere, ties in with the two poets also here dealt with. Enough then that *Writers in a Landscape* deals with two pairs of writers, namely Edward Thomas and Richard Jefferies, and John Cowper Powys and Thomas Hardy; and also, that it embodies all its author's familiar concerns and values. The lasting memory of childhood places, the palimpset of rural England, the care and tact at each decided judgement. It is a fine, disciplined book, and very serious; flavoured too much with the latter for some no doubt, but with

Hooker's characteristic combination of broad principle and close attention to detail evinced on every page. Most of all it occupies what Donald Davie once called the presiding territory of Hooker's poetry: 'the emotion that we have when we recognise some particular terrain as home'. This too seems to be what compels Foss and Cavaliero equally. Followers of Hooker so far will not be disappointed, while for new readers *Writers in a Landscape* is not too late a starting point.

Yet a theme runs through it which, bearing in mind Hooker's own poetry of place too (not under review here), is relevant to the other two books here reviewed. Grossly oversimplifying of course, Edward Thomas falls short as a prose writer in lacking Jefferies' 'art of seeing'; the microscopic details, in particular, of Jefferies' descriptions of rural people, scenes, incidents, plants, textures of soil and wild life. In his early career Thomas 'attempted to transcend the limitations of the aesthetic vision by peopling nature with mythological presences' (64). Thomas's late melancholic body of poetry finds a voice by being at least partly inturned, something that Jefferies seldom turned to. Although rather differently — for John Cowper Powys evoked mental and physical nuance as closely as most when he chose — Thomas Hardy too founded his massive novels upon the 'noticing' he underlined in a famous poem.

Peter Foss and Glen Cavaliero both express what they love in the belief that seeing it full frontally is the road through to its essential spirit. This is abnormally difficult in an age which values a poetry of the askance, the streetwise phrase, awareness of the in-your-face as ephemeral, and detail as proof of where you are coming from rather than as symbol of the invisible but pervasive. Both poets long for an earlier poetry, write it with considerable sensitivity and resource, and are alert too for chances to include a more current patois. If we are still left a touch uneasy, it may be because their very integrity at times blocks out the messy layering of current Britain — its writing and its life — by the latest round of all that work, transport, technology, communications and such have imposed on us.

Foss picks his subjects carefully and serially: 'Iris', 'Child', 'The Picture', 'Mwnt', 'Hinckley Displayed', 'Stockerston', 'Bilstone Gibbet' — these last are from the Leicestershire where he long lived.

'Stockerston' begins:

> Nestling close as though grown there
> On the wooded hill, this hall, this church;
> Alike removed from human care
> And long survived our will to search.
>
> But search we do. A lane through hills
> From corner and cottages leads us there;
> Randomly the landscape yields
> Sheep and pasture, earth and air.

This poem like its predecessor 'Hinckley Displayed' is a fine quatrain with something of T. S. Eliot's own quatrain voice hanging round it ('Hinckley Displayed' has some unimprovable closing stanzas). But the short sentence beginning the second stanza only tells what we would have liked evoked; and there is little random about what the landscape randomly yields. 'Aubade', a more personal poem, begins thus:

> In the white dawn where the window's screen faced us,
> crazed with the night's frost in late October,
> we woke, in love, to the same spare concerto.
>
> Along the passages these sounds of Mozart
> like resolutions of all fear and folly
> merged with the morning's drone and crying kettle.
>
> From gantry doors where the bleak concrete stairwells
> defined the contours of the fractured city,
> there crept the children that the streets devour.

In some ways an ideal Mozart, autumn and love merge with kitchen and cityscape very cleanly. But it takes an act of will to hold them together; the problem remains. In some poems Foss takes on the contemporary vernacular more frankly — 'Home From Home', 'Donkeywise' — but usually the experience is elevated before he starts, and the poetic then aspires to rise to that level.

Glen Cavaliero illustrates the matter even more thorough-goingly. For this reviewer he recalls the precision of Charles Tomlinson,

Vernon Watkins and George Barker; many of his poems are so finely-tuned that it seems perverse to be other than grateful for them. In some of the longer ones such as 'The Passing of the Gods' and 'A Norwich Triptych' (with its superb third section on Dame Julian) the depth, extent and saturated long-time meditation that precedes them is evident and enviable. But a premise lurks, that language, today, can still be trusted as co-valent with the spiritual experience entered and conveyed. It is as though we can rely on the old grammar and lexicon to match our deepest experiences in the age when such communication, for so many, is most found in film, electronics, body-language and much else. Here is the end of 'Wetherham Clock':

> At dusk those hills take shape together,
> a limber curving line that seems to measure the earth's
>   music.
> Old Man, Brim Fell, Swirl How, the Carrs
> and thrusting out before them Wetherham, proud skull
> presiding over valleys where the work
> is Wetherham work, old as the mountain's bones
> and never done. Made under planetary laws,
> these drystone walls and homesteads
> gather to a purpose past conceiving, as above
> the raven hunter wheels among the rocks.

If in cultural correctness the mountain is 'made under planetary laws' it can hardly have 'bones' or 'measure the earth's music', whatever that is. Yet I still don't doubt Cavaliero's belief that its 'purpose' is 'past conceiving'; the poem earns that bit entirely. But in many poems, the network of words is so wrought as to risk lifting off its subject like an independent crust.

So what? both these poets may retort. Maybe we must wait a couple of generations to see whether such poets — Cavaliero deeper and more accomplished, Foss more impassioned — will survive when the rock-and-roll set have subsided. I left these collections somewhat unconvinced, yet like Hardy at the end of 'The Oxen' — 'hoping it might be so'. Maybe.

John Powell Ward

The Sixpenny Strumpet [*containing* In Good Earth, God, The Two Thieves, *and* The Sixpenny Strumpet]
T. F. POWYS
edited by IAN ROBINSON, assisted by ELAINE MENCHER, with a textual history by J. LAWRENCE MITCHELL
Harleston, Norfolk: Brynmill, 1997, 437pp., £25.00, ISBN 0 907839 41 X

The publication of this book is not only a welcome but an important literary event. It comes from a discerning small publisher but, by rights, a major publisher should have done the job years ago. Few scholarly editions, in these days when new 'texts' of established (and already available) 'classics' are two a penny, can claim to have rescued three central works by a major, though neglected, writer; even fewer to have given us another one ('The Sixpenny Strumpet') for the first time ever. Robinson's edition will not sell as many copies but it is much more significant than most of the Penguin Classics one is ever likely to buy. (The main reason that its author is not better known is that it is so difficult to find copies of his books to read — perhaps he should be put in *samizdat?*)

Yet the *TLS* heralded this event with a particularly muddle-headed review, pigeon-holing its author as a 'fine stylist' but a 'problematic thinker'. Readers who know his work will realise how unthinkable such a distinction is, even more so for him than for any good writer. They will not need to read far to see that they are in for an uncommon treat. but for the *TLS* Powys is simply an 'eccentric writer'. This *canard* has by now become a cliché, as necessary to vague criticism as bread sauce used to be to chicken. The rest of us will probably find an adjective such as 'original' less patronising (though even eccentricity is not to be sneezed at a time when so many of our novelists spend so much of their time in looking over their own shoulders at each other). Originality, however, has never been the best way of selling books.

Indeed, it seems almost otiose to try to *say* anything about a tale like 'In Good Earth', so perfect is the fit of its form to its meaning.[1] Every word counts and there is not a word in it that is there merely to draw attention to *itself*. Powys's profound simplicity is quite unlike the slicker kind of simplicity that Hemingway is famous for, the kind where simple words are used to contrive a striking effect of self-conscious directness. Powys's plain style is neither mannered nor *macho* as Hemingway so often is. If his form (like many of his characters) is deliberately limited that is because he instinctively thinks in terms, not of the arresting detail, but of the total effect of the work as a whole. It is because a story like 'In Good Earth' rests on a firm bedrock of clear, simple language that it is able to grow so surely and steadily in power towards its conclusion. The fable is allowed to speak for itself and there is no call for the prose to point out where it is going. This is why a Powys tale rarely falls off at the close, why (unlike so many novelists) he is so good at *endings*. One can always see him thinking out the whole story as he tells it. Something similar can be found in a few novelists (Stendhal and Jane Austen spring to my mind) but it is surely a rare quality, one that is almost in contradiction to the novel's inclusive nature as a form.[2] Moreover, even some of the greatest novels — *Bleak House*, for instance, or *L'Education Sentimentale* — can seem very *written* beside Powys at his best. Ian Robinson's indispensable 'Afterword' to *The Sixpenny Strumpet* shows in detail how long an apprenticeship he had to go through in order to achieve such simplicity. It did not come easily to him, like singing to a bird, as is sometimes supposed, nor was it merely the fruit of passive immersion in the language of the King James Bible. To pare English down to its bones as he did entailed an immense intellectual and spiritual commitment and then, on top of that, untold hard work. Flaubert only learnt to do something similar in *Bouvard et Pécuchet*, a novel he left unfinished at his death. In saying this, however, I do not mean to make inflated claims for T. F. Powys but simply to emphasise how unusual his fiction is, how unlike that of most novelists one can think of. His readers, ever since John Cowper Powys, have always known this but one wonders whether his originality has ever been acknowledged as positively as it deserves to be.

   As with many of Powys's writings, the germ of 'In Good Earth' is Biblical (in this case the Parable of the Sower) though in his version the Biblical story is virtually reversed and it turns out that it is 'the poor earth that God loves'. In other words, we may be given a new parable but we certainly don't get a sermon. Thus, the violent ambition of

John Gidden, who mistakenly seeks for the 'good earth' in worldly possessions, is not seen in any censorious spirit. On the contrary, we find ourselves in closer and closer imaginative touch with his greed and, consequently, feel almost as devastated as he is when it is disappointed. Only by participating in this shock (as no preacher would) is Powys able to understand his final renunciation and his decision to make do with his father's barren and debt-ridden farm. Yet if the moral of *magnitudo parvi* is implicit it surfaces without any moralising. It is one thing to opine that the 'good earth' lies in (or beyond) the grave but quite another thing to give the thought emotional reality and a 'local habitation and a name'. When we begin 'In Good Earth' we suppose that we are in for a cautionary tale but by its end we find ourselves in territory that is close to tragedy.

If I could, I would like to try to show this by quotation but, to do the story any justice, I would need to quote much more than there is space for here. In fact, to quote merely a dozen or so lines would almost be a species of vandalism because the story's strength lies in the way it is sustained over its whole length, building inevitably into a whole. You cannot illustrate its intensity properly just by quoting a single step in it, however intense that particular moment may be. There is not, in fact, very much even in *Mr. Weston's Good Wine* itself to equal the mounting pitch of its narrative. I am reminded rather of another novella from the same period at the end of Powys's career, *The Only Penitent* — so much so that I am almost tempted to suggest that the essence of his art really lies not so much in his novels as in his shorter fictions. Suffice it to say that, in general, the latter bring out more strikingly the sheer gift for story-telling that is at the heart of all of his most concentrated writing. Beside 'In Good Earth' a novel like *Unclay* looks, for all its interest, rather diffuse and drawn-out. The best parables can afford to be short. In a good Powys tale it is almost impossible to separate the meaning from the context or the setting. If this makes his work sound schematic in summary that is simply because of what cannot be summarised at all, the pacing and modula-tion of the narrative rhythm as a whole. With most fiction it is possible to pick out highlights and purple passages or moments that seem especially significant (we can all call many of them to mind) but with

Powys's best tales it is impossible to do this without damaging one's sense of them as artistic wholes. One seldom finds one's self thinking, 'This is a good bit' or 'This bit doesn't quite come off' as one often does with Scott or Dickens or Lawrence. One has the impression that Powys thought more deeply about the overall shape of his fictions *as he was writing them* than most novelists do. One can't imagine him ever getting so absorbed in one particular page as to forget, in the way Hardy sometimes did, that, however beautiful, one page can never be more than just one link in a chain.

The remarkable story called 'God' is a good illustration of the way what some readers of Powys think of as his whimsy (how could a story whose hero believes that God is embodied in his father's top hat possibly be as serious as *Jude the Obscure*?) is really a vehicle for a kind of metaphysical wit. The fable enables him to explore serious issues without falling into a serious manner (like Hardy). Both Robinson and John Williams have noticed the parallels between 'God' and Powys's own childhood and also with the last years of his own father's life but, because it is a fable, it is never autobiographical in the way a book like *David Copperfield* is: real life dressed as fiction and, in the process, re-arranged and even romanticised. The personal memories are simply its raw material, sources but not a *raison d'être*. The tale is just as arresting if we fail to recognise them. The religious experience at the centre of it is never presented simply as personal experience. Indeed, the whole point of the fable (and the 'whimsy') is to transcend the merely personal. The bizarre conceit of the top hat is actually a means of generalising what is private in the story's inspiration. Thus, we don't think of John Chew's schooldays in the light of the time his creator spent at Dorchester Grammar School, in the way David Copperfield's time at Murdstone and Grinby's makes us think of Dickens's drudgery in the blacking factory. John's experience may be odd but it is not special. Moreover, it is not really John who is the main character but God himself. The reason that John is necessary to bring this about is simply that, for Powys, God is always an experience and never just an idea. In other words, the story is only speculative in the way that art is speculative. Powys's famous statement that 'a belief is too easy a road to God' (in *Soliloquies of a Hermit*), so often taken as expressing an idiosyncratic kind of mysticism, is more than just that: it also implies his commitment to art over dogma in a way that is close to Lawrence's dictum that 'art-speech is the only speech'. To see 'God' simply as a sport is to miss the way its fable is, in essence, a way of thinking imaginatively. The alleged whimsy turns out in the end to be inseparable from the story's seriousness.

Notwithstanding Powys's reputation as an 'allegorist' (a novelist who is more moralistic than other novelists) it seems, then, that he turned to fiction because it was the only way in which he could express his moral thought with sufficient subtlety. As Robinson points out, in choosing to write novels and tales he was also giving up 'prophecy'. He did not evolve a vision of the world and then apply it *through* fiction, as Bunyan might (crudely) be said to have done. It was only *by* writing fiction that he could discover what he had to say in its full complexity. The single vision of 'prophecy' was too restrictive to allow enough room for all the obliquities and qualifications that were intrinsic to his actual way of thinking. This is why *Soliloquies*, admirable as it often is, reads like a personal testament whereas the best fiction comes over as fully-fledged self-expression. It would be impossible to reduce *Mr. Weston's Good Wine* to a bald paraphrase of its thought. How could one boil down even Mrs Vosper's spitefulness or Mr Grunter's gruffness, let alone the moment at the Folly Down inn when time stops, to an *idea*? What is told can no more be separated from the way it is told than in a novel by Jane Austen. Similarly, any attempt to pin down a tale like 'God' would be doomed to miss its strange blend of comedy, pathos and religiousness. Its simplicity and economy, like the 'whimsy', are themselves part of its saying. Most writers who tackle such large questions as 'God' does, produce large books (*The Idiot*, for instance) but Powys is concise and direct. His simplicity, in fact, is an integral part of his subtlety, as much part of the thought as is the naive humility of the hero. A novel of the length of *A Glastonbury Romance* which said the same things would not have the same meaning.

That is, in Powys, it is always hard to say anything clear about God. There is a spiritual motive for his brevity and simplicity. His tales are, as it were, the polar opposite to something like Milton's head-on treatment of God and Heaven in *Paradise Lost*. It is perhaps no accident that the novel of his that comes closest to being portentous, *Unclay*, should also be his longest. Unlike Milton, one of his great qualities as a writer is *tact* and tact, such as we find in *Fables*, is twin-brother to brevity. It is this that makes his work so hard to paraphrase: its meanings have already been pared down to their essentials in the art itself. Hence, the religious power of *Mr. Weston's Good Wine* lies not so much in what it says about God as in what it refrains from saying. Powys understands that, on this subject, it can never be the novelist who gets the last word. Behind the affable, accessible wine merchant there looms a shadowy figure of immense but reserved power. All the novel can offer is glimpses of Him, glimpses that are impressive precisely because they are so fleeting. Mr Weston *has* to be ordinary. Powys cannot afford to let him hog the limelight like Milton's God. I have always thought of this as the most cogent reason for thinking that Powys himself believed in God: he believed in Him enough to think of Him as indescribable. But he had no personal hot-line to God as some mystics do. A ubiquitous God-figure like his Mr Jar is nearly always humble, almost too human, seen, except in flashes, 'through a glass darkly'. By no means all religious writers, even the best ones, have been this humble or this realistic.

However, I would not want these remarks to be taken as yet again directing attention back to *Mr. Weston's Good Wine*: they are equally germane to many other works by Powys. That book is a wonderful one but the fact that it is the only one of his books to have consistently remained in print has been a disaster for the reputation of the others. It has meant that many readers who have read and admired it feel entitled to claim to know what T. F. Powys is like. In reality, extracting the kernel from the nut is not so simple. No one could claim to know his work without at the least reading a good deal of his shorter fiction too. He is one of the most natural short story writers in the language, one whose thought instinctively takes a condensed form without its ever having to be forced into it. I myself suspect that he probably had to force his genius more to write at novel-length. This is not the least of his many differences from his older brother. Unlike him, he had a spontaneous feel for the pleasure that a good tale can give simply by the grace of its shape. I don't mean, in saying this, that his fiction is therefore mannered or merely aesthetic but that it shows a rare gift for finding the right form for a particular idea. If John Cowper has a genius for elaboration, for dotting the 'i's and crossing the 't's until they glow, Theodore's genius was for concentration. Form came almost as naturally to him as it did to Jane Austen. The kind of economy that Henry James valued so highly and took years to refine in his own work, the ability to keep the focus on the real subject, was, as it were, implicit in the way Powys saw life in terms of fundamentals.[3] This is why he shows so little interest in trying to depict the changing surface of society in the way nearly all novelists do. In other words, there may well be a point in suggesting that he was really a writer of tales first and a novelist only second, not unlike Kafka, another creator of parables.

The real significance of the publication of four novellas of the quality of those which comprise *The Sixpenny Strumpet* is that it leads one to ask whether the novella and the shorter tale were not Powys's most natural forms as a writer. I would suggest, for example, that the level of achievement of his shorter fiction is in general much more consistent than that of his novels. In a way, this thought can even be applied to *Mr. Weston's Good Wine*, perfectly rounded as it is. There is a sense in which that novel takes the form of a series of condensed episodes that can seem almost intact in themselves. Its chapters often read almost like short stories. This is not to disregard the presence of the story-teller himself, moving from one story to another, or the pervasive presence of Mr Weston or the unifying theme of his two kinds of wine (love and death) but one cannot help noticing that the greatest tales, such as *When Thou Wast Naked*, do not need to rely so much on such things and are perhaps all the more intense because they can dispense with them. *Mr. Weston's Good Wine* seems to me, at least, more of a *tour de force*, more a feat of construction, than any of the tales in *The Sixpenny Strumpet* do. It too is very much a work of art but its art is perhaps a more conscious and calculated thing. The novel is still a remarkable one but its art is more like that of other novelists, such as James, than that of the tales is.

'The Two Thieves' at first reads like a simpler, more moral tale than the others but it soon turns out, as it often does in this author, that a

227

seemingly simplistic tone is actually a way of springing a surprise on the reader. Readers of fiction are, after all, only too ready to moralise themselves — as Powys knows very well. So, as soon as we settle down to the confirmation of our own moral certainties, we find ourselves plunged into a world that grows increasingly dark and paradoxical. The subject is a tragic one — the birth of evil — but there is a characteristic impishness in its treatment that we would scarcely expect to find in a tragedy. Again, the story begins from a text ('Watch therefore; for ye know not what hour your Lord doth come' from *Matthew*) but it proceeds, simply through the telling, to squeeze more meaning out of it than the reader could ever have suspected it of holding. The idea, put crudely, is that God is a thief and it is only by stealing souls that he can give a human thief like George Douse a hope of redemption. My word 'idea' is, of course, a reductive one: the dramatic way the tale enacts its meaning has its own peculiar stark power but its clarity is not on the level of any rational moral analysis. The action is ingenious but much more convincing than it sounds, starting as it does from the impoverished but greedy Douse's improbably marrying an heiress (whom he then proceeds to abuse). The story hinges on three kinds of theft that look similar but are actually quite different from each other, those of Douse, the Pedlar and Mr Jar (or man, the devil and God). This may sound rather Bunyanesque but it is less abstract that it seems. The story will perhaps appeal more to readers who value Powys as a creator of parables than as a shrewd observer of village life but it never reads at all like a sermon in disguise. It is both too disturbing and too comic for us to take its moral insights as merely didactic. From its opening juxtaposition of the squalid soul of George Douse with the fantastic, folktale-like figure of the Pedlar, it keeps us in a constant state of expectation. We may perhaps anticipate that Douse will end by hanging himself but the striking image of his exchanging clothes with a pauper in his final despair is sobering and shocking. We feel too implicated by it to view him with any sort of moral complacency. The moment has, rather, a kind of ironic grandeur. 'The Two Thieves' also contains some alarming descriptions of Douse's cruelty to his wife which some readers will set down to the author's presumed sadistic streak and others will take more as signs that he has a sense of tragedy. Suffice it to say that Powys always writes with particular intensity when he writes about cruelty. He had a keen sense of the brutish side of human nature. No doubt he could not have properly shown what Douse did to his wife without understanding the kind of pleasure he took in doing it. He sometimes shows a special relish in punishing evil-doers himself — Mrs Vosper, for instance. But such things entail much more than simple moralising. What distinguishes 'The Two Thieves' is the powerful psychological realism that it is able to draw from the apparently schematic mode of allegory. It is a way of by-passing all that rich detail of everyday life that we usually expect to get from fiction.[4]

The text of 'The Sixpenny Strumpet' has been painstakingly established by Ian Robinson and Elaine Mencher from manuscripts in Dorchester and Texas. Since no definitive version survives their work does not claim to be authoritative, though in some respects it may be truer to Powys's intentions than many of his published works were. But the editor has to make certain choices without any means of being sure that they are the ones the author would have made. Moreover, Powys is notoriously difficult to edit in that he set out his work in short paragraphs, almost like poetry, but often neglected to indent at the start of a new paragraph. This said, we are given a scrupulous text of what is a remarkable story, one in some ways unlike anything else its author wrote. Its overdue first appearance is therefore a double bonus. It is not entirely clear why the story was not published at about the same time as the other ones in this volume (they were all written in 1930–31) but Robinson suggests that Chatto and Windus may have been chary of bringing out the tale of a village prostitute (to the local parson, among others) who ends up as the bride of Christ, at a time when the Home Secretary had more than a little in common with the rich hypocrites who persecute her. The fact that the tale alludes to Christ's words to the woman taken in adultery does not mitigate the bluntness with which it illustrates everything that a middle-class public would have found shocking and unpalatable in His teaching. In the aftermath of the Wall Street Crash not many readers would have cared to be reminded that it was the poor who would inherit the earth.

One sees why Robinson admires 'The Sixpenny Strumpet' so much.

It is a parable but it is also embedded in an unusually realistic picture of rural poverty. Nuttycoome has none of the timeless feeling of Folly Down; the action is precisely located in the late nineteenth century, in the time of Gladstone and Spurgeon and Joseph Arch. As a whole, Mary Triddle's story has a beautiful unrelenting drabness to it that is more reminiscent of the tone of *Fables* than of *Mr. Weston's Good Wine*, though it is a more sustained piece of writing than any of *Fables* is. It moves from realism to its symbolic conclusion in a particularly seamless and natural way. Furthermore, Powys shows us poverty through the eyes of the poor, not from the perspective of horrified middle-class pity that is more usual in English fiction since *Oliver Twist*. (Powys knew what being poor was like.) In this respect, the story suggests that his range as a social observer may be wider than it is often thought to be. Nevertheless, I am not yet sure that 'The Sixpenny Strumpet' belongs on quite the same shelf as 'In Good Earth' and *The Only Penitent*. It strikes me as being more swayed by the urgency of its own moral message than they are. If it has a comparable moral power it perhaps lacks their artistic tact.

Though 'The Sixpenny Strumpet' has a similar rough simplicity to the other late novellas its simplicity was perhaps more hard-won, carved as it was out of especially intractable material.[5] The humour of its opening pages, for instance, has a cautious, almost crabbed indirectness:

> the rich ruled the poor in the grandest manner, presenting to those in need, a weekly dole of two shillings and sixpence, and a loaf of bread; or else, did any refuse such luxury, a home in the workhouse.

Or:

> Though good people enough, the Triddles had never bothered Mary about Religion, but when she was a child, and still lived in Suffolk, her Mother taught her to repeat on Sundays the Lord's Prayer.

These sentences are so dead-pan that they seem guarded, even sly. Yet if Powys keeps his cards close to his chest it is not simply out of impersonality. At other moments one feels real hatred in his comic descriptions of the great ones of the earth. As the story progresses, however, its tone becomes more resigned and almost mournful though even then the prose can have a salty frankness that reminds one more of Fielding than of any Victorian novelist. For example, 'A fine fancy is lust, a flea that can get into any man's ear.' The parable of the stranger on a donkey who rides into Nuttycoombe to claim Mary as a bride emerges out of these things too; there is nothing pious about it. Nonetheless, by the ending of the tale the comedy of the opening has been hushed. The noble stranger, laden with symbolic hot cross buns, may seem incongruous but he is too serious a figure — too much of a dignified rebuke to the inhabitants of Nuttycoombe — to provoke laughter. By contrast, in the great final scene of *The Only Penitent*, where Mr Jar begs Mr Hayhoe's pardon for the world he has created, both characters are as comical as they are symbolic, the one apologetic and the other heroically ingenuous. If that scene goes beyond tragedy it is because there is a role-reversal in it that comes straight from comedy. The religious fulfilment at the end of 'The Sixpenny Strumpet' is less complex than this. For this reason, its symbolism therefore seems rather less resonant, more like a demonstration. Not that this diminishes the sheer boldness of Powys's conception, a boldness that has not dated and still puts the averagely sinful reader on the spot. Nor does that reader need to be a Christian in order to respond to the story's religious feeling.[6]

I am quite prepared to have to eat my words about the stature of 'The Sixpenny Strumpet' once I come to know it better but I suspect that it will always seem somewhat different from the other late novellas. Robinson himself sees it as 'more purely Christian in feeling' than most of T. F. Powys is. This may not be a literary reason for admiring it but it does suggest how original it is for a fiction written in the 1930s. Here is an author who is in many ways a modern, whose work could not conceivably have been written in the nineteenth century, not even by Hawthorne, creating a story that , in its way, out-Bunyans Bunyan. The nearest thing to its closing pages that I can think of is the passage in *The Pilgrim's Progress* where Christian crosses the river and 'the trumpets sounded for him on the other side'.

There have been other religious novelists in our century but none who would have embodied such a ringing parable within such a bleak tale of bygone rural squalor. Robinson invokes Wordsworth but none of his fallen women are as prosaic as Mary Triddle is. And the characters in Graham Greene and Mauriac who suffer in Christ are invariably not humble innocents but educated sinners. Powys's prose still has a sort of contemporary immediacy but few writers since Tolstoi in his late tales have drawn so deeply on the Bible for artistic inspiration for fiction.[7] That is something one expects to have to go back as far as Blake and beyond to find. No doubt this can restrict Powys's range as a writer (and his popularity!) but it is also a pointer to the singular imaginative purity of his best work. It would be rash to suppose that the Bible provides a less lasting source than contemporary society does, even to those for whom it is only a collection of fables.

David Gervais

NOTES

[1] John Cowper Powys thought it a 'magnificent story' and 'equal to Mr Weston' when he read it in 1932 (Robinson, 409).

[2] Orwell's remarks on Dickens's weakness for the 'unnecessary detail' apply to many of the great novelists of the period before Powys and, of course, to John Cowper too.

[3] James learnt the value of concentration from Balzac but was himself as much an elaborator as a condenser – as his late prose style amply confirms.

[4] Powys's gift for allegory should not blind us as to how well he knew the every-day life of rural Dorset. John Gidden and Mary Triddle evoke more clearly the actual poverty depicted in, say, Sturt's Bettesworth Books than the more fiction-alised poor of Jefferies and Hardy do.

[5] Powys wrote to Charles Prentice at Chatto & Windus that, '"The Only Peni-tent" is certainly the best story to begin with. It was by far the most easy to write. Though I had a secret liking for the Strumpet, because I found her the harder perhaps.' (Robinson, 385)

[6] My one slight doubt about Robinson's edition is that its very thorough account of Powys's debt to the King James version might encourage some readers to think too narrowly of him as an Anglican writer. His religious vision could also embrace both Rabelais and Nietzsche and *Fables* takes a view of created things that perhaps comes as near to Eastern religions as to Christianity.

[7] The Bible provided Powys with political as well as spiritual inspiration. In the period between Blake and Lawrence it was still a radical book, drawn on by many writers who saw society through the eyes of the poor – as it was to some of the poor themselves.

'I Am Myself Alone': Solitude and Transcendence in John Cowper Powys

JANINA NORDIUS

Göteborg, Sweden: Acta Universitatis Gothenburgensis, 1997, 208 pp.

It has been a curious experience, writing a review of Janina Nordius's book *Solitude and Transcendence*, and at the same time preparing my last conference paper for publication in this current issue of the *Journal*. We approach John Cowper Powys from opposite directions. Dr Nordius makes it clear in her book that she wishes as far as possible to ignore the personality and concentrate on the philosophy and the novels. My training in psycho-mythology and my experience of John Cowper from immersion in his diaries, make it almost inevitable that I come at the writings from the writer himself. I respect her decision as I hope she honours my perspective. And synchronistically, we end up treading the same circle around the central mystery of Powys — what I call his 'alienation' and she calls his 'solitude'.

Her book sets out to prove three main points: that Powys's 'fictional inquiry into solitude … constitutes an integral structure in all his major novels'; that his 'philosophy of solitude — whose main tenet is that it is both possible and desirable to make solitude a source of personal happiness — is continually being tested against the fictional reality of his novels'; and that there is change and development in his philosophy with each novel. (Nordius, Abstract)

After succinctly summarizing his 'philosophy of solitude' as he formulated it in *In Defence of Sensuality* (1930) and *A Philosophy of Solitude* (1933), Nordius goes on to a detailed examination of six novels in which Powys explores various aspects and implications of this philosophy: *Wolf Solent*, *A Glastonbury Romance*, *Weymouth Sands*, *Maiden Castle*, *Owen Glendower* and *Porius*.

Powys's 'philosophy' of solitude is founded on his acceptance that we are 'completely alone in the midst of a universe that cares nothing' (*In Defence of Sensuality*, 197). Our response to this 'metaphysical horror' (DS, 107) can be denial, or retreat into gregariousness. Powys suggests affirmation: instead of trying to escape our 'inherent loneliness' we must 'not only accept it, but find our unique and singular happiness in it' (*A Philosophy of Solitude*, 43). Paradoxically, the only way to achieve a modicum of personal happiness is for the individual to cultivate his own physical and mental solitude. Since there is no possibility of relation with other human beings, the 'way' he proposes is a solitary close communion with nature and the elemental world. This, he argues can bring comfort, sometimes happiness, and in rare moments, ecstasy.

Nordius begins:

> One of John Cowper Powys's master-narratives is the story of solitude and its overriding importance to individual human life. His major works present a continuous inquiry into this area — into solitude as an ultimate condition of existence, into solitude as a transcendental notion, but also into the many different ways solitude might manifest itself practically in human experience. (1)

In all the novels, the moral question raised by the deliberate cultivation of mental and/or physical solitude — its intrinsic 'selfishness' — is in the foreground. Powys asks in his Foreword to *In Defence of Sensuality*, 'how far has the individual the right to be what is called selfish? How far has he the right to concentrate on his own solitary awareness of existence and make this alone his life-purpose?'

Nordius convincingly argues that the 6 novels she examines can be seen as 3 pairs, in which different aspects of solitude are explored. In *Wolf Solent* and *A Glastonbury Romance* Powys centres on the conflict between the individual's need for solitary withdrawal and the presence of suffering all around him. Nordius points out that 'both novels feature the struggle between the two ideologies that Powys refers to as "the philosophy of the saint" and "the philosophy of the ichthyosaurus"'. She sees the latter as 'a provisional version of Powys's philosophy of solitude' (230).

> [T]here are only two basic alternatives, in adjusting ourselves to this essential cruel world. The one is *to be a Saint* ... to devote your life ... to the alleviation of all sentient suffering.... The other is to try to forget the suffering as completely as you

can, and to devote your life to a defiant enjoyment of as much happiness ... as you can snatch or can create. (DS, 251–2)

The ichthyosaurian motto is 'enjoy-defy-forget' and it constitutes the core of his philosophy of solitude. Nordius argues that Powys constantly used 'the fictional reality' of his novels to test the viability and the implications of this philosophy.

Nordius suggests that the conflict is staged as an internal conflict in the hero of *Wolf Solent* and externalized in *A Glastonbury Romance* — with Sam Dekker playing the role of the saint and John Crow the ichthyosaurus, and makes the point that, while Powys does not avoid either the horrors of existence or the problems that the pursuit of ichthyosaurian solitude gives rise to, these two novels celebrate the power and the joy that comes from the pursuit and practise of solitude. John Crow's celebration of his own aloneness is exultant:

> 'I am myself,' he thought, 'I am myself alone.' His mood ... became ... more and more anti-social and more and more inhuman ... 'What I really am is a hard, round stone defying the whole universe.... It's a lovely feeling to feel absolutely alone, watching everything from the outside, uncommitted to any-thing ...' (*A Glastonbury Romance*, 370)

He continues:

> Why should I accept the common view that you have to 'love' other people? Mary belongs to me; but sometimes I wonder whether I 'love' even Mary.

This leads back to the fundamental question of 'selfishness'. How can one attain this 'lovely feeling' in a world where relationships with other people are inevitable, and how does this 'solitude' impinge on the happiness or fulfilment of others?

The relation between love and solitude is one that Powys comes back to again and again. Powys in *In Defence of Sensuality* admits that 'to establish a compromise' between love and solitude is 'Life's most difficult task.' (DS, 10) As even Wolf realizes, love is an emotion that 'demands a response.' (*Wolf Solent*, 55) In the next two novels, *Weymouth Sands* and *Maiden Castle*, 'the bone of contention ... is, ultimately, solitude as a subjective preoccupation, dialectically opposed to partaking in close relations with other people.' (230)

In *Weymouth Sands*, 'love and the loss of the lover are the prominent motifs', and 'the drawbacks of solitude and loneliness become more prominent.' (103–4) Certainly there are moments when some of the characters experience a rush of happiness in solitude, usually triggered by the contemplation of nature or the inanimate. Magnus Muir, for example, desperately unhappy in his loss of Curly, catches sight of a derelict piece of cork lying on the sand and 'a rush of happiness, so intense, so overwhelming, took possession of him, that he was as one transported out of himself' (*Weymouth Sands*, 478) But the separation and disconnection between characters is constantly stressed in this novel. Nordius, in a telling metaphor, says that the characters 'live closely side by side, each single person is enclosed in his own self, as if it were a hard shell that he cannot or does not want to break through ...' (118) What was a cause of exultation in John Crow has become a cause of desolation in *Weymouth Sands*.

In *Maiden Castle*, it is Wizzie, Dud's girl, who acts as the major critic of the philosophy of solitude that the Powys-hero shares with his author: 'By paying so much attention to his solitary sensations and absorptions in the not-self ... Dud No-man neglects the real world around him, and in particular the needs and pains of Wizzie.' (135)

Nordius believes that 'although *Maiden Castle* presents the most severe attack on Powys's philosophy of solitude, the novel 'also features the final consolidation of this philosophy.' (231) This is because while Dud is depressed when Wizzie leaves him, his 'strategy to exorcise the pain of loneliness is not to alleviate it by looking outward ... but to accept and intensify his inescapable existential solitude in order to transform it into happiness.' Dud has lost his subjective pleasure in solitude and he has lost Wizzie. So he falls back, or goes deeper, into an 'impersonal solitude' where he can find 'a sense of communion with a collective past' (159–60).

Thus she sees *Maiden Castle* as a transitional novel with a shift in emphasis: the sense that the solitary individual has to defend his own solitude is dropped for the larger, less subjective 'sense of being a medium for the continuity of human life on earth'. In *Owen*

Glendower and *Porius* this is, she believes, the dominant aspect of the writer's vision of solitude.

Nordius has an enlightening section on visible and invisible solitudes, concentrating on Glendower as prince and outlaw. But her most interesting point is the suggestion that in the Welsh novels, Powys has found a way of overcoming the sense of absolute aloneness. This is by way of trances, dreams and reveries which 'call forth a solitary experience of a shared collective heritage' (195). She refers to Catharine's enchanted forest tapestry and Meredith's trance at the end of the novel: 'Experiences like these, where solitary communion with past generations provide spiritual sustenance for life in the present are what ultimately emerges as the most valuable solitude.' In *Porius*, although the characters are still 'alone' this new perspective of 'impersonal solitude' allows 'what seems a new acceptance of outer, practical reality' (200):

> What is essentially new in Powys's approach to solitude in *Porius* … is the narration from within 'impersonal solitude'.…
> In so far as new stories appear, they can, significantly, be seen as expressions of the new 'confusion' of inner/outer, stressing human cooperation and peaceful coexistence rather than the importance of solitude. (213)

If she is correct, and certainly the hero Porius arguably represents this 'new story', it is nonetheless a bleak resolution. The emphasis has shifted from Wolf's maxim 'enjoy–escape' to Porius's 'endure–forget' the horrors. Solitude has drifted from enjoyment to endurance.

There are brief epiphanies. In one scene, the princess Tonwen and her lover Cadawg are riding together through the forest which is traditionally the place where man confronts his aloneness. And there, for a brief time before death, two people know that they are <u>not</u> alone but guarded by 'shared memories'.

> Not a wolf, not a fox disturbed the silence, not an owl, not a night-hawk. Nothing was audible but the steady hoof-fall of the dapple-grey, thudding upon moss soft as sleep … and they felt as if all the years they had been friends together were

returning on soundless wings to reassure them, to let them know that in this their supreme moment they were not alone, but that all their shared memories like guardian spirits were about them .... *(Porius,* 351)

There are a lot of deaths in *Porius* and I wish that Nordius had pursued a brief comment she makes toward the end of her chapter on this novel. She says that as well as the old versions of the philosophy of solitude we are given a new story — death. 'What is death' asks Powys, 'if not the consummation of loneliness?' (DS, 102) Death is the ultimate reality and the ultimate solitude — the ultimate escape from the conscious self and the horrors. Porius believes that the individual has as much right to indulge in this ultimate solitude as in any other kind of solitude.

★ ★ ★ ★

Dr Nordius's book raises two problems for me. The first one is the difficulty of relying on Powys's books of 'philosophy' as a basis for an analysis of his novels. Her premise of the importance that the role that solitude plays in the novels is absolutely right, and her analysis of the different kinds of solitude and the implications of them in 'fictional reality' is enlightening. But as early as page 57 she admits to the problem that no doubt other Powysians have come up against time and time again — that he is not 'rigid in his definitions' and that 'the distinction between the saint and the ichthyosaurus becomes at time so blurred as to almost collapse'. While what he said in his various books of philosophy were clearly important aspects of his life-illusion, they were never meant by him to be closely analysed by scholars. He intended them for what they are: 'a good book for forlorn spirits to be helped by'. (25 May 1932) Powys in his diaries makes it clear that they were written because his American publishers knew that they would sell well; they appealed to a certain mass readership. Phyllis called them, and the readers of them, 'these little Cults for funny ones — these Pigeon Roost sermons.' (12 July 1933)

Virtually all his 'philosophy' books were written in haste. Referring to *The Art of Happiness,* he wrote in his diary 'This book shall go to the limit of my peculiar points of view. The title has been carefully selected by Mr Schuster. The contents will be hastily concocted by the author …' *In Defence of Sensuality* was 'concocted' in less than 5 months, and *A Philosophy of Solitude* in 6 months, while writing *Weymouth Sands* at the same time.

And when Powys came up against 'real reality' (as distinct from his 'fictive reality' he too sometimes wondered what he really meant.

> Monday 5 November 1934   Ailinon! Ailinon! A difficult day! … After breakfast I gave myself an ENEMA & then trouble of a serious kind came upon us. For the ENEMA did not act. I had been too long & it had got all hardened in my bowels and refused to budge. … I came up with a terrified countenance & the T.T. tried the other kind. No good! Then she went to the Chemist who suggested after looking in big books a certain proportion of Turpentine. But I was shy of this: I went to bed & prayed to St Theresa & thought of my book on Happiness & about what the bloody hell I really meant by 'Be Happy or Die' & the Ichthian Process.

He was not a philosopher, although I am sure that his 'philosophy' books contained much of what he believed. Nor do I think that his novels were a fictional working out of philosophical ideas. The work of art, I believe, is an act of metamorphosis. T. S. Eliot described this as 'the struggle which alone constitutes life for a poet — to transmute his personal and private agonies into something rich and strange, something universal and impersonal.'

This is the second problem, which I referred to at the beginning of this review. Nordius's approach is to 'keep the "real-life" Powys out of my present discussion as far as possible.' (7) My approach is that of a literary psychologist. Both approaches are valid, and ideally, together should provide greater illumination of a work of art than is possible by one approach.

For example, much of what she says about love and solitude is valid and valuable, and needs no life gloss. But some things that puzzle her cannot be explained by reliance either on the philosophy or on the text, because they are the outcome of specific situations in the artist's own life. For example, she is puzzled by the radical shift in the treatment of solitude from *A Glastonbury Romance* to *Weymouth Sands*. In *A Glastonbury Romance*, she sees an 'extreme affirmation of solitude' but in *Weymouth Sands* 'the picture of solitude ... is, if not totally negative, at least considerably deflated.' (102)

She also recognizes *Weymouth Sands* and *Maiden Castle* are a pair, and that in them 'the criticism of the philosophy of solitude ... [is] delivered from a viewpoint of "feminine realism"' (230) But, with respect, her understanding of the internal psychology of these shifts would have been enhanced had she been aware, or allowed into her analysis, the 'real reality' that Phyllis Playter, John's companion, is as much Christie, Mary and Wizzie, as JCP is Wolf, John Crow, and No-man.

May I suggest that 'the narratorial attitude to this kind of solitude is radically changed' because Phyllis had a much greater hand in the writing of *Weymouth Sands* than in any of his other novels, and her attitude to solitude was more pessimistic, or, to use Nordius's word, 'realistic'?

Nordius also notes, as have other critics, that in *Maiden Castle*, 'roughly at mid-novel we have a shift of the point of view': the narrator turns from Dud's point of view to Wizzie's. 'By letting the reader experience No-man from Wizzie's point of view, the narrator conveys his most mordant criticism of D.'s egotism ... ' (152). He sees, in other words, the 'practical implications of No-man's solitude' (146).

With the publication of *The Dorset Year*, we will see how closely events of 1934–35 are reflected in the novel itself. It will add, I believe, to our understanding of the conflict between love and solitude in *Maiden Castle* to know that while it was being written, Phyllis was in a state of revolt against many things, but most of all, questioning as never before whether she could live with this solitary man. The novel was continued after their move to Wales in 1935. It might be useful to quote from some unpublished entries to show precisely how the switch in narrator point of view came about and when.

> 23 July 1935 ... The T.T. read to me — I adore it when <u>she</u> reads aloud my chapter — & I was amazed how well she did it

— the close or end of chapter V — leaving them on the way to Maiden Castle at last! But then a very upsetting, foundation-shaking event occurred — namely the T.T.'s renewed Distress over the Wizzy part of my book & my hero's masculine reaction to little Wizzie's nervous outbreaks. The T.T. placed this masculine cold-blooded detached unsympathetic reaction to Feminine Anger side by side with all those Pan-ergic & in Spite-of-All Stoical shifts & tricks in the Art of Happiness & she got hold of the agitating notion that all my Socrates self-Control & all my 'Aequam Memento rebus Arduis servare Mentem' protective-cement or self-evoked 'Stillicide' as I call it wherein in self-righteous self-control the male soul tries to keep itself guarded from the up and down surging of the Feminine Ocean-tides like a Barnacle under the foam, gathering sea-grit & sea-sand and rubble to protect its interior softness & vulnerability like a Caddis-worm in its coat of stick-mail — I say that all this philosophic evoking of 'Stillicide' as I call it — was a mean base and profoundly revengeful Hit-Back at the Feminine. She felt that in Wizzie's moods & in the relations between her and Dud-Dud I had betrayed this struggle and this detached self-righteousness that refuses to quarrel but conceals a deep grudge & brings it out in Books which is, she feels much worse than any personal immediate anger or even a blow!

11 August   … Worked fast and furious at Chapter VI which has now reached its 100th page. I don't know how far this chapter will please the T.T. or indeed whether she'll want to hear another chapter at all so upset does this book make her! But I keep assuring her that it is only Begun!! This is chapter VI and if my life is spared I purpose to compose 12 chapters & I am going to make Wizzie my mouth-piece soon in order that Dud-Dud's attitude to women shall no longer dominate the book. We shall see how that pleases her.

1 Sept   … I returned to revising Chapter VI which is my final chapter with poor old Dud-Dud as the chief mouth-piece.

After this with a daring plunge I am going to strain it all — a la Henry James — thro' the personality of poor little Wizzie.

2 Sept ... I have had slow work in finishing Chapter VI because I have been so anxious to make Dud-Dud's thoughts clear before turning to Wizzie in the next chapter. I keep adding 'Insets' to it in order to strengthen Dud-Dud's position.

5 Sept ... I must read Chapter VI to her today. <u>Will</u> she like it? After this I shall leave Dud-Dud, please God & take Wizzie as my <u>centre-point</u>. No — she hates this chapter VI. Ailinon! Ailinon! In fact she has come to hate this whole book. In fact she has hated all my writing since I finished <u>Weymouth Sands</u>. <u>Why is this?</u> <u>She does not know.</u>

7 September ... I hope today the T.T. will do up my Chapter VI & get it off to be typed by Mrs. Meech. Now I am free to begin with Wizzie. ... I began Chapter VII. This memorable moment in my Book when I leave the thoughts — so monotonous to the T.T. — of poor old Dud-Dud & transfer myself to what is going on in the mind of the enigmatic Wizzie — Well! we shall see how this works out. It is a new departure for me.

9 October ... Have read Chapter VII — but it's <u>no good</u>. She really does condemn this whole book as <u>unreal</u>.

16 October ... [A] long afternoon at Revising chapter VII — under the strictures of the T.T.

I could continue in the same vein, by pointing out that what Nordius calls 'the new narrational "shamelessness"' in *Owen Glendower*, where scenes of sadism and violence avoided in *A Glastonbury Romance* are now written without censorship, has not so much to do with his philosophy of solitude as with traumatic personal and psychological experiences in the dark months after the outbreak of World War Two.

But nothing of the above detracts from the achievement of Janina Nordius's close reading of these novels. This brief review cannot do justice to her densely written analysis of Powys's philosophy of solitude. Her book is a significant step forward in our understanding of this solitary artist who made art out of his aloneness.

Morine Krissdóttir

Our Lady of Europe
JEREMY HOOKER
Enitharmon Press, 1997. 136 pp., £8.95, ISBN 1 900564 15 7

When I first met Jeremy Hooker he was living in Wales, and I subsequently read his work in Anglo-Welsh journals. The subject matter of *Our Lady of Europe* covers the Low Countries, other parts of Europe and the Middle East. Many of the poems are inspired by works of art. When poets turn to galleries for stimulation it often means that they are searching for their elusive muses in a strange land, where they clutch at technical terms such as etching, and misapply them to the horror of the visual artist.

In Hooker's case, his genuine enthusiasm, sensitivity and knowledge shines through. He is an admirer and expert on the work of David Jones, a man who was equally talented in two arts; a rare thing in this country, though common in China and Japan.

On the cover of the collection is a detail from a photograph of a sculpture by Ossip Zadkine, one of my favourite sculptors. Hooker has written a powerful poem on this work. It is entitled 'Rotterdam: Zadkine's De Vervost Stad' and begins:

> Bronze Atlas, with a mortal wound.
>
> But still powerful;
> a contorted giant, hands raised
> reeling in agony. Not defeated.
>
> He is the city that will live again
> when a bird builds its nest in the place
> of his burnt-out heart.

Hooker identifies the figure with the city when it was in pieces but undefeated in World War Two. He goes on to link it with a friend who watched the sculpture being constructed and who carries responsibilities that made him part of the city's well being.

I should have liked fuller notes to guide me through some of the poems. I fear that I have missed some of the intended nuances. I very much enjoyed a short poem 'Beginning Again' which I quote in full:

> Walking in the New Year
> blinded with splinters
> of rain, almost blown
> off the dyke into the sea.
>
> There is no one behind us
> in all the wide land
> but a frantic scarecrow
> dressed in a black suit
> and running, running, running.

This is a lucid succinct poem free of obscurity and ambiguities and without a superfluous word. The picture it creates is as clear as a Japanese print. 'Splinters of rain' recalls the work of Hiroshige. The lines have the clarity and economy present in the best Haiku and Tanka. I return to it with increasing pleasure.

In the section *A Troy of the North*, 'William Barents's Last Voyage' is as sharp and bleak as the regions it describes. On the Dutch coast where Hooker now lives he finds echoes of the Hampshire coast where he spent his childhood. This feeling is well described in 'Nostalgia'. In other poems he describes the Dutch landscape paintings that British collectors have bought since the seventeenth century, where the sky dominates the scenes.

'Blinded', a striking poem about a stone sculpture that he comes upon in a clearing, shows his ability to translate the visual into the verbal. The line 'The head was rounded and more pathetic than brutal' is a telling one and brings one up short. Having myself written poems about Rembrandt and Van Gogh I found it easy to turn to his; he melds the artist with the art. On returning to Wales he recalls 'Strata Florida' and dedicates the poem to Wynn Thomas. In another that he dedicates to his Dutch wife, he describes her among the Hart's Tongue ferns that grow by the tower in the Abbey's ruins.

Another section's title is *Motherland* and includes a poem dedicated to Gerard Casey called 'Homer Dictating', where he recalls Rembrandt's *Homer* — the light of the sacred is upon him — 'a pale watery gold'. *Written in Clay* includes poems on Berlin, Brittany, Verdun and Arras; the last refers to Edward Thomas. 'An Ode to Antonio Gaudí' attempts to put into words the extraordinary decoration that it part of his cathedral. Hooker ends with the lines:

> He died, the great work
> unfinished
> and because of that
> more natural, more
> a place to play in,
> and laugh and cry
> and wonder at the maker,
> man-child and his praise
> in the body of Creation
> that begins and has no end.

I can't help remembering Rimbaud's remark that a work of art is never finished, it is only abandoned.

'Verdun' includes a reference to 'Our Lady of Europe' to whom a chapel on the battlefield is dedicated. *Crossways*, another section, celebrates a visit to Palestine, where he writes poems linking the Holy Places with the biblical events and the people, flora and fauna that he finds there. He looks with a sharp eye at the details and creates clear pictures of the landscape and townscapes, and the inhabitants going about their business in what must often be an unbearably tense atmosphere.

> An old Arab
> leading a donkey
> laden with toilet rolls
> down the track past Absolom's Tomb.

This is from 'Jerusalem Sketchbook'. In Bethlehem he sees:

soldiers at roof-top gunposts,
Arabs selling fruit in Manger Square

In the section called *Earth Song Cycle* he has poems both topographical and mythological, set in the classical and Byzantine world. He juxtaposes a 'Hymn to Demeter' with a description of the orthodox Easter ceremony in a poem called 'Christ is Risen'. From the 'Hymn':

— and let us be where
earth and waters meet
and make for you a song.

From 'Christ is Risen':

Once more a cry
sounds where a cry
has echoed
over cornfield
and olive grove
across thousands
of years. Again
the cave stands open
and the faithful see.

Does this poem imply that there is little to choose between all forms of worship? If so, would it were true that the rest of the world felt the same. May Our Lady of Europe, be she Christian or Heathen, prevail. She is certainly called upon in times of stress. I noticed that the Communist reared Russian in charge of the *Mir* space station cried out 'Mother of God' at the time of the crash.

Patricia Dawson

NOTES ON CONTRIBUTORS

RODNEY AITCHTEY is an author with a specific commitment to ecological issues. His work has appeared in *Fourth World Review*, *New European*, and *New Welsh Review*, among others; and he has an essay in the book *Deep Ecology and Anarchism* (1993).

MICHAEL ALSFORD is a Senior Lecturer in Contemporary Theology at the University of Greenwich. His published work includes essays on science fiction.

PATRICIA DAWSON is an artist and writer whose interest in the work of J. C. Powys over many years has influenced aspects of her own work.

MORINE KRISSDÓTTIR was until recently Chairman of The Powys Society. Her most recent publications include *Petrushka and the Dancer* (the diaries of J, C. Powys, 1929–39) and *The Dorset Year, The Diary of John Cowper Powys June 1934 to July 1935*..

H. W. FAWKNER is Professor of English Literature in Stockholm University. His book, *The Ecstatic World of John Cowper Powys*, was published un 1986.

PETER FOSS is a writer and painter. His book on the Battle of Bosworth, *The Field of Redemore*, has been republished this year; his book on the diary of Joseph Moxon, 1798–99, *A Truly Honest Man*, is due out shortly; he is also editing the letters of Frances Gregg to Oliver Wilkinson.

DAVID GERVAIS is an Editor of *The Cambridge Quarterly* and Honorary Fellow in English at Reading University. His publications include *Literary Englands* (Cambridge University Press); he is currently working on a book on Shakespeare and Racine.

TIMOTHY HYMAN is a painter and writer. He is an Honorary Research Fellow at University College London.

ROBERT B. KUNKEL, who died on cancer on April 29th 1998, was an American lawyer and active Quaker, discovered The Powys Society only recently. He showed his enquiring enthusiasm in his detailed investigations into aspects of *Porius for the Society.*

CHARLES LOCK is Professor of English at the University of Copenhagen.

STEPHEN POWYS MARKS is an architect, editor and writer, and is the Honorary Treasurer of The Powys Society. He has contributed extensively to Powys studies, especially in the *Newsletter*, and to other publication work of the Society.

PAUL ROBERTS is the Chairman of The Powys Society, and was previously editor of *The Powys Society Newsletter*. He has written widely on Powysian topics, including a study of G. Arnold Shaw.

JUDITH STINTON was the writer/researcher responsible for the new galleries for 'A Writer's Dorset' at the Dorset County Museum. She has written six books, including *Chaldon Herring: The Powys Circle in a Dorset Village.*

SUBI SWIFT is a Senior Lecturer at St Mary's University College, Twickenham. Her PhD thesis, *A Descriptvie Power*, was on J. C. Powys and the visual arts.

JOHN POWELL WARD is a poet and writer on language and literature. He is the editor of Seren's Border Lines series, which has now published Herbert Williams' biography of J. C. Powys.